THE COMPLETE IDIOT'S GUIDE® TO

World Mythology

by Evans Lansing Smith, Ph.D., and Nathan Robert Brown

ALPHA

A member of Penguin Group (USA) Inc.

ALPHA BOOKS

Published by the Penguin Group

Penguin Group (USA) Inc., 375 Hudson Street, New York, New York 10014, USA

Penguin Group (Canada), 90 Eglinton Avenue East, Suite 700, Toronto, Ontario M4P 2Y3, Canada (a division of Pearson Penguin Canada Inc.)

Penguin Books Ltd., 80 Strand, London WC2R 0RL, England

Penguin Ireland, 25 St. Stephen's Green, Dublin 2, Ireland (a division of Penguin Books Ltd.)

Penguin Group (Australia), 250 Camberwell Road, Camberwell, Victoria 3124, Australia (a division of Pearson Australia Group Pty. Ltd.)

Penguin Books India Pvt. Ltd., 11 Community Centre, Panchsheel Park, New Delhi—110 017, India

Penguin Group (NZ), 67 Apollo Drive, Rosedale, North Shore, Auckland 1311, New Zealand (a division of Pearson New Zealand Ltd.)

Penguin Books (South Africa) (Pty.) Ltd., 24 Sturdee Avenue, Rosebank, Johannesburg 2196, South Africa

Penguin Books Ltd., Registered Offices: 80 Strand, London WC2R 0RL, England

International Standard Book Number: 978-1-59257-764-4
Library of Congress Catalog Card Number: 2008920882

10 09 08   8 7 6 5 4 3 2 1

Interpretation of the printing code: The rightmost number of the first series of numbers is the year of the book's printing; the rightmost number of the second series of numbers is the number of the book's printing. For example, a printing code of 08-1 shows that the first printing occurred in 2008.

Printed in the United States of America

Note: This publication contains the opinions and ideas of its authors. It is intended to provide helpful and informative material on the subject matter covered. It is sold with the understanding that the authors and publisher are not engaged in rendering professional services in the book. If the reader requires personal assistance or advice, a competent professional should be consulted.

The authors and publisher specifically disclaim any responsibility for any liability, loss, or risk, personal or otherwise, which is incurred as a consequence, directly or indirectly, of the use and application of any of the contents of this book.

Most Alpha books are available at special quantity discounts for bulk purchases for sales promotions, premiums, fund-raising, or educational use. Special books, or book excerpts, can also be created to fit specific needs.

For details, write: Special Markets, Alpha Books, 375 Hudson Street, New York, NY 10014.

Publisher: *Marie Butler-Knight*
Editorial Director: *Mike Sanders*
Senior Managing Editor: *Billy Fields*
Executive Editor: *Randy Ladenheim-Gil*
Development Editor: *Megan Douglass*
Production Editor: *Kayla Dugger*
Copy Editor: *Tricia Leibig*

Cartoonist: *Steve Barr*
Cover Designer: *Bill Thomas*
Book Designer: *Trina Wurst*
Indexer: *Tonya Heard*
Layout: *Brian Massey*
Proofreaders: *Terri Edwards, John Etchison*

This book is dedicated to the heroes of legend, who taught me that the only evil in the world is when good men do nothing; and to the "goddesses" of my life ... you have always been my guides through the labyrinth. —Nathan Robert Brown

I dedicate this book to the memory and inspiration of Joseph Campbell. —Dr. E. L. Smith

Contents at a Glance

Contents

Appendixes

Introduction

You know you've said it, or heard someone say it, at least once in your life: "That's just a *myth*." Likely, what he or she meant to say was "That's not *true*." The belief that myth means fiction is a common misconception of those unfamiliar with the study of mythology. Before you begin reading this book, there is something you need to understand—myths have nothing to do with fact or fiction, but with *truth*.

One way to understand what is meant by *truth* is to consider the myth of the "Boy Who Cried Wolf." Have you ever once felt compelled to question the historical validity of this tale? Probably not. Chances are that no such incident ever happened. So why do we still tell it to children? Because we are trying to help them understand that habitual lying makes it hard for people to believe you when you *are* telling the truth. So you see, the "Boy Who Cried Wolf" story is one of truth, whether or not it is actually fact. Fact doesn't matter, as it has no affect whatsoever on the value of a myth.

Also, please understand that when religions are referred to as myths in this book, this does not mean that they are not true. Most mythologists are firm believers in the existence of God. However, they often hold a much broader view. So please do not be offended if texts from your religion are referred to in this book as myths. The word myth is not being used to mean "fictitious" or "untrue," but to refer to tales of metaphorical value and universal truth.

Since the dawn of language, mythology has been an outlet through which humanity expresses its understanding and perception of its existence on this planet, and within a far greater cosmos. Myth is humanity's way of expressing fears and joys, existence and environment, as well as the workings of a divine entity that can barely be understood within the limits of physical reality.

This book offers an overview of mythologies from across the globe. From the indigenous tribes of the Americas to the ancient Cradle of Civilization that is now called the Near and Middle East, myth is a constant element of human culture. The myths of different civilizations, though separated by such obstacles as time and geography, consist of common themes that bind us together as a species.

This book promises an extensive though still partial overview of a subject that is far more diverse and vast than most people realize. The oldest myths of which we know date back to around 3500 B.C.E. and are probably even older than that, considering that most myths are passed along verbally before being written down. So as myths have continued to multiply throughout the last 5,500 years, there are literally thousands upon thousands of them in existence. Sometimes, there can be more than one version of a particular myth, story, or folktale. As a result, any book that covered every facet of world mythology would likely be too heavy to carry. However, we have certainly tried to get as close as possible to providing a complete picture of world myths that may act as a gateway through which you will begin to understand the multitude of myths that our species has produced during the last five millennia.

The characters and myths covered within this book are separated into parts and chapters that address themes and types, instead of by geographic location, allowing you to obtain a working understanding of how the myths and/or heroes of one culture may be compared to those of another. This book will also explain many of the profound breakthroughs and discoveries in the disciplines of mythological studies during recent centuries.

To study the myths of just a single culture can be a challenge. To study the myths of the world, however, can be a complicated and somewhat overwhelming task. This book effectively condenses the tales, characters, concepts, subjects, and important events of world mythology. By reading this book, you will be able to easily reference information from literally hundreds of myths, without spending the countless hours it would take to read all of them. More than just stories, more than just superstition or religion, myths are the keys to unlocking the hidden recesses of our minds, the unknown potential of our bodies, and the timeless enigma of the soul. Through myth, you may begin to understand how these parts of the self connect us to a being that is far beyond the limited capacity of understanding that is physical reality.

How to Use This Book

To offer you the most effective possible reference for the comparative analysis of world mythology, the myths in this book have been separated into four main parts and further broken down into chapters by theme and type:

Part 1, "Gods and Goddesses," are the creators that formed us from the dust of the earth. They are the destroyers that ravage humanity with pestilence, war, and death. They are the torturers that wrack the bodies of the wicked with pain. They are the merciful saviors that rescue us from our own dark natures. On the ancient battlefield, they were our allies as well as our adversaries. They are our gods. Whether existing in the domain of a transcendent Heaven, a dark and frightening underworld, a world of immortal glory where the brave live forever, or on the cloud-hidden mountaintop of Olympus, these gods stand as a representation of humankind's evolving perception of a divine being that we may never be able to fully understand.

Since man's first steps into the great unknown, which was then no further than the horizon, heroes have walked among us. **Part 2, "Heroes,"** discusses the perilous journeys, violent battles, and courageous deeds that have granted them immortality in legends of valor and songs of glory. They are the models of men, displaying amazing amounts of courage, honor, and skill, at levels which others may never reach but continue to strive for. Whether the half-divine sons of gods or simply human warriors of uncommon valor, they stand as a testament to the potential of Man. They represent the hope of a man that, when it matters most, will prove to be greater than he appears, braver than he feels, and stronger than he ever thought possible.

Who said that a woman's place is in the home? Whoever they were, they must never have met these ladies of adventure in **Part 3, "Heroines: Women of Myth."** These brave women of the shield and spear walk the paths of warriors, heroes, and men, very often bringing even the gods to their knees in submission. From the legendary warrior-women of the Amazon to the wrathful and defiant Lilith, the first wife of Adam, these women prove that their place is most certainly not in the home, but on the roads to glory and immortality.

In the darkest recesses of the human psyche lurk the greatest fears of the imagination, covered here in **Part 4, "Monsters, Creatures, Demons, and Dangers."** These creatures are angels and aids, beasts and abominations, which can serve as humanity's greatest hope or bring about its most certain doom. Some can be helpful yet mischievous, such as the Tengu, winged demons said to have conveyed the secret arts of death to the legendary ninja warriors of Japan. Others are destructive, such as the Chimera of Greek mythology. Still others represent our own fears about our most hidden desires, such as the blood-consuming vampires or mind-shattering banshees of the western mythological traditions. Whether angel, demon, imp, or monster, you don't want to get on their bad side.

Sidebars

Mythology is a vast subject, and it can be easy to become confused. Here are explanations of the sidebars that have been provided to offer you readily available explanations of key ideas, concepts, objects, and terms in the realm of world mythology.

Myth and Metaphor

These sidebars explain and identify the metaphorical and archetypal significances of mythic character types, events, relationships, and situations.

Sword and Man

These boxes give you in-depth explanations of the backgrounds, uses, meanings, appearances, and/or significances of weapons, tools, objects, and so on in myths.

Avoiding the Labyrinth

These sidebars offer clarification for easily confused concepts, characters, events, and/or words in mythology due to common misperceptions or similarities in names, spellings, purposes, and/or actions.

Immortal Words

These sidebars offer definitions, meanings, and explanations of mythological terms, words, objects, and/or names that are obscure or of non-English tongues.

Acknowledgments

Nathan Robert Brown's acknowledgments: First and foremost, I would like to thank Dr. Smith for taking on this project with me. You have been an inspiration to me, and I have been truly humbled by this experience. I would also like to thank Randy Ladenheim-Gil, executive editor, and Megan Douglass, development editor. You have all been truly valuable in the creation of this incredible project.

Dr. E. L. Smith's acknowledgments: My thanks to my co-author, Nathan Brown, who wrote this book. His diligence and creativity in the face of the most daunting of challenges has been, and will remain, a great source of inspiration.

Trademarks

Part 1

Gods and Goddesses

They are the creators that formed us from the dust of the earth. They are the destroyers that ravage humanity with pestilence, war, and death. They are the torturers that wrack the bodies of the wicked with pain. They are the merciful saviors that rescue us from our own dark natures. On the ancient battlefield, they were our allies as well as our adversaries. They are our gods. Whether existing in the domain of a transcendent heaven, a dark and frightening underworld, a world of immortal glory where the brave live forever, or on the cloud-hidden mountaintop of Olympus, these gods stand as a representation of humankind's evolving perception of a divine being that we may never be able to fully understand.

Chapter 1

In the Beginning ...

In This Chapter

- ◆ Primal myths from around the world
- ◆ Similarities/archetypes of creation myths
- ◆ Civilizations with altered creation myths
- ◆ Primal myths that deny the existence of a Creator

At the root of all mythology is the primal myth, a tale from which all later myths follow. The myths of creation are often seen as the most sacred, primarily because of this relationship. The primal myth is the ground upon which all myths of that tradition must stand. Therefore, if the creation myth is shattered, it is often feared that the entirety of the tradition will fall apart as well. As the civilizations of our world began to share their myths with one another, the parallels they revealed were often shocking. As you read this chapter, you may begin to notice these parallels. Please note that this book does not seek to bring into question anyone's religious beliefs, only to present information.

Making the New World

Native American primal myths offer a wide range of interesting examples. Although the creation myths of some native tribes are centuries old and have, for the most part, remained unchanged (such as the Wyot's), other native tribal myths (such as the Okanagon's) were altered as a result of the overpowering and sometimes enforced influence of the invading white men. Sadly, these "white-influenced" creation myths often replaced the originals, causing them to be lost to the passage of time. Still other Native American primal myths (for example, the Cherokee's) carry a sad theme of uncertainty in many details of the "who" and "how." The loss of these details is likely the result of constantly being uprooted from their lands by European settlers, relocated by the military, and forced by the government into programs meant to "civilize" them. It is no wonder that parts of their cultural myths were lost.

This chapter should be viewed as a basic overview of Native American primal myths. Had *all* primal myths from *every* Native American tribe been included, this section alone would be hundreds of pages long.

The Wrath of Above-Old-Man (Wyot)

The Wyot were a people from regions of what is now the state of California. Their creator god is referred to as Above-Old-Man. The primal myth of the Wyot explains how Above-Old-Man was terribly disenchanted by his first attempt at creating mankind. The method by which he created them is not specified. The first people created by Above-Old-Man were covered with fur and unable to master the skills of speech. Plainly speaking, these first people were more akin to animals than mankind. Of note in the Wyot primal myth is Above-Old-Man's use of a great flood/deluge to destroy the creation he grows angry and unhappy with.

Myth and Metaphor _____

Reference to a great flood/deluge is a common theme in ancient world myths. Stories of a massive flood exist in Native American, Sumerian, European, Semitic, and African cultures. Much of the scientific community dismisses the idea that such a great flood was a real event in the planet's history. However, some theorize that extreme flooding could have occurred near oceans, rivers, or other bodies of water (where most early civilizations settled). Although it's unlikely the *entire* surface of the earth was ever *completely* underwater, it's important to note that, to early/primal man, the world stopped at the end of the horizon. If all they could see was water, then to primal man, the "world" had flooded.

As Above-Old-Man floods the land, Condor weaves a basket and, along with his sister, takes refuge inside. The pair survives the flood by staying inside the protection of the basket. When the flood ceases and the waters begin receding, Condor and his sister seek out land and remaining animals. They discover that all the first people are dead and gone. Among the animals, they find that the winged ones are nearly all that survive—pigeons, doves, and so on.

Condor, though never specifically referenced as a god, seems to assume a creator-god role. Oddly enough, it is at this point in the tale that Condor's sister becomes displeased when he refers to her as "sister." After walking away to consider this, Condor returns and calls her "my wife." A testament to the power given to words, this simple name shift changes their relationship entirely, from brother-sister to husband-wife.

Their union results in pregnancy and a new form of human is born, followed by many more. Above-Old-Man witnesses this and is pleased with the new people, even though they do not seem to be directly of his creation. These new humans are not covered with thick fur, and they are able to master the skills of speech. As a result, Above-Old-Man allows this new species of human to remain and does them no harm.

Golden People of the Red Clay (Okanagon)

The Okanagon tribe dwelled in regions of what is now the northwestern United States and southwestern Canada/British Columbia. Before the arrival of whites, the Okanagon were a hunting and fishing culture. It's quite possible that at one time the Okanagon had a far different creation myth than the one presented here. However, as whites settled into the lands of the Okanagon, the tribe could not help but be influenced by them in a number of ways. White agricultural influences led them to shift culturally from a migratory hunting and fishing people to an agricultural society. Apparent in this creation myth is how the tribe's mythology and cosmology were influenced by the Christian ideologies of whites, causing them to change their original creation myth to match these ideas and explain the existence of peoples with varying skin colors (which had probably not been addressed by their original primal myth).

In the existing Okanagon primal myth, God (whom they refer to as "The Chief") creates seven worlds—three above, three below, with the earth at the center. In the myth, it is acknowledged (but not confirmed) that this cosmological arrangement *might* have been suggested by the white men, but that it is now accepted as truth. The myth also states that the Okanagon believed the planet was originally a female entity. This reference to a feminine primal figure could be an acknowledgment of an Earth-Mother-Goddess figure from the original Okanagon creation myth (however, as the original primal myth has been forever lost, this can't be confirmed). She is given no specific name in the myth, but is referred to here as Earth Woman for the sake of readability and clarity.

God/The Chief transformed Earth Woman into the earth, using her parts to make up various areas of the planet. The directions, as well as what exists in those directions, are established in the myth at this time. Heaven is westward, as this is the direction in which The Chief places Earth Woman's head, while pointing her feet to the east. Earth Woman's flesh is used to make the soil, and it is from this soil that The Chief created the people of the earth, primarily the American Indians.

> **Myth and Metaphor**
>
> The concept of a female/ mother goddess figure being used to make up the earth is not exclusive to Native American myths. You will see this in Babylonian myth when Marduk performs a similar act. He dismembers his mother, Tiamat, and uses the pieces of her corpse to create the world.

Because the soil from which the Indian people were created was red clay, the myth states that this explains why Native Americans are red-skinned. Because other non-American Indian races (more specifically in the myth, blacks and whites) were created from different-colored soils, this explains why they are of different skin colors.

The myth ends with the claim that Native Americans are an exalted people as a result of their red skin color. Red clay, the myth explains, is closely related to the element of gold. This leads to the idea that Indians are directly related to gold. Therefore, the myth claims, the red-skinned races are finer than other races that have been made from other soils.

Beaver's Grandchild (Cherokee)

The Cherokee once called home the mountain ranges of the American South. However, when the U.S. government discovered that these territories were rich with gold, they relocated the tribe west by way of military force. This "trail of tears," still marked in areas of Oklahoma, claimed thousands of Cherokee lives.

The Cherokee creation myth portrays the earth as a great island that was raised up from a vast, endless ocean. At the four corners of the land are cords from which the earth is suspended by a sky canopy of solid rock. One day, the myth tells, the cords that hold up the world will break, the earth will sink, and only water will remain.

Above the earth, in the upper world called *Galun'lati*, a water beetle named Dayuni-si (meaning Beaver's Grandchild) went down to the endless ocean and, unable to find anything on the surface, dove to the bottom. He emerged from the depths with soft mud, which grew and solidified to become the land. The Cherokee myth explains that later the land was fixed to the heavens with cords. However, the myth also states that it is unknown just who fixed these cords or how, specifically, it was done.

Uncertainty is an ongoing element in the Cherokee creation myth. For example, the myth states that plants and animals were created first but also states that it is not known by whom. The myth goes on to tell how the animals are told by this unidentified entity (a creator god whose name had likely been lost or forgotten) to remain awake for seven nights. A great majority of them fail this task. The only animals to succeed are the panther, owl, and a handful of others. As a reward, these animals are granted the power to move about in darkness as though it were daylight. This explains why these animals are nocturnal hunters. Among the plants and trees, only the spruce, laurel, holly, pine, and cedar are successful. In reward, they are granted the gift of remaining forever green. As a result, these trees are the evergreens while others must lose their leaves or needles in the fall and remain bare throughout the winter.

 **Myth and Metaphor**

In the *Epic of Gilgamesh*, the hero Gilgamesh and his companion Enkidu endure a similar trial of remaining awake for seven nights.

Man and Woman are created later, after the animals and plants. Again illustrating the theme of the Cherokee uncertainty of origin, the manner in which humans came into being is not explained in the myth. The first man and woman of the Cherokee, in similar fashion to those in the Wyot primal myth, were brother and sister. In contrast, however, there isn't a role/name shift that causes them to become husband and wife. Instead, quite an odd act takes place. The brother strikes his sister with a fish (possibly a Cherokee symbol of fertility and/or prosperity) and tells her to create more humans. The sister immediately becomes pregnant and gives birth seven days later. She continues birthing a child every seven days, until concern arises (though *who* is concerned isn't named) that if this continues there will be too many people for the world to contain. So it's decided that women will only give birth once a year.

Creation Myths of the Apache

The Apache are perhaps one of the most well-known Native American tribes, primarily due to their skills as warriors and for their amazing horseback riding abilities.

Although often thought of as a single tribe, the Apache were actually divided into a number of sub-tribes by the time they entered the southwestern United States near the onset of the eleventh century C.E. These sub-tribes branched off from four main groups, the basic primal myths of which are still extant—Lipan, White Mountain, Chiricahua, and Jicarilla. The primal myths of the White Mountain and Chiricahua Apache tribes are provided here.

The White Mountain people of the Apache still reside on a reservation in Arizona. According to their primal myth, the earth was created not by gods but by the work of four people. When their work was completed, the god of the east wind, Black Wind Old Man, thrust himself against the earth three times, making it solid and creating thunder. The four workers continued to further improve the face of the now-solidified Earth. Then the thunder god, Black Thunder, came and gave the earth "veins." He then lashed at the surface until water began pouring from the gashes he'd made. After several trial-and-error attempts, these four creator people positioned the sun and moon into correct and appropriate positions. It is interesting to note that these four workers are not given names, nor are they identified as gods in any way.

The Chiricahua primal myth was heavily influenced by the Christian ideologies of whites, primarily that of divine retribution. In their primal myth, the earth is populated by humans who are not aware of God (referring to the Judeo-Christian God). They prayed to the gods of the mountains, and to Wind, Lightning, and Thunder. The Judeo-Christian God, the myth tells, punished these people with a great deluge. Only a handful of living creatures survived by climbing to the top of the White-Ringed Mountain (located near Deming, New Mexico), the only place not immersed by the flood.

After the waters receded, the last two men were presented with a gun, along with a bow and arrow. The man who was given the first choice took up the gun and became the White Man, leaving the other with the bow and arrow. He became the American Indian. The myth states that, had the second man been given first choice and taken up the gun, then he would have been the White Man, suggesting that the present situation in which the American Indians found themselves could have been reversed.

A New Father God (Mayan)

The Maya Indians of South America were conquered by foreign invaders from Europe by the close of the sixteenth century, first fighting Cortez and later Pisarro. Unfortunately, the original religious texts of this once great civilization have been forever lost to the sands of time. The modern Mayan creation myth (of the Guatemala Mayan tribes) stands as a testament to a culture forced to surrender to the beliefs of their conquerors.

Tezcatlipoca, a "Mayan-ized" re-creation of the Christian Jesus, is referred to as Our Father God. He was born of a virgin and destroyed the ancient heathen kings. His wrath resulted in the destruction of the old world and the creation of a new one for the Mayan peoples, whether they wanted one or not. The Mayan epic, *Popul Vuh*, offers a more extensive Mayan creation myth.

The Nameless God

The Inca, as with the Maya, were also conquered by European invaders during the sixteenth century. The upper social classes of the Inca worshipped an unnamed primary god who was the creator of reality and the source of all things. The Inca would refer to this primary god only by his title, *Wiraqoca*. This primary god, as a result of his unknowability, was offered no shrines and was served by no specific cultic group.

The religion of the populace (that practiced by those of low social rank) was focused on lower gods, who were viewed as little more than servants of this primary god. The gods worshipped by the common folk, then, were little more than servants to the greater, single entity worshipped by the upper class. This was done perhaps to show how the structure of the Incans on Earth was a reflection of the divine structure of their deities' hierarchy.

Forging Africa

As in many vast geographical areas, Africa is a land rich with a diverse number of tribes, cultures, and/or ethnic groups. Each of these groups has their own set of beliefs, their own gods, and most have their own unique language(s). Although a basic collection of African primal myths is given here, there exists a multitude that would fill a book themselves.

Chameleon's Father, Spider's Friend (Yao)

Mulungu, god figure of the Yao people of Mozambique, was father to Chameleon. Though Mulungu and Chameleon participate in the myth, it doesn't claim either is directly responsible for the creation of human beings. The myth tells how, one day,

Chameleon finds two miniature beings in his fish basket while retrieving it from the river. He takes them to his father, Mulungu, who says to put the creatures on the ground so they will grow. Much to the horror of Mulungu, the creatures not only grow, they begin killing and eating any living being they please.

Myth and Metaphor

God's/gods' abandonment of the earth is a common theme in the African creation myths. In contrast to man being expelled from Heaven or paradise due to a transgression, it is the divine figure that chooses to abandon Earth and return to Heaven in a number of African primal myths. In some African primal myths (such as that of the Barotse in the next section), man is first banished from paradise but continues to commit terrible acts that eventually lead to the gods' abandonment of the planet.

In fear of these violent creatures (humans), Chameleon retreats to the trees, where he continues to live to this day. The animals flee for their lives to the wild areas, the jungles, and the forests. Disgusted and heartbroken by the acts of these humans, whom he unleashed upon the world, Mulungu retreats from the earth with the aid of the Spider. Spider spins a ladder to the heavens with his web. The gods who lived on Earth ascended this ladder, after which it was destroyed and humans were forever abandoned by them.

The Unreachable Sun (Barotse)

The creation god of the Barotse (also called Lozi) people of Africa is called Nyambi. Nyambi is a typical creation god, having brought into existence all the living things during his time on Earth in the first days. Nyambi first lived on the planet along with his wife, Nasilele. One of the last (if not *the* last; the myth is not specific) creatures Nyambi creates is Kamonu, the first man. Kamonu learns by observing Nyambi, as a son mimicking the actions of his father.

Sword and Man

Though the spear can be seen as a phallic symbol, it is also symbolic of the often-destructive nature of human beings. Here, the fact that Kamonu creates a weapon with the skills he is taught is significant because it illustrates how man's natural inclinations toward violence go against the will of god(s). Although the god in this myth (Nyambi) creates life and the means to sustain it, Man (Kamonu) creates the first weapon, which is meant only to destroy life, instill fear in others, carry out wars, and/or commit murder.

Kamonu observes Nyambi forging steel, and thereby learns to do so as well. However, instead of creating farming tools with this skill, Kamonu creates a weapon (a spear). He kills an antelope and is temporarily banished for his actions. He is later allowed back and encouraged by Nyambi to cultivate the earth by farming. He does so for a time but later resorts back to violence, killing buffaloes and elands that enter his garden. Nyambi and the other gods abandon him, but on Earth Kamonu keeps finding ways to follow them. Finally, Spider creates a ladder which Nyambi and the other gods ascend, leaving Earth and the killer, Kamonu, behind forever. Kamonu tries to reach them by building a tower to Heaven (similar to the Old Testament story of Babel), but fails. In the end, he is left to view Nyambi from afar, now in a different form as the unreachable sun.

The Vomiting Creator (Bushongo)

Bumba is the creation god of the Bushongo (also called Bakuba) people of Zaire, who reside along the Congo River. Bumba's act of creation is not quite voluntary. In the dark void that is the beginning, he is all that exists until one day he begins heaving and retching.

First, Bumba vomits up the sun. The waters recede in the heat, exposing the lands; next are the moon and stars. He continues to retch, and spews forth nine creatures—Pongo (eagle), Koy (leopard), Yo (small fish), Ganda (crocodile), Kono (tortoise), Tsetse (lightning), Nyanyi (white heron), Budi (goat), and a beetle. The last creatures to be vomited out are men, of which there are many. However, one is different. His skin is white, similar to Bumba's (this color is likely used as a symbol for the sun/light, or perhaps purity). The nine original creatures create others similar to themselves. Bumba now leaves the completion of the world to his three sons—Nyonye Ngana, Chonganda, and Chedi Bumba. Most of his sons' creations, however, are either useless, inadequate, or fatal (Nyonye Ngana, for example, is killed by his own creation, the white ants). Before leaving Earth in the hands of men, Bumba banishes Tsetse (the "firemaker" who is now lightning) into the sky and teaches humans how to make fire.

The Son of Mebe'e (Bulu)

The creation myth of the Bulu people of the Cameroons is similar to some Native American myths in that it attempts to explain through myth the plight of the African blacks under occupying whites (first the Germans, then the French and British).

Although Mebe'e (He who bears the world) is the supreme god of the Bulu, his son Zambe is credited with the creation of Man, the chimpanzee, and the gorilla. These three creatures were originally the same, and each were given divine gifts by Zambe and left to sit by a fire.

Of Man, one is black and one white. Both are given a book of knowledge by Zambe. White man's eyes are irritated by the fire and smoke. However, he cherishes and protects his book. Black man stirs the fire, but neglects his book. Chimp and Gorilla both abandon their gifts to climb for fruit. When Zambe returns, he disfigures Chimp and Gorilla and banishes them to the forests for neglecting their gifts. Black man, who neglected his book, is cursed to be deprived of knowledge and forced to work and toil all his days. White man, the only one of the group to protect and care for his gift, is blessed with knowledge and understanding. Because he was bothered by the fire, he is made to no longer need it (which is why blacks had to warm themselves at fires while whites seemed to not need to).

Fathers of the East

Some of the most complex, philosophical primal myths come to us from the regions of India and Asia. In these myths, it is not unusual for more than one story or theory about the creation to be presented within one text. However, for the sake of brevity, the more original of these primal myths is provided.

Purusha's Sacrifice (Indian)

The *Rig-Veda* is a collection of more than 1,000 religious hymns that were written down in Sanskrit sometime between 2000 and 900 B.C.E. The tenth book of the *Rig-Veda* explains how the body of Purusha (meaning primal man), which has a thousand eyes and feet, is sacrificially used to make up creation. Three quarters of his body is used to make up the immortal world of the heavens, while one quarter is used to construct the planets along with the social classes, creatures, plants, and animals that exist on those planets.

Avoiding the Labyrinth

In other religious texts of the Hindu Dharma religion of India, it is basically understood that *Brahma* is responsible for the creation. Brahma is the chief deity of the Hindu trinity of the Trimurti godhead, which consists of Brahma (the creator), Vishnu (the sustainer), and Shiva (the destroyer).

The Myth of P'an Ku (Chinese)

As in a majority of creation myths, the Chinese assert that in the beginning there was only a void of chaos, a *"no-thing."* From this void, the myth explains, arises a cosmic egg from which is born the powerful and fertile god P'an Ku. This primal god is described as four times the size of a normal man, completely covered with hair. Rising out from his head are two immense horns. From his upper jaw protrudes a pair of long and thick tusks. In his hands is an *adze* (a set of tools similar to a hammer and chisel). With these tools P'an Ku sculpts out the world, bringing order from chaos in the way that a sculptor creates a polished form from a rough stone.

Immortal Words

Do not confuse the word **"no-thing"** with the English term "nothing." Though similar in meaning, they are not the same. No-thing means that no thing yet existed as it does now. However, existence existed, so to speak, within the chaotic void. Therefore, no-thing cannot be the same as nothing, because even for there to be a void would be "something."

P'an Ku first creates the world and its inhabitants. He then instructs mankind in skills that will ensure survival. However, similar to the sacrifice of Purusha in the *Rig-Veda*, the world is not whole until he dies. Through his death and the sacrifice of his physical self, his creation is finally made perfect.

Avoiding the Labyrinth

In Western myths, horned beings are often considered evil or demonic. However, in Chinese tales, horns are associated with magical or supernatural powers. Therefore, although these horns are often symbolic of great power, the wielder of this power is not necessarily an evil force or being.

The Creators of the Kami

Nihongi means "Chronicle of Japan," and is the official religious text of Shinto, the national religion of Japan, which worships the sanctity and power of the natural world and the deified personifications who represent that world. Perhaps due to Chinese influence, the *Nihongi* states that in the beginning is a chaotic void of no-thing. This void, however, is created by the heavens and fashioned into a cosmic egg (again bearing similarity to the Chinese P'an Ku myth). This egg separates the heavens (by drawing out the purest parts) from the newly formed Earth (made up of impure parts).

A total of eight deities are formed by the operations of the heavens, both male and female. The two gods most involved in the creation myth of Japan are Izanagi no Mikoto (male-who-invites) and Izanami no Mikoto (female-who-invites). Seeing that there is no land below them, they thrust the jeweled spear of Heaven into the ocean. As the spear was removed, the brine at its tip dripped off and solidified into an island called Ono-goro-jima (the spontaneously-solidified-island). This creation causes Izanagi and Izanami to decide to become husband and wife and to create further lands and countries. Izanagi turns left and Izanami right. They encircle the globe and meet on the other side. Upon meeting, Izanami speaks to her husband first. It displeases him that she speaks before him, so they repeat the process and this time Izanagi speaks first. This somewhat ritualistic encounter leads to their first intercourse. From their consummation are born the other islands of Japan. Lastly, they create a lesser order of deities, known as *Kami*, from which many of the living things of the earth are born.

The Kojiki

The *Kojiki* actually predates the *Nihongi*, but was compiled less than a decade before by Yasumaro Futo. It contains the earliest writings of the Shinto religion and also appears to have been heavily influenced by Chinese ideas. In the chaos that is the beginning, Heaven and Earth separate. This text refers to the three deities of creation's beginnings (who are also named in the *Nihongi*)—Kuni-toko-tachi, Kuni no sa-tsuchi, and Toyo-kumu-nu (all the Mikoto class of deity). However, as in the *Nihongi*, the act of creating the lands and life is credited to the divine couple of Izanami and Inanagi, who were created by these first three deities.

The Lords of Europe

Among European myths, perhaps the most well known are those produced by the ancient Greeks and the Roman Empire. However, Europe is a continent rich with many diverse cultures, each with its own mythological tradition.

Sons of Light and Darkness (Celtic)

Heaven and Earth, according to the Celts, were originally giants. Heaven lies upon Earth in copulation, from which numerous offspring are born—some are gods (beings of light or "sons of Heaven") while others are gigantic Titans (beings of dark or "sons of Earth"). Between these children of polar opposites, there comes to be much animosity. With Heaven and Earth so close together, their children soon became cramped and uncomfortable. Soon, one of the Titans murdered his father, used the world-giant's mutilated corpse to create the firmament, and crowned himself king of the Titans. The bright god beings refused to allow him to rule over them, and the Titan king's own son (who had been unexplainably born as a being of light) led the armies of the bright gods against him. The Titan king was defeated and left to wander creation alone.

Avoiding the Labyrinth

The Titans that are mentioned here should not be confused with the Titans of Greco-Roman/classical mythology. In this case, the word Titan is used to name the beings of darkness that were the patricidal sons of Earth. These Titans are not the sons of *Kaos/Chaos* (or Gaia and Uranus) told of in classic Greek and Roman myths.

As a result of the earth world–giant's murder and mutilation, the creation was struck with a great deluge. With the aid of one of the Titans, a single pair of humans survives in a special ship he builds for them. After the flood, a new king is appointed for the gods—Father Sky. In the winter and at night, the king of the Titans (the same who built the ship to save humankind and believed by some to be the same who murdered Father Earth) reigns until he does battle with the coming of the bright Father Sky. He is always defeated by Father Sky, which is why darkness always gives way to light and winter to summer. On only one occasion is it written that the Titan almost triumphed over Father Sky, terribly wounding him. However, the gods employ the aid of the great spearman, Sun-hero, who was the son of a wise man. This alliance between the Sun-hero and the gods brought an end to the bright gods' great cruelty and animosity toward man (because man was seen as a creation of the Titans, sons of Earth).

Sons of Borr

In the beginning there is only Ymir, the ice giant (from whose blood the race of dwarves is later created), overlooking a great and grassless void. Then the god Borr

Yggdrasil is a great ash tree that grows through and thus connects the realms of Niflheim (underworld ruled by Hel, goddess of death), Midgarth (land of men), Utgard (land of elves and giants), and Asgard (realm of the gods). There are a variety of activities constantly taking place along different parts of this tree, many of which are covered throughout this book.

and his wife Bestla create sons, the sky gods. Among them, three are primarily responsible for the creation of humankind—Odin, Lodun, and Honir. The generation of Odin (the sons of Borr) shapes and fashions Midgarth (also said Midgard, or "middle Earth"). The earth was fashioned when Odin and his siblings killed and dismembered Ymir, and then used his corpse as the material of creation.

The myth, which claims to be the words of the priestess Vala, states that the gods were content and productive until the arrival of the fates, three daughters from Jotunheim (the race of giants) who take up residence at the roots of *Yggdrasil*, the World Tree.

Ovid's Metamorphosis

The creator god of Ovid, who wrote a collection of myths titled *Metamorphoses*, is unnamed. It states that in the beginning there was only the potential for existence, but all the forces and energies of existence were unbalanced and therefore chaotically at war. This chaos is brought to order when the anonymous "God, or kindlier nature" spontaneously appears and brings order out of chaos, creating the universe and living creatures, including mankind.

Orphic Creation Myth

The Orphic tradition is a variation of the Olympian religion of Homer that sprang up sometime between 600 and 500 B.C.E. somewhat as a result of heavy influences from the religious ideas of the Iranians. The Orphic myth states that, in the beginning, Zurvan, the god of time, created a silver egg. From this egg emerges Phanes-Dionysus, an androgynous god who bears the seeds of all which is later created, including other gods.

Avoiding the Labyrinth

Phanes-Dionysus should not be confused with Dionysus, the Olympian god of wine and madness. Though associated in name, they are not one and the same god and, in fact, the myths surrounding them are quite different. The Olympian Dionysus was not a primal god.

Phanes-Dionysus first begets Nyx (Night). With her, he then creates Gaea (Earth), Uranus (Heaven), and Cronos. First, Uranus is lord of the world, but later is replaced by Cronos.

Creation in the Cradle of Civilization

The Middle East is often referred to as "The Cradle of Civilization." This title is due to the fact that the most ancient civilized societies known were born in this region of the world, and the ideas and advancements of these cultures spawned a new era in human history. In this section, you will find myths from the civilizations of the Sumerians, Babylonians (located in what is now called Iraq), Assyrians, Persians, Iranians, Israelites, Egyptians, and others.

The Old Testament

The creator god of the biblical Old Testament came to be called Jehovah, or Yahweh, by the Jews. His name is represented by the symbols YHVH. In the beginning, all was void until this god called out for there to be light. For seven days, YHVH fashions existence and the earth, creating the first man, Adam, on the sixth day. Eve, the first woman, is fashioned from Adam's rib.

Avoiding the Labyrinth

In some traditions, there is debate regarding the claim that Eve was the first and only woman created by God in Eden. In some Judaic myths, the first woman is Lilith, who is banished from paradise (Eden) for refusing to lie beneath Adam during sexual intercourse. There are also some myths that make brief mentions of a second female whom YHVH destroyed before finishing, as Adam was repulsed after witnessing her insides as YHVH formed her.

The Evolution of Atum (Egyptian)

Atum, the original creation god of Heliopolis (city of the sun), was portrayed as rising from the primordial waters to fashion order from chaos. By around 2400 B.C.E., when the Pyramid Texts were recorded in Hieroglyphics and the creation myth therefore was finally written down, Atum had come to be associated with Ra (or Re), the Egyptian sun god.

According to the myth, Ra rises from the waters of chaos in the form of Neb-er-tcher ("Lord-to-Limits," which is but one form that the sun god takes). This arrival into existence causes Atum/Ra/Neb-er-tcher (remember, all these names refer to the same god) to receive a fourth name, *Khepera*, meaning "He who comes into existence." In the original language of the myth, the word *Kheper* appears often and means "to come into being." Being the only existing entity, Ra masturbates in his hand, mating with himself. He pours the ejaculate into his mouth, using it as a womb of sorts, and (after a very long time) gives birth to his son Shu (god of air) and daughter Tefnut (goddess of moisture and order). These offspring somehow allow Ra to have two eyes (originally, Ra had but one eye), and his original eye (which behaves as an independent entity) is angry to find it has been replaced. To satisfy the original eye, Ra places it in his forehead. Seeing his new offspring, Ra weeps and from his tears are created men and women. The union of Shu and Tefnut (basically, air and water) gives birth to Seb (Earth) and Nut (Sky), who later become the parents of the Egyptian gods Osiris, Isis, Horus, and Set.

The Rise of Ptah

Around 3000 B.C.E., the ruler Menes united Egypt, creating a new capital city in Memphis (away from Heliopolis, the city of the sun that is associated with Atum/Ra). Menes favored a god named Ptah (who up until this time was simply the god of destiny/fate), a primarily Memphite deity, and therefore sought to destroy the sun god religion of Atum by replacing it with one of his own. He therefore gathered Ptah cult theologians and had a new myth written, one that was performed as a ritualistic play of sorts (with the ruler playing the role of Horus). This story claimed that it was Ptah, not Atum, who was the creator.

Myth and Metaphor _____

The alteration of myths and religious texts is not as uncommon as one might think. Throughout history this has been done for the purpose of political or monetary gain, or as a way to ease an assimilated culture's conversion to a new religion due to linguistic or perceptual conflicts. For example, in Christianity, the word "hell" was adopted to refer to a biblical underworld of damnation. However, as you might already know, "Hel" was the name of the Nordic goddess of death who ruled the underworld beneath Yggdrasil. The belief that hell is a purely biblical term is a common misconception.

In this new creation tale, Atum (the original creator god) was said to be the son of Ptah, and therefore lesser in power and standing. In contrast to Ra's act of masturbation, Ptah must only speak and, by his words, the universe and all things that exist come into order. The Ptah cult also does its best to both integrate and usurp the god Osiris (quite a popular god at the time) into the myth by claiming that this god had drowned long ago and his body was buried in the city of Memphis.

The Rise and Fall of Apsu (Babylonian)

In the Babylonian creation epic of the *Enuma Elish*, the god Apsu exists in the sweet waters of primordial chaos while the goddess Tiamat exists in the bitter waters. Lying together amongst chaos, they beget the divine entities of creation (the first four of which are coupled polar opposites)—Lahmu and Lahamu (silt and sludge), Anshar and Kishar (Sky and Earth), Anu (god of Heaven and authority), and Nudimmud, also called Ea (god of the waters and wisdom). As these divine offspring grew, they began to form order out of chaos. They also began to rebel against their parents, Apsu and Tiamat.

Mummu (the mists and clouds and patron entity of chaos) councils Apsu, telling him that something must be done to bring down his rebellious offspring (who are a threat to him, because they are bringers of chaos). He, Apsu, and Tiamat conspired to kill the young gods. Tiamat, however, is overcome with maternal love for her children, and backs out of the plan, causing it to fail. In the end, Ea (Nudimmud) in his wisdom, slays his father Apsu and imprisons Mummu. More on this creation myth can be found in Chapter 2.

The Least You Need to Know

- Primal myths are the foundation upon which all future myths of a culture must stand.

- Primal myths are often treated as the most sacred.

- The occurrence of a great deluge or flood is a common theme of ancient myth, and is the result of either a prehistoric meteorological event or due to its significance as an archetype in the collective human psyche.

- A common motif in primal myth is the dismemberment and/or use of the body of a goddess to create the world.

Rebels, Usurpers, and Troublemakers

In This Chapter

◆ Why there were wars for domain over Heaven and Earth

◆ When latter-generation gods usurped the thrones of their parents

◆ What the difference is between rebel gods and rebellious characters

◆ Why these types of tales and characters are so prevalent in mythology

Just as people do, the gods have their own fair share of bad boys, murderous sons, rebellious daughters, pranksters, and troublemakers. Sometimes these gods get a bad reputation for being usurpers, thieves, and bringers of mischief. The truth, however, is that myths would often be rather boring without them. Mythology often works under the principle of balanced opposites. As you saw in Chapter 1, there was not order in the universe until there was first chaos. In similar fashion, for there to be peace there must be conflict. There can be no good without evil, no light without dark. For law and order to arise, there must first be lawlessness. These gods serve the chaotic side of this universal balance.

Coyote, Eagle, Rattlesnake, and Raven (Native American)

Four animal totem gods stand out prominently in American Indian myths as the bringers of misfortune and trouble—Coyote, Eagle, Rattlesnake, and Raven. They are often portrayed as rebellious and stubborn tricksters who, by their foolish actions, cause harm, not only to others but to themselves as well. Though often they are the bringers of mischief, they are also portrayed at times as the protectors of humankind and the guardians of creation. Although these animals are often portrayed as servants to trickster gods by many other cultures around the world, it is primarily the American Indians who portray them as gods.

The Trickster Coyote

Coyote is a common incarnation of the rebellious trickster god in the native myths of the Americas. For example, the Aztecs called their trickster god of music and the dance Huehuecoyotl. Although a trickster by nature, Coyote is also often seen playing the role of culture hero. He may be called Coyote, but he behaves and speaks like a human being. Often, this is attributed to the fact that the myths claim to have taken place in a time preceding humans, when the animal totems walked the earth in the same way people do now.

Coyote's behavior may be obnoxious and quite ridiculous, but his tales often serve to convey some sort of moral lesson. Simply put, Coyote is used as an example of how one should *not* behave. Tales are often told to children of Coyote's outlandish actions to show them what *not* to do. In this manner, Coyote (though troublesome in nature) actually serves to minimize discord within the tribes that tell of his exploits.

Eagle, Cunning Defender of Creation (Salinan)

Eagle, in a myth of the Salinan tribe of California, saved creation from destruction. The Old Woman of the Sea, enraged by her jealousy of Eagle's power, attacks creation with a flood that she pours from a great basket in which she kept the sea. Borrowing whiskers from the Puma, Eagle is able to lasso the basket, which ends the flood and causes the Old Woman of the Sea to die. Having defeated his jealous rival, Eagle then repairs the world by recreating the lands. He then fashions humans out of *barsalilo*, a special wood, after purifying himself with others in a sweat house. As with

Coyote, Eagle is a rebel in his defiant nature against the Old Woman of the Sea, as well as a culture hero through his defense of and gifts to all creation and humankind.

Rattlesnake, Enemy of Coyote (Maidu)

In one Maidu tribe myth, Coyote's power is limited when the order of the universe is set in place. He is made finite, and though he is able to fashion likenesses of humans, he cannot make them live and move. The Maidu refer to their creator as Earth-Initiate. He is generous and kind, giving humans an existence of prosperity that is free from hardship. They need only put out baskets every night, and each morning the baskets will be full of food. There was no sickness and no death. Then Coyote arrives and decides that people should have to work for their food, be stricken with illness, and eventually be fated to die. So Coyote convinces the people to hang up their baskets and have a foot race. Among the racers is Coyote's only son.

Meanwhile, one man named Ku'ksu remains in his abode. Soon, Rattlesnake comes to him and the two agree that Coyote's actions would ruin the perfect world of ease that they all enjoyed. After speaking with Ku'ksu, Rattlesnake hides himself to the side of the runners' path and is poised to strike. When Coyote's son passes, Rattlesnake strikes out with his poisonous fangs. The boy dies quickly. As a result of this first death, the perfection of man's easy life is indeed ruined. Life ceases to be easy and the people are made to speak different languages and ordered to separate into numerous tribes by Earth-Initiate. This division of language and location eventually leads to misunderstandings, disagreements, and the horror of tribal warfare.

A Bird of Ill-Omen (Kiowa and Crow)

Crow, according to the Kiowa tribe (and many others), did not always have black feathers. The Kiowa myth tells of how the Crow, when he had white feathers, ate the eyes of Snake. This act caused his feathers to turn black. One Sioux-related tribe came to be known as the Crow tribe due to a translation of a French word, *Absa'roke*, which means "crow" or "bird people." Crow is similar to Coyote in that most of the ills that befall him are of his own making.

Africa's Lords of Mischief

The rebellious, foolhardy, trickster types of gods are a prevalent motif among the myths of the African peoples. In such a difficult, harsh, and sometimes fatal environment, it is no wonder that this would be so. Mistakes could easily mean death to many of these tribes and, much as with Coyote and Crow in Native American myths, these mischievous god figures gave examples of both what one should not do and explanations of why such hardships befell them.

Cagn (Bushman)

Cagn is a primary character in many myths of the South African Bushman. He was the first being to be created by the gods, but is not human. In fact, he displays a number of godlike abilities such as basic creation powers (though he is not the Bushman creator god). He did not create existence, but did create many of the things within it by verbally calling them into being and ordering them into place. Cagn created the animals. Then, in true trickster fashion, he creates the traps and weapons with which humans can kill and eat them.

By giving a magic stick to his son, Cogaz, Cagn helps transform a tribe of large snakes into humans and they become his subjects thereafter. Later, Cagn sends Cogaz out to gather sticks for bow-making. Cogaz is assaulted by baboons. Their attack is motivated by the infuriating knowledge that these sticks are being used to make bows to kill them. Cogaz is beaten to death by the baboons because his father is asleep at the time and unable to protect him. Cagn later brings his son back to life and he continues to go on a number of adventures and misadventures.

Sword and Man

The giving of a magic stick to Cogaz by Cagn could be viewed as symbolic of a father passing on to his son the ability to procreate and reproduce. When the snakes are touched by the stick, they become human. By popping out of their snakeskin, the phallic (masculine) nature of the snake is transformed into a womb (feminine).

Hat of Two Colors (Yoruban)

The Yoruba peoples of West Africa have a trickster god named Eshu. He is the messenger to the gods, both valued and despised for his mischievous ways, generosity, and cruel method of teaching people a lesson. Eshu is considered the most important of the four warrior gods of the Yoruba, called the Orisa (or Orisha).

The trickster Eshu often acts as a mentor, bringing both elation and misery to his students. One myth tells of a mischievous journey where Eshu wore a large, tall hat that had one red side and one white side. He passes between two friends who are walking side-by-side. One friend sees only the white side of the hat, while the other sees only the red side. Later, the two friends begin talking to one another about the man in the hat who passed between them. One claims the man wore a white hat, while the other argues that it had been red. The argument turns to shouting, and shouting soon comes to blows. Each man screams his insistence that he is right about the color of the hat. Eshu is delighted at the mayhem he has caused. After the two poor men have beaten each other into bloody and exhausted pulps, Eshu approaches them and reveals that his hat is both red and white. Both men were right … and both men were very, very wrong. Eshu found joy in knowing that men would turn to violence over something as mundane as the color of a man's hat.

King of Story (West African)

Another example of the cultural hero trickster is Anansi of West African mythology. In some myths, Anansi discovers how to cause rain to douse fires, and reveals this wisdom to the world after first attempting to keep it to himself. The most popular Anansi myth among the majority of African cultures tells of how Anansi became the King of Story. In the myth, he approaches the Sky God (the African equivalent of Zeus in that he is lord of all gods) and requests to be crowned King of Story.

The Sky God gives Anansi a seemingly impossible task, hoping to satisfy his request without actually granting it. He tells Anansi if he is able to capture a jaguar with dagger-teeth, hornets with stingers of fire, and a fairy never seen by the eyes of men, then he would grant him the title King of Story. Anansi sets out to accomplish his mission. He soon captures the jaguar, whom he persuades to play a fake game that requires the predatory cat to be bound. He tricks the fire hornets into believing it is raining and tells them to take shelter in a large gourd. Lastly, he tricks the fairy never seen by the eyes of men by trapping it with sticky tar. He brings these trophies back to the Sky God, who has no choice but to crown Anansi King of Story.

Rebels of the West

The rebels of Western myths, as with their counterparts, cause trouble and make mischief while still serving a purpose in the grander scheme of things. Their purpose may be to benefit man, despite the fact that they face opposition from other gods for such actions; they may act as allies to other, more heroic deity figures; or they may serve as a monkey wrench thrown into the plans of men as divine retribution for the sins of their pasts.

The Bringer of Fire (Greco-Roman)

Perhaps one of the most widely recognized rebel gods of classical Western mythology is Prometheus. Although he did a number of things to the benefit of humankind (such as the creation of human beings!), the deed for which he continues to be most familiar is bringing knowledge of fire to Earth. He creates humans out of mud (a common method for human creation in many myths) while another god, Epimetheus, makes the animals. The goddess Athena gives humans souls.

Zeus lays out a limited number of gifts to be bestowed upon all living things these two gods create. Unfortunately, while Prometheus is carefully shaping the humans, Epimetheus uses nearly all of the most precious gifts, bestowing them upon the beasts (which is why certain animals have better hearing, keener eyesight, or faster legs than humans do). Prometheus, feeling that humans are being shortchanged, goes to Zeus to ask for a special gift for the humans … fire. Zeus refuses. Fire is reserved for the gods alone, lest it make humans too powerful. Prometheus defiantly steals some fire from Zeus' hearth and takes it to the humans. Many humans are saved from the winter cold and the sharp jaws of nocturnal predators by this stolen gift.

As punishment for his disobedience, Zeus has Prometheus chained to a rock. Every day, an eagle (though, in some versions, it's a vulture) flies down, pecks into his side, and begins devouring his liver. At night the eagle flies away, and Prometheus's liver regenerates, only to be devoured again the next day. In one of the myths of Hercules, half-god son of Zeus, he shoots the liver-eating eagle/vulture in return for information Prometheus has on the location of certain sacred apples. The torturous bird slain, Prometheus is released and allowed to return to Olympus.

Loki, Brother Discord (Nordic)

Loki is the brother of the Norse god Odin (by oath more than blood), and quite the troublemaker. He is son of the giant Farbauti and the giantess Laufey. The Aesir gods treat him as one of their own, though they are often at odds with him due to his troublesome nature. He is associated with the element of fire and has the ability to fly and change into a number of different types of animals. He can even change his *sex!* He is resourceful in his tricks, but also a culture hero, much as the tricksters you've already seen. Despite his annoying behavior, he is valued because he is partly responsible for the magnificent war hammer that was bestowed upon Thor, Odin's son. He was also the one who rebuilt the walls of Asgard. Of course, often he was only being useful because he was the one who caused the destruction in the first place. Loki's tricks grow more malicious, and over time the Aesir gods find it more difficult to control him. Of course, because he is also somewhat of a close compatriot of the god Odin, they leave him alone.

> ### Sword and Man
>
> Loki slays Balder by making a dart out of mistletoe. Myth states that all plants (including trees and, therefore, wood) had taken an oath never to harm Balder … all but the mistletoe. Even worse, Loki convinces Hodr (Balder's blind brother) to throw the dart that kills him. Mistletoe was also thought by some cultures to have certain mystical properties.

However, one of Loki's pranks results in the death of Balder—god of light and one of Odin's most beloved sons. Realizing enough is enough, the gods decide that something must be done. Even Odin, a longtime friend of Loki, agrees. Adding insult to injury, Loki (disguised as an old woman giant) refuses to weep for Balder even after the goddess Hel agrees to return him from death if *everyone* in the world weeps for him.

The Aesir gods' punishment comes down hard on Loki, who has by this point become more like a demon of evil (no longer just a trickster with a playful nature). They chain Loki to three enormous boulders: one under his shoulders, one under his knees, and the third under his groin. This keeps him prone and weighted down so that he might do no more harm. However, the myth also says that one day Loki will break free during the *Ragnarok* and lead the giants in war against the gods.

> ### Immortal Words
>
> Ragnarok is the Norse version of Armageddon. The first stages of the Ragnarok cycle are said to have been put in motion by Loki's murder of Balder.

Against the Rising Sun

In India and China, the monkey is often portrayed as the stubborn and arrogant trickster. The Japanese Shinto god of mischief is the anarchy-prone, sea-and-storm god Susanowo (also, Susano-o). In Hindu Dharma, the most mischief-causing god is a beloved musician named Narada. These characters have become well known for bringing discord to both the gods and people of the Land of the Rising Sun.

The Monkey King

Sun Wu Kong is the Chinese name for "Monkey King," as he has come to be referred to in the West. Chinese author Wu Ch'eng-en, at a time when the Chinese dynasty had all but outlawed new ideas, chose to write down the exploits of the Monkey King in a book called *Journey to the West*, sometimes referred to by Westerners as simply *Monkey* or *Monkey King*. Sun Wu Kong is perhaps the most unique rebellion figure in Asian mythology, primarily because he was not born a god. Instead, he was born of a stone egg that had been in existence since the dawn of time. He emerges and bows to the four corners of the earth. From this point forward, Monkey proves to be a handful. He quickly designates himself king of the monkeys and, for a time, he is happy. Soon, however, Monkey becomes discontent in the knowledge that he will continue to grow old and eventually die.

Monkey leaves his subjects and embarks on a series of adventures to ensure his immortality. First he meets a Tao Patriarch, who teaches him the arts of magic and shape shifting. Eventually, however, the Patriarch banishes Monkey for being arrogant. Next, he travels to the realms of the Ocean Dragon Kings, from whom he rather rudely and meanly acquires an enchanted cudgel as well as a magical hat, shoes, and clothes. Next he succeeds in becoming immortal by erasing his own name (and those of all his original monkey subjects) from the Book of Life and Death. Now immortal, he travels into the Kingdom of Heaven, domain of the great Jade Emperor, and demands to be given a god's title. Unable to kill him, he is given a title and heavenly position (without pay) to guard the Jade Emperor's Sacred Peaches (which grant power and immortality). He fails miserably at this task when he eats the peaches, making himself even stronger and more secure in his immortality. He also crashes the Jade Emperor's banquet hall and drinks all the wine and food, along with a special elixir made by Lao Tsu. Having caused such trouble, Monkey flees Heaven and is pursued by the armies of the Jade Emperor.

This rebellious monkey-turned-god continues to run amok until he is stopped by the lord Buddha himself. He tricks Monkey by challenging him to jump across his hand. Monkey, in his arrogance, attempts to jump across the world. When he lands, he sees five pillars. He urinates on one and writes his name on another. Upon returning, Buddha informs him that he failed and holds up his hand for Monkey to see. On one finger is written Monkey's name, and another finger smells of urine. Monkey realizes that during his great leap, he never left the boundaries of Buddha's palm. Monkey must concede defeat and Buddha has him trapped under a mountain and bound there with a special incantation for a number of centuries, forcing him to meditate and read

Buddhist texts in an attempt to stem the wild Monkey's uncontrollably rebellious and arrogant nature. Although this helps, Monkey continues to be rebellious and arrogant (even now) ... he is just a bit wiser and slightly less of a troublemaker. Later, as penance, Monkey serves as bodyguard to the Buddhist pilgrim Tripitaka on his journey to the West to retrieve the sacred scrolls of the Buddha. He does so with the aid of two other penitent creatures—Pigsy, a reformed cannibal with a bottomless stomach; and Sandy, a fish spirit with a *very* absent sense of humor.

This Chinese version most likely originated from the tale of the Monkey in a collection of Buddhist fables entitled *The Jataka* (or *Jatarka*) *Tales*.

Susanowo

In the Japanese religion of Shinto, one of the most troublesome gods was Susanowo, mischievous god of storms and the sea. Born from the nose of Izanagi (see Chapter 1 for more information on Izanagi), he has the sea as his domain. His sister and consort is Amaterasu, goddess of the sun. Susanowo is considered primarily evil in nature. However, he has also been known to be brave in addition to being a reckless and hot-headed anarchist.

Susanowo strikes both sea and land with storms, turning the sky black. Doing this too often, however, brings down the fury of the 8 million deities upon him, the single title for the many kami gods of Shinto. Susanowo's constant antagonizing of the kami, especially Amaterasu, bring about his downfall. As punishment for being such a nuisance, Susanowo is stripped of his mighty beard and thick, clawlike fingernails. He is separated from all that he owns and banished from the realm of the gods. There are many myths about his time wandering the earth after his banishment. None of these myths is more well known in Shinto than Susanowo's slaying of an eight-headed snake called *Koshi* (or *Yamata-no-Orochi*; see Chapter 17). After tearing this monster to ribbons, he discovers a powerful sword, *Kusanagi-no-Tsurugi*, within its belly. Susanowo, in his many adventures, is also credited in Shinto myth with the Japanese conquest of Korea. Later Susanowo has a son, Okuni-Nushi, who turns out to be a reckless troublemaker (like father, like son). Eventually, Okuni-Nushi tricks his father out of his possession of the *Kusanagi-no-Tsurugi*.

Immortal Words

Kusanagi-no-Tsurugi is the Japanese title for a magical sword, which translates as "blade of cutting grass."

Gossiper of the Gods (Hindu)

Narada is a beautiful and beloved musician among the gods of Hindu Dharma mythology. In fact, he is loved by all who are in existence—gods, demons, and men alike. However, he has one quite troublesome vice … he talks too much when he should not, about things of which he should not speak. His loose tongue often reveals the truths and secrets of the gods and demons to the opposition, telling demon secrets to the gods and divine secrets to demons. As these two sides are natural enemies, one can imagine the amount of trouble that Narada's careless disclosures can cause.

Rebel Children

In the myths of the Middle and Near East, gods are often challenged by their children. Sometimes, they prevail. Other times, they are murdered by their patricidal offspring. Often, such myths are thought of as archetypal representations of the tumultuous relationship between fathers and adolescent sons, parents and children who are nearing adulthood. These relationships mirror, though on a far grander scale, the various pitfalls that can occur in human familial relationships.

A War in Heaven (Judaic)

Lucifer, technically, is not and has never been a god, so to speak. At least, his role in the Judaic tradition has never been on par with the one YHVH god of this monotheistic religion. Lucifer is created by YHVH as the most beautiful and powerful of all angels—his name means "light bringer," but he is also referred to as "The Morning Star." Despite being blessed above all other angels, Lucifer becomes displeased with God and his creation. Some myths say he grew jealous of humans after YHVH showed them favor by giving them souls.

Avoiding the Labyrinth _____

One common misconception is that Lucifer is cast into hell after losing the war in Heaven. In fact, the word "hell" was added to the Christian Bible during the Christianization of Europe (which, obviously, was quite some time after the original myth had been written down). Hel, in fact, is the name of the Norse goddess of death who rules over the underworld. The myth states that Lucifer is, in fact, given domain over the realm of Earth. When you consider that Lucifer's home up until this point has been the blissful and perfect realm of Heaven, being banished to the painful and terrible realm of physical reality would be the most cruel punishment imaginable.

Lucifer gathers an army of rebels, sparking a civil war between the angelic ranks of Heaven. YHVH, seeing this, appoints the archangel Michael as General of Angels. Michael and the loyal angels battle Lucifer's rebels and defeat them. As a result, Lucifer and his compatriots are cast down from Heaven into the realm of Earth.

The Son Who Would Be King (Babylonian)

After slaying his father Apsu (see Chapter 1), Ea takes Damkina as his wife and they give birth to a son, Marduk, who is exceedingly strong. He has four eyes that see all and flash violently with light. His four ears hear all, and a tongue of fire lashes from his mouth. (A born leader and warrior, to be sure.)

Tiamat, you will remember, retreated from her husband's plan to kill their children. However, she apparently had not expected any of her children to kill Apsu. She becomes enraged by the murder of her husband, and creates a demonic creature named Kingu, whom she marries and appoints Supreme Commander of Wars. This act robs her son Anu of the authority originally given to him, as she replaces him in station with Kingu. She then begins to birth a new generation of monstrous children—the Worm, Dragon, Mad Dog, and Man Scorpion, to name just a few—with whom she intends to exact revenge on Ea and his siblings.

Among the children of Apsu, none succeed in stopping the advancing horde of their mother's new brood, who are protected by her magic and led into battle by the terrible Kingu. Even Anu and Nudimmud (Marduk's uncles) fail in the face of such terror.

Marduk steps forward, offering to lead them into battle against Tiamat, Kingu, and their army of abominations. He asks for one thing in return—to be proclaimed superior to the other gods and ruler of all. The other gods concede to his request; Marduk is quickly crowned and a throne is created. His reward fulfilled, Marduk leads the other gods (now his subjects) into battle and slays Tiamat by crushing her skull with a war hammer.

Myth and Metaphor

Marduk, as mentioned in the following section, was the first King of Babylon. This myth was likely conscripted as a way to establish the legitimacy of Marduk's kingship as well as to validate his divine authority.

During the battle, the victorious children of Apsu and Tiamat capture Kingu and his monstrous compatriots. Using Tiamat's corpse, Marduk puts into order all that is still in chaos. He creates and places the world, stars, clouds, and all things in the cosmos. However, he still feels something is needed and decides to create Man. Marduk and his siblings know that at least one kindred (a child of Tiamat) will have to be sacrificed to create this kind of life. They confront those captured by Marduk, demanding to know which of them instigated their mother into such behavior. All captives point the finger at their brother, Kingu. The victorious gods hold Kingu down and slice open his arteries. From his sacrificial blood, humans are created so that they might act as servants to the gods. This final creation task accomplished, Marduk gives each god a specific task, purpose, or station for which they are to be responsible. He then creates the majestic city of Babylon. Marduk, son of Ea, by his brave deeds, becomes Lord of Gods and King of Babylon.

The Least You Need to Know

- Ancient/obsolete gods are often replaced with new gods in myth by being killed or usurped by their own offspring.

- The trickster in myth is not purely problematic, and often serves a secondary role of culture hero.

- Troublesome and foolish gods are often used in myth to convey examples of how not to behave and what not to do.

- Though he is not a god by definition, the fallen angel Lucifer meets the criteria of a troublesome spiritual entity.

- Narada is a unique god among those of this chapter, as he is loved by all for his beauty and musical skills despite the trouble he causes.

Gods Among Us

In This Chapter

- ◆ When and why gods take human form
- ◆ What Messianic figures are and why they are mortal
- ◆ Why half-god heroes are not considered avatars
- ◆ Why there are avatars versus incarnate gods

A god who walks among us in human/physical form *chooses* to do so. There are times when it is necessary for a divine being to enter physical reality in the body of a mortal. These gods often transubstantiate (change from nonphysical/spiritual to physical form) or incarnate (arrange to be born as infants to human mothers) so that they may reach our plane of existence. Sometimes these gods come among us through ritualistic invocations that result in a type of divine possession, whereby a god enters the body of a human host. Though they often exhibit inhuman strength, divine wisdom, and supernatural abilities, they are *not* immortal (in the physical sense, anyway). If these gods were made to live in the physical realm forever, it would prevent them from returning to their rightful places in the realms of ascension. These gods have come to right wrongs, restore law and order, convey wisdom, and/or save humankind from destruction (often, this means saving us from ourselves).

Half-gods/part-gods are not included in this chapter (see Chapter 9). A half-god is born with godlike qualities as a result of genetic pairing. They have no choice in this, as they have no control over the nature of their births. Often, half-gods have tormented lives that end in tragic deaths.

Gods, Chiefs, and Men

Often, in the myths of the native peoples of South America, tribal leaders were deified. This was likely done to validate authority and to foster a healthy fear of a divine coercive power. The laws of the leaders were the laws of a god, and therefore needed to be followed to avoid the wrath of divine retribution. However, in cases such as those provided in the following sections, this deification continued after their deaths.

Traveling God of Peru (Incan)

Viracocha's full Incan name is quite a mouthful, Con-Ticc-Viracocha-pachayachachic. He was the creator as well as the most powerful god of the Peruvian Inca. In typical creator god fashion, Viracocha once flooded the earth to destroy the first peoples, who are said to have been a race of giants. When the waters receded, he created a new race of humans that continues to inhabit the world. Though a creator god, he is very much a god that is said to have walked among humankind.

At the height of the Incan Empire (around 1200 to 1400 C.E.), it is said that Viracocha walked among the peoples of what is now Peru. As he traveled from village to village, Viracocha spread wisdom and created moral as well as social order. Viracocha was the greatest of teachers to the Incans, bringing them the arts of agriculture, industry, song, and language.

King of Sharks (Hawaiian)

Nanaue, the Shark King (or Shark Man), is a god that lived among the people of Hawaii. From the ocean, the Shark King catches sight of a gorgeous maiden. As she walks away, he quickly transforms himself into a human man so that he might follow her. He is adorned with a cape of feathers, the apparel of a king.

Upon his arrival, the people are pleased to welcome the king of a foreign people and they hold a lavish luau in his honor. As the young men begin to play their games, the Shark King joins in. He is the victor of every game, impressing the girl of his desires.

Soon, the two are married and move into a house near a waterfall. When the girl becomes pregnant, the Shark King dives to the bottom of the waterfall's pool every single day, creating a special place that will be of future use to his unborn son.

Sadly, just before the child's birth, the Shark King must return to his ocean kingdom. Before leaving, he gives strict instructions to his wife—his feathered cape must always be kept around the boy's shoulders. After the boy is born, the girl realizes why her absent husband had instructed her to do this. On the boy's back is a mark in the shape of a shark's mouth. This mark gives the only clue the girl needs to realize the truth of her husband's identity. Later, the Shark King's son, who is named Nanave, will have his own trials to face in the world of men (see Chapter 9).

Walking Gods of Africa

In Africa, it was not uncommon for the king of a tribe to be worshipped and spoken of as a god. To list all such kings would require a book all its own. The examples provided in the next section, from the Baganda and Uganda of Africa, originate from observations written down in Sir James Frazer's book *The Golden Bough*.

Lubare

Sir James Frazer was one of the first scholars in the English-speaking world to write about the god Lubare of the Baganda tribe. In his writings, Frazer told of how the Baganda tribe of Central Africa worshipped a god that they believed inhabited Lake Nyanza. The Baganda believed that this god sometimes inhabited the body of a man or woman. In such a form, the incarnate god was treated with both fear and reverence by everyone in the tribe, including the king and tribal chiefs. When this divine possession occurred, the human vessel was seen as being the god. For safety and to show honor to the possessed individual, he or she would be taken about a mile and a half from the lake, and resided there until the next new moon by when the god would have to complete the fulfillment of his sacred duties. Once the crescent moon appeared in the sky, the king and all his subjects were at the command of the divinely possessed individual, which they called a *Lubare* (god). A Lubare was given absolute power in a number of tribal matters between the time of the crescent and new moon—spiritual rituals, decisions of war and peace, and changes or additions to tribal policy.

God in the Priests of Uganda

In Uganda, there was no stated belief in the transubstantiation of gods from spiritual to physical form. Instead, a god would be invoked by a priest until the spirit of the divine possessed his body. Sir Frazer wrote of this in his work *The Golden Bough:* "In Uganda the priest, in order to be inspired by his god, smokes a pipe of tobacco fiercely till he works himself into a frenzy; the loud excited tones in which he then talks are recognized as the voice of the god speaking through him."

Living Gods of the West

In the West, the gods who came to Earth are often the cause of pregnancy. In the ancient Western mind, the gods had the same carnal needs as human men, so they often ventured into the physical realm to fulfill their lustful desires with human women. As you will see in Chapter 9, these godly "one-night stands" are responsible for some of mythology's greatest heroes … as well as some of its greatest abominations.

Priestesses of Apollo

At the Oracle of Delphi, Apollo was said to inhabit the bodies of Apollonian priestesses. Because he was, among other things, the God of Truth, he never spoke deceitfully. As a result, it was believed that Apollonian priestesses would also speak only the truth, and people came from all over the civilized world to consult the priestess oracles of Apollo.

The Many Faces of Zeus

Zeus might be the first mythological "sex addict," coming to Earth to have sex with its most beautiful women anytime the mood struck him. Unfortunately for Zeus as well as the women he seduced or raped, his wife Hera became a vengeful and bitter goddess as a result of his extramarital exploits. Two particular sexual dominations of Zeus are the most well known.

Europa is the daughter of King Agenor of Phoenicia, and said to be beautiful beyond measure. One day, as she is gathering flowers near the water's edge, Zeus catches sight of her. He transforms himself into a bull and descends to Earth. He then kidnaps Europa by throwing her on his back (still in the form of a bull) and carrying her across the ocean to the Greek island of Crete, where he rapes the girl. After he's had his fill of Europa, Zeus leaves her in Crete. Before he leaves, Europa gives birth to three half-god sons. She later marries Aserius, King of Crete, who adopts her sons as his own.

The last mortal woman to be impregnated by Zeus is Alcmene (also spelled Alcmena). At the time, Alcmene loves and is married to Amphitryon. While her husband is away, Zeus appears to Alcmene in the disguised form of Amphitryon, who is said to be on his way home from avenging the deaths of Alcmene's brothers. Wanting more than the usual short night, Zeus orders Helios the sun god to rest his chariot for 24 hours. This allows Zeus extra time in which to enjoy his pleasures with Alcmene. This union results in the birth of Herakles (called Hercules by the Romans), the legendary yet tragic half-god hero of classical mythology. For more information on Hercules, refer to Chapter 9.

Father of a Conqueror (Zeus-Ammon)

Alexander the Great, who conquered the known world in his short lifetime, is said to have truly believed that he was the half-god son of the Pre-Hellenic hybrid god Zeus-Ammon. Zeus-Ammon was an integration of the Greek thunder god Zeus and a similar Egyptian deity named Ammon (also spelled Amun). Alexander's mother, Olympias, was a priestess of a Dionysian snake cult. Alexander's human father figure, King Phillip II of Macedonia, is said to have often avoided sharing his bed with Alexander's mother, primarily because she had a habit of keeping snakes in her bed.

It is thought that Olympias encouraged Alexander to see himself as a half-god, telling him that Zeus-Ammon had come to her in the night and impregnated her through intercourse. In reality, it is also thought that the so-called "Zeus-Ammon" who visited her was more likely the priest of a Zeus-Ammon cult wearing a ceremonial mask. From a mythological perspective, however, this would be among the instances that the god Zeus-Ammon came down to Earth to give seed for the birth of one of the greatest conquerors of all time.

Avatars of the East

In the East, there are a multitude of instances where a divine being takes human form. For example, in the Hindu Dharma faith, there are 10 avatars of Vishnu, sustainer god of the Trimurti. These avatars occur when Lord Vishnu manifests himself by way of incarnation to restore peace to the world and/or to reestablish order when, for whatever reason, the cosmic balances of existence have been disrupted.

In order, the 10 avatars are Matsyavatara (Fish), Kurma (Tortoise), Varaha (Boar), Narashima (Lion-Man), Vamana (Dwarf), Parasurama (Axe Rama), Rama (Warrior and Ideal Man), Krishna (Charioteer), Buddha (Enlightened One), and Kalki (Apocalypse). According to myth, nine avatars have already appeared throughout human history. One avatar, Kalki, remains to be seen. His appearance will mean the merciless and violent destruction of evil.

The Dwarf Avatar (Hindu)

Vamana is the fifth avatar of Vishnu. When Bali defeats Indra and takes control of the three worlds, the other gods (in fear of Bali/the *asuras*) appeal to Vishnu for aid. Vishnu's response is to incarnate into the dwarf Vamana. Appearing before Bali, who is pleased to see a holy man of such small stature, Vamana is granted any request. Vamana requests that he be granted domain over whatever land he could traverse in three steps. Seeing how short Vamana is, Bali agrees. Unfortunately for him, the dwarf avatar of Vishnu manages to cross the entire universe in only three steps. Bound by his word, Bali must surrender all existence to Vamana.

Immortal Words

In the Vedic texts, the **asuras** and **devas** are said to be separate classes of gods that eventually come to oppose each other. Some have come to believe that this battle represents a conflict between the religious beliefs of the Iranians and Hindus. The asuras are thought to represent the Iranian gods while the devas represent the Hindu gods.

In another version of the myth, a battle takes place between the asuras and *devas*. The asuras arrogantly submit a challenge to their deva adversaries that they will willingly surrender whatever can be covered by one of them in three steps. Vamana, avatar of Vishnu, steps forward and, as in the other version, crosses the entire universe in three steps.

Rama with the Axe

Parasurama is the sixth avatar of Vishnu, preceding prince Sri Rama of the *Ramayana* (see the following section). Parasurama's name means "Rama with the axe." Born a Brahman to Jamadagni and Renuka, his *dharma* (a word which roughly translates as destiny/purpose/law) is to rid the world of the Kshatriya (warrior caste). Though he is a Brahman by birth, Parasurama is also born with an aptitude for the Kshatriya arts of combat.

Parasurama's father, Jamadagni, possesses a blessed cow called Surabhi. This cow produces infinite amounts of food, enough for Jamadagni to feed his entire army as well as all the people in his kingdom. One version of the Parasurama myth (there is more than one version of how these events transpired) states that when a Kshatriya king named Kartavirya hears word of the magical cow,

Sword and Man

The combat arts of the Kshatriya are taught to Parasurama by Lord Shiva, destroyer god of the Hindu Trimurti, who gives Parasurama the axe (parasu) for which he is named.

he desires it to further his power and riches. He marches his army to the gates of Jamadagni's kingdom and demands that the cow Surabhi be surrendered to him. Enraged, Parasurama attacks Kartavirya and his men, overpowering the Kshatriya warriors. Before the fight is over, he cuts off King Kartavirya's head.

In revenge for the death of their father, the sons of the Kshatriya king murder Parasurama's father. Blind with hate for all Kshatriya, the avatar goes on a bloody crusade to rid the world of all Kshatriya kings, as well as their sons/heirs. He accomplishes this task 21 times over, decimating the Kshatriya and destroying them again when they begin to regain their numbers.

Avoiding the Labyrinth

Some who are not of the Hindu Dharma faith have trouble understanding how or why Rama, an avatar of Vishnu, would fight and kill Parasurama, who's also an avatar of the same god. Due to Vishnu's omnipresent nature, he's more than capable of being more than one person at the same time. Therefore, the lives of some avatars overlap or happen simultaneously. Avatars manifest for specific dharma(s), so their lives are designed to lead them in directions that will fulfill their purposes. After the power of the oppressive Kshatriya had been significantly diminished by his 21 crusades, Parasurama had served out his dharma.

Even after crushing the power of the Kshatriya 21 times over, Parasurama still harbors a terrible hatred in his heart for all warriors of the Kshatriya caste. Not until the arrival of Rama is Parasurama's lust for vengeance satiated. Prince Rama of Ayodhya, son of King Dasarath and seventh avatar of Vishnu, kills Parasurama during a confrontation with a flaming arrow from the powerful bow of Vishnu.

The Champion Prince of Dharma

Prince Rama is the legendary hero of the Hindu epic *Ramayana*, a title which translates roughly as "Power of Rama." This book was written by Valmiki, a sage. The exact time period in which *Ramayana* was written is unknown, though there are a number of conflicting theories.

Thousands of years before, King Ravana of the Rakshasa demons had secured an agreement with Lord Brahma that his death could only come at the hands of a human. Because humans are far weaker than Rakshasa demons, Ravana thought that this boon made him immortal. He was wrong.

Rama is the seventh avatar of Vishnu and vanquisher of Parasurama. Though he defeats Parasurama, this is not the reason Vishnu decides to assume the Rama avatar. According to *Ramayana*, the purpose of the Rama avatar is to kill Ravana and rid the world of the terrible Rakshasa demons, which he does with the aid of the Monkey Lord Hanuman and his monkey army, all of whom are incarnate gods. When Ravana kidnaps Rama's beautiful wife, Sita, he unknowingly sparks the chain of events that lead to his destruction.

 Sword and Man

Lord Shiva's enormous and mighty bow (though unstrung) was in the possession of Sita's father, King Janaka. Brahmans proclaim that Sita will never marry a man incapable of stringing it. Many would-be suitors attempt this test, but are unable to so much as lift the bow, let alone string it. Knowing that Sita should be his wife, Rama takes up the challenge of Shiva's bow. To the amazement of all present, he lifts and strings the bow with ease, proving himself to be Sita's prophesied husband. A similar myth can be found in the tales of Odysseus, when he strings his bow in the presence of his wife's suitors, all the while disguised as a beggar.

In Hindu Dharma, Prince Rama is the perfect Hindu man. He accepts all fortune in life as it unfolds, good or bad. His wife Sita, likewise, is seen as the perfect Hindu woman. To this day, Rama and Sita are used as role models for children of India. It is not uncommon to hear parents and teachers advise children to "Be as Rama" or "Be as Sita."

Charioteer of Arjuna (Krishna)

Lord Krishna is the eighth avatar of Vishnu and the charioteer of the Prince Arjuna in the battle-torn Hindu epic *Mahabharata* (which is the longest epic tale known to the world, being approximately eight times longer than the combined lengths of Homer's *Iliad* and *Odyssey*). One long excerpt from the *Mahabharata*, referred to as the *Bhagavad-gita*, is a pre-battle scene in which the charioteer Krishna reveals his divine nature to the hero prince Arjuna (see Chapter 10). This results in a moment of divine revelation for the young archer, learning his charioteer is a living god. Krishna, more than any other avatar, is seen as a symbol of the divine lover. Many myths tell of how, as a young man, Krishna enjoyed playing his flute and seducing village girls. He is also perceived as an avatar of humor and wisdom, as well as a bringer of peace. Krishna's death sparked the beginning of the fourth age of man, an age of darkness called *Kali Yuga*, in which we currently live.)

The Final Avatar

Hindu myth states that Kalki will be the tenth and final incarnation of Vishnu. His appearance will spark the destruction of all evil on Earth. Specifically, by "evil" this prophecy likely refers to human desire, which the ninth avatar Buddha explained to be the root of all suffering. Hindu mythology/prophecy states that Kalki will appear at the end of the *Kali Yuga* (Age of Dark/Death/Destruction, literally "Age of Kali"). He will descend from the sky so that he is seen by all on Earth, riding a white horse and wielding a fiery sword.

Due to the fact that the avatar Kalki has not yet appeared on Earth as Vishnu incarnate, there are no specific myths or epics that tell of his exploits. Primarily, Kalki is an avatar of prophecy. As a result, *what* Kalki is prophesied to do is granted more importance than *how* he is going to do it. When he does come, there will be an amazing tale to tell.

Myth and Metaphor

A common element in prophetic mythology is that a god (for example, Vishnu for the Hindu and Jesus for the Christian) will return to Earth to usher in a period of strife and destruction that will be followed by a grand age of renewal, peace, and righteousness. This archetypal occurrence is likely spawned by the idea that, eventually, humankind will go too far in its transgressions, so much so that a god or messianic figure will return to wipe the world clean, so that creation may be started again "from scratch."

The Bodhisattvas

Though Hindu Dharma considers the Lord Buddha as the ninth avatar of Vishnu, Buddhists do not believe this is so. The Buddha was born the son of a prince of the Shakya Nation in the ancient city of Kapilavastu in what is now Nepal. Before his enlightenment, at which time he became the Buddha (The Enlightened One), his given name was Siddhartha Gautama.

Immortal Words

Shakyamuni is the Japanese name for the Buddha, taken from the word "Shakya," the nation of Gautama's birth.

Gautama lived a life of ease and luxury, never stepping beyond the walls of his father's palace. His father wished that his son might never know suffering. One day, when Gautama was in his late twenties, he slipped away from the shelter of the palace walls. At this time, the young prince saw three visions—a man suffering, a man dying, and a dead man. In some versions of the myth, he has a fourth vision of a monk or ascetic. Shocked by these sights of human mortality and pain that he has never known, Prince Gautama seeks to find the truth of its cause as well as how it might be stopped.

These visions of suffering and death lead to what is now called the "Great Renunciation." Prince Gautama gives up his right to rule his father's kingdom, leaves his wife and child, and rides out of the city of Kapilavastu in search of enlightenment. Of course, Gautama's father does not wish him to leave and would prevent his son's departure if allowed. However, one myth states that the powers of heaven (or the gods, depending on which Buddhist sect is telling the myth) allow the former Prince of Shakya to leave the city in the dark of night by making it so that his horse's hooves do not touch the ground. As he approaches the city gates, the powers of Heaven open them without making even the slightest sound.

When the Buddha died, it is said that he chose not to remain in heaven. Instead, the Buddha returns to Earth from time to time, often reincarnating as more than one person at a time, in order to show others the path to enlightenment. These reincarnations of the Buddha are called Bodhisattvas, or "Those who have arrived at the *Bodhi*."

Immortal Words

Bodhi is the name commonly given to the tree under which the Buddha sat and meditated while being assailed and insulted by the powers of evil, who hoped to convince him to abandon his search for truth and enlightenment. The followers of darkness threw stones and darts at Gautama, only to watch their missiles transform into flowers before they could strike their target.

Gods Arrive in Fertile Crescent

Gods who walked among the peoples of the near and far east often did this to enforce religious reformation. In the harsh environments of the ancient Near and Middle East, violence was an everyday reality. The validation of order and authority offered by religious mythology was a valuable tool.

The Saoshyans Messiah

In Zoroastrian mythologies, originating in approximately 660 B.C.E. in Ancient Persia, the Messiah figure is called the Saoshyans. He will appear on the last day as the final savior of the world in its struggle between the forces of good and evil. The benign forces are associated with the creator god, Ahura Mazda (or *Ohrmazd*), god of truth and light. The evil forces are represented by his twin, Ahriman, god of lies and darkness. The two do battle throughout the course of history.

To assist humanity in its struggle, two previous savior figures appear (Oshetar and Oshetarman), each at the end of thousand-year cycles of history that lead up to the last battle, when Saoshyans defeats the forces of the evil Ahriman for all time, and effects a universal resurrection and judgment of the dead. Each of the three savior figures are miraculously conceived by a virgin who swims in a lake where the Prophet Zoroaster's semen is preserved after his death. The final victory of Soashyans brings about the restoration of the world in its original splendor, a glorious state referred to as *Fraskart*.

Father of Horus (Osiris)

The story of the death and resurrection of Osiris is among the oldest and most important of all Egyptian myths. The story was not written down until Roman times, when Plutarch told the tale as a key to the understanding of the mysteries of Egyptian religion, very popular during his day. But the imagery of the tale goes back to ancient inscriptions on the walls of temples and tombs, and to the hieroglyphs of the Books of the Dead. These were papyrus scrolls placed in coffins alongside the mummy. Their function was to guide the soul of the deceased into and through the underworld.

In the story, Osiris, a God-King of Egypt, is killed by his wicked brother Set, who lures Osiris into a coffin one night during a wild party. When Osiris lies down in the coffin, 72 conspirators nail the coffin shut and put it onto a barge in the river.

The barge floats up the Nile and comes to shore at a palace near Abydos, where royal servants are attracted by the divine fragrance of the coffin. They take it and stand it erect in the courtyard of the palace, where an Erica tree grows up around it.

Meanwhile, Isis (Sister-Bride of Osiris) goes in search of her murdered husband, coming eventually to Abydos. Disguised as a mortal woman, Isis gets a job as nursemaid for the Princess, who has just given birth to a baby boy. Every night Isis anoints the baby with oil, and puts him into the fire, with the intention of making the boy immortal. While the child sits chirping in the flames, Isis turns into a swallow, and flies in circles around the coffin of Osiris, embedded in the trunk of the Erica tree. As she flies, she emits shrieks of lamentation, which eventually awakens the sleeping Princess. Coming into the nursery, the Princess is shocked by the sight of her baby sitting in the fire, and screams, breaking the spell. Isis appears in the full radiance of her divinity, and berates the Princess, explaining that her boy would have been immortal if she hadn't intervened.

Isis then asks a favor of the Princess: "Would you mind if I took my husband back? He is buried in the coffin inside the tree in the courtyard." Isis then cuts the coffin out of the trunk of the tree, and puts it back onto the barge. The couple floats down the Nile until midnight, when Isis hovers over the body of her dead husband, and brings Osiris back to life with the powerful flapping of her angelic wings. They make love, and a child is born: Horus, the hawk-headed deity, son of the Lord of the Resurrection and his wife Isis. Ancient Egyptian sculptures show Isis nursing the baby Horus on her lap, sitting in the seclusion of the reed marshes along the river, where she has gone to escape the vigilant wrath of Set.

Set, however, eventually discovers that his plot to kill his brother Osiris has been foiled. He tracks Osiris down with the help of his 72 conspirators, kills his brother a second time, and scatters the dismembered pieces of the god all over Egypt. Wherever a piece falls, tradition says, a temple to Osiris is built.

Horus, meanwhile, sets off to recover the dismembered pieces of his father's body, hovering like a hawk high over the desert and the river. All pieces are found and put back together, with the exception of the phallus, which has been swallowed by a fish! A wooden prosthesis is used in its place, and Osiris is reborn as the Lord of Death and Resurrection. We see him sitting in the throne room in the Egyptian Books of the Dead, with his sisters Isis and Nepthys behind him, and a row of cobras with their hoods inflated around solar disks above him. Osiris holds a shepherd's crook and royal scepter in his hands.

In other images, from the tombs and temples, Osiris is shown as the Lord of the Staircase, in the sixth hour of the soul's nightly journey into the underworld. In the background we see his wicked brother Set, who has been turned into a black pig and is being driven off into the wilderness.

The Sacrificial Son

The story of the son of God who comes down from Heaven to redeem the human soul from bondage to original sin gives us two marvelous versions of the Messianic conquest of death.

In the first, Jesus is conceived by the Virgin Mary after God appears to her in the form of the Holy Spirit (symbolized by a dove). The miraculous conception of the hero is a universal theme of world mythology. So also is the Infant Exile of the hero, which occurs in the New Testament when Joseph and Mary flee the wrath of Herod, taking the baby into Egypt. Jesus will of course eventually return to Jerusalem on Palm Sunday, and complete his Messianic mission by sacrificing himself on the Cross of Golgatha.

After the Crucifixion on Good Friday, another version of the descent into the underworld and the conquest of death occurs. Although not to be found in complete form anywhere in the New Testament, the story developed during the Middle Ages into one of the most famous themes of Christian art. The story is known as the Harrowing of Hell, and it is about the descent of Jesus into hell, where he goes after the crucifixion to rescue the patriarchs of his ancestral lineage—which stretches all the way back through the House of David to Adam and Eve.

The story originated in a theological problem: according to the strict teachings of the Medieval church, only souls born after the life of Jesus were eligible for salvation. Were the patriarchs and prophets of the Old Testament therefore damned to hell for all eternity? To counteract this absurd proposition, the story of the Harrowing of Hell came along. In the story, Jesus is shown smashing down the gates of hell to rescue Adam and Eve. In some pictures, Jesus is shown standing on the crossed doors of the gates, fending off the devils who attempt to thwart his mission. And, in all the paintings, Adam is depicted as an exhausted old man, while Eve looks fresh as a daisy.

All this occurs between the Crucifixion on Good Friday and the Resurrection on Easter Sunday. After the Resurrection, Jesus returns to Heaven, from which his journey began, there to remain until the Second Coming on the Last Day. Then the forces of evil will be defeated for all time; there will be a universal resurrection of the dead, followed by the last judgment and the restoration of the Paradise lost when Adam and Eve ate the apple—thus initiating the hero journey of human history, which begins and ends in the same place.

The Least You Need to Know

♦ Half-gods cannot be considered as avatars or incarnate gods.

♦ Incarnate gods/avatars do not always serve the same particular roles.

♦ In myth, deified heroes and leaders, Hindu avatars, gods incarnate, messiahs, and transubstantiated gods are all considered gods that walked among men.

♦ The method by which a god comes to physical reality often depends on how the culture of that god views the separate natures of the physical and spiritual realms.

Chapter 4

Bringers of Mercy, Love, and Fertility

In This Chapter

- The gods and goddesses of mercy who bring succor and aid to the tortured souls of the world
- The deities that bring the vibrant green of life and fertility
- The hand of mercy and cycle of fertility
- The evolution and expansion of the Hindu god of mercy to an Asian goddess of mercy

We could all use a little help every now and then. Ancient humanity was no exception to this. Whether seeking peace, salvation from strife, relief from pain, or just a good crop, humans call out to the gods of this chapter for help.

They offer much and ask little in return other than our devotion and respect. From the moody playfulness of the pipe-playing Pan, to the merciful hands of the beautiful goddess Kwan Yin, our survival and livelihood rest with them. May these gods have mercy on us all.

Mercy and Fertility in the New World

The deities of both mercy and fertility among the indigenous tribes of the Americas and Hawaii were the helpful bringers of peace, knowledge, and plentitude to the people. Their arrivals often signified a new age of prosperity and peace. These gods abhorred violence and force, valuing instead order, production, and reason.

The Gift-Bearing Hunchback (Hopi/Pueblo)

Kokopelli (also spelled Kokopolo) is usually seen in the form of an insect Kachina of the Pueblo Hopi tribe, and is associated with agricultural fertility. He is depicted as a hunchback, and several long, odd appendages protrude from his hump. The appendages may be the result of Kokopelli's association with the dragonfly. His so-called "hump," however, is not actually a hump at all but a sack in which he keeps gifts to bestow upon humans.

A hunter by nature, Kokopelli often seduces young maidens and/or brings bridal moccasins to them. The earliest pictographs of Kokopelli were in the image of a human male figure killing sheep with his bow. Though many of the Kachina are said to hunt, Kokopelli is one of only a few that are portrayed almost exclusively as such.

Surfer of the Rainbow (Hawaiian)

Lono descended to the earth on a rainbow to marry Laka, sister of Pele. He is a god of music and fertility as well as mercy and peace, and one of the four original gods of Hawaiian mythology that existed before the creation of the earth. The yearly festival honoring Lono, called *Makahiki*, begins in October and ends in February. During this time, waging warfare (unless for defense from attack) or working (aside from that which is necessary for survival) is forbidden, or *kapu*.

The god Lono, while among men, created laws, annual taxes, and a number of games. Eventually, he is said to have boarded a canoe and departed for Kahiki with a promise that he would one day return to the people of Hawaii on a great canoe called *Auwa'alalua*. When Captain James Cook came to the Hawaiian Islands with his large ships, some believe that the locals may have mistakenly believed that he was a reincarnation of the god Lono, returned to bring new knowledge to the people.

Life and Forgiveness in the Old World

In the Western world, gods and goddesses of fertility were shown special attention. Often, even the most primitive of Western cultures carried out special ceremonies and rites at certain times of the year to appeal to the gods of mercy, compassion, and fertility for new or continued prosperity, peace, and abundance.

A Piper God (Greek)

Pan is said to be either the son of Hermes and Dryope or the result of an interlude between Hermes and Penelope, wife of the epic Greek hero Odysseus. In the second version, it says that Hermes came to Penelope in the form of a giant ram, and perhaps is intended to explain why Pan's body from the waist down is that of a goat.

Pan is a lower-level god of fertility and the herds, whose origins came from the Arcadian tribe of the Greeks. Aside from having the shape of a goat from the waist down, Pan also sports a pair of goat ears. From his forehead protrudes a pair of goat horns that are depicted in a variety of lengths, from long spiraling horns to short buds that barely clear his hairline. As a pastoral deity, Pan has done as his station requires by inventing a special musical instrument (all Greek pastoral deities had their own special instruments): the panpipes. In most depictions, Pan is shown dancing joyfully while playing his panpipes.

Pan's symbol is the phallus, so you might imagine that his sexual appetite is quite impressive. He often spends his active hours playing his pipes and pursuing nymphs and young women. He also has quite a confusing nature. Despite his playfulness, he also acts as the leader of all satyrs. Despite his love of noise and revelry, he also enjoys moments of solitude in the quiet serenity of nature.

Myth claims that, at noon each day, Pan often seeks out a shady and quiet place of refuge for his daily nap. Therefore, forest travelers took special care to be quiet during the middle hours of the day in fear that they might wake him. Though Pan is a playful and sexual god, he is apparently quite grumpy when prematurely awoken from his nap. Myth says that he has the ability to strike any human with fear by bellowing out with his incredibly loud voice. Some myths say that any human who hears the shout of Pan will be cursed with terrible nightmares for the remainder of his or her lifetime.

Originally, Pan was a god specific to the Arcadian people of Greece. However, his popularity increased over the years and spread throughout Greece. Myths about him soon became abundant. He is said to be a close friend to Dionysus as well as Cybele, one of the last gods of Greek tradition to be widely worshipped. Eventually, Pan went from being a simple god of livestock and shepherds to the god of nature as a whole. In fact, in the Greek language, the word *pan* was eventually used to mean "nature."

Immortal Words

Panic, a word meaning an overwhelming fear that robs one of one's senses, originates from the name of Pan. The Arcadians claimed that before their battle with the Persians at Marathon, Pan promised that he would scatter the enemy forces. They claimed that Pan had made good on his promise, breaking the enemy line by striking the Persian forces with "Panic Fear." Of course, having the skilled forces of the militaristic Spartans on their side probably helped.

One of the last and youngest myths surrounding Pan is one that claims to have been passed verbally for nearly 2,000 years. Written records of this myth are rare and hard to verify. However, if true, then the story has survived the last two millennia, passed along primarily by word of mouth. This myth states that on the day of Jesus of Nazareth's (the Christ's) crucifixion, a lone ship was sailing past the island called Paxos in the Ionian Sea. As they passed, the crew clearly heard a voice come from the island, shouting out "Our great Pan has died!"

Avoiding the Labyrinth

The myth of the cry from Paxos announcing the death of Pan, as well as that of all the "old gods," was likely an early bit of propaganda created by the Roman Empire around the time of Constantine. As the Roman Empire adopted the religion of Christianity, stories such as these aided them in the peaceful removal of the old religions. Simply put, new religions often phased out old religions with a technique that involved creating a new myth or story that said something along the lines of, "My new god destroyed your old god," or "Your old god was banished by my new god."

When this ship later arrived in Rome, the crew conveyed the story to others. Last, the myth claims that from every corner of the empire reports began pouring in that every oracle in the land had gone silent. This has led some to believe that the voice heard from the island of Paxos was likely that of an oracle priest of the Pan cult.

Mysteries of a Goddess (Greek)

Of Greek deities, the goddess Eleus (also spelled Eleos) was worshipped exclusively by the Athenians. The only known altar erected to her was located in the *agora* of Athens, and it is mentioned in a number of Greek historical and mythological texts. Eleus is the female personification/deification of mercy and compassion.

Immortal Words _____

The term **agora** comes from the Greek root *ageirein,* meaning "to gather." An agora can be used to mean a place of congregation in general. In ancient Greece, however, this word referred specifically to a public marketplace. This is the root of the modern word "agoraphobia," which is the fear of going outside or into public.

That Eleus's name only appears as a goddess of the Athenians is somewhat odd. However, one explanation for this is that the goddess's name was changed, or that other Greek cities began associating her with the earth goddess Demeter, when she was absorbed by another culture. One supporting piece of evidence for this is the well-known existence of a mystic cult that flourished for years in the ancient world. They were referred to as Eleusinian, because the home temple of the cult stood in Eleusina (also spelled at times as Eleusis), a rural township fewer than 20 miles south of Athens.

Every year, special initiation rites were held for candidates of the cult. These rites have come to be referred to as the "Eleusinian mysteries," and their practice is believed to have begun sometime around 1500 B.C.E. They are named as such due to the shroud of mystery surrounding what took place in the rites and training of members in the order.

Myth and Metaphor _____

The fact that only the Athenians worshipped Eleus is of note, considering that throughout the history of polytheistic cultures it is common to see deities with such beneficial traits as Eleus's absorbed by the pantheons of neighboring tribes, civilizations, and/or cultures.

Eleusinian initiates were sworn to lifelong secrecy and outsiders were strictly barred from witnessing what took place. In fact, during the initiation rites, the only people allowed to attend were those directly linked to the Eleusinian order—priests, priestesses, initiates, and hierophants. The goal of all members in the Eleusinian order was to achieve what was called *epopteia*, a state that could be seen as akin to enlighten-ment in Buddhism. Those who achieved this state were eligible to become Eleusinian *hierophants*.

Immortal Words

The word **hierophant** now refers to a member of a religious organization who brings together the congregation and leads them into the "presence of the holy." However, in Ancient Greece, this word specifically referred to the highest priests of the Eleusinian order, those who had mastered the mysteries of Demeter and could therefore interpret the mysteries of existence and signs from the gods.

In at least one myth, it is said that Herakles fought to gain initiation into the Eleu-sinian so that he might undergo mental and spiritual training. Such training was needed for Herakles to succeed in the last of his 12 labors, bringing Cerberus out from the domain of Hades. He was denied at first, however, because he was not an Athenian citizen, which was a requirement for initiates of the Eleusinian order.

Herakles was eventually able to gain partial entry into the order by being made an honorary citizen by his close friend Theseus, the King of Athens. Even this, however, was not enough to allow Herakles access to all facets of the Eleusinian mysteries. His final purification rites, for example, were held outside the city of Eleusis. The name of the order as well as the specificity of its membership, exclusive only to Athenian citizens, give clues that lead to the assumption that this order has close ties to the goddess Eleus.

The Fertile Goddess of Fire (Irish)

Brigid (also spelled Brigit, as well as a number of other ways) is perhaps one of the most important and valuable goddesses in Irish mythology. Brigid is the daughter of Dagda, the benevolent god of the Old Irish mythological tradition. To the Irish, Brigid wears a number of hats, so to speak. First and foremost, she is said to be a fire goddess. However, she is in no way restricted to this single role. In addition, she is goddess of poetry, wisdom, fertility, agriculture, livestock, blacksmithing, crafts, and all the arts of the household.

In later years, Brigid appears in texts of the Gauls and the British under the names of Brigh, Brigindo, and Brigantia. After the sainthood of Saint Brigit in the sixth cen-tury C.E., the personality and traits of Brigid were transferred to the female saint.

Legacy of Amida Buddha (Asian and Indian)

Amitabha, Amida Butsu, Amita, and Amida Buddha are all names for the merciful Buddha of Infinite Light, one of the Five Buddhas of Contemplation in Mahayana Buddhism. Throughout the years, the figure of Amida Buddha has all but replaced that of the original historical Buddha, Prince Siddhartha Gautama, or Shakyamuni, in *Mahayana* Buddhism. He is the Buddha of divine grace, embodying the most pure and powerful aspects of the Buddhist tradition.

Immortal Words

Mahayana is a sect of Buddhism that is unique in its belief that becoming a Buddha, by transcending Karma and reaching enlightenment, is achievable. This sect of Buddhism places emphasis on showing love and respect for all living things in creation as well as on showing compassion for the sick, poor, and unfortunate. Mahayana also expanded the idea of worship in Buddhism, making the image of the Buddha—a representation of the human potential to achieve Buddha-hood—into something that can be directly worshipped.

Amida, most importantly, presides over the realm of Sukhavati, the heavenly afterlife of eternal bliss. Sukhavati is probably the closest thing Buddhism has to the Western perception of Heaven. Ironically, it is even called the Western Paradise of Amitabha. However, Sukhavati is simply a merciful removal from the cycle of Samsara (life-death-rebirth) even though one has yet to transcend one's karma.

Immortal Words

Zen, or *Ch'an*, Buddhism was founded by the monk Bodhidharma (he is called Potitamo in Japanese) who came to China from India to spread the teachings of the Buddha. He also founded the Xiaolin (Shoalin) Temple, the birthplace of Kung Fu. Zen focuses on the practice of meditation to reach enlightenment. Zen made its way to Japan sometime during the twelfth century and soon became a popular religion among the samurai class. Eventually, Japanese Zen split into two main sects: the Rinzai, which was founded by the monk Eisai; and the Soto, founded by a student of Eisai's named Dogen. Unlike Mahayana Buddhism, the Buddha is not directly worshipped in Zen Buddhism.

The Jodo sect of Buddhism introduced the idea of Sukhavati naming Amida Buddha as patron deity over it. Over time, the samurai followers of *Zen* began to view Sukhavati as a heaven for warriors, similar to how the Teutonic warriors viewed

Valhalla. In contrast to the Vikings, however, the Japanese samurai saw Sukhavati as a heaven where warriors were forgiven of bad karma caused by the blood they shed with their swords during life.

Aiding Amida Buddha in his works are two very special and widely beloved *Bodhisattvas:* Avalokitesvara and Mahasthama. By the merciful acts of these Bodhisattvas, any human being who invokes the name of Amida Buddha may be granted salvation from karma and gain entry into Sukhavati, the Western Paradise of Amitabha.

Immortal Words

Bodhisattvas are people who have transcended karma and achieved enlightenment. In other words, they have reached Buddha-hood. However, they choose not to go on to the bliss of Nirvana. Instead, these people choose to postpone their well-earned eternal bliss to return to Earth through reincarnation so that they might help others on the path to enlightenment.

A Son Born of Tears

Avalokitesvara, also called by his shorter name Avalokita, is depicted in the mythological tradition of Mahayana Buddhism as the son of Amida Buddha. When Amida witnessed the suffering of humanity, he shed a single tear, which came to life and took the form of Avalokita. In the beginning, Avalokita was portrayed as standing around or below a Buddha figure, along with either four or seven of his fellow Bodhisattvas. Being the son of Amida Buddha, Avalokita's home is in Sukhavati, the Western Paradise of his father. When the present age of existence comes to a close (FYI—the Buddhists, as with the Hindus, agree that we are currently living in the last age of humankind's current existence), Avalokita will appear to humanity in one last reincarnation, to act as the thousandth and final Buddha of this existence.

Avalokita has become the most valued figure in Tibetan Buddhism. In Tibet, Avalokita has completely overshadowed his father, Amida, in importance and is the primary focus of worship. In fact, he had been made the national patron deity of Tibet. The Dalai Lama, spiritual leader of Tibet and head of Tibetan Buddhism at his palace in Lhasa, is said to be the reincarnation of Avalokita. In artistic depictions, Avalokita is portrayed as human in appearance, holding a lotus in one hand while making signs of blessing with the other.

Avoiding the Labyrinth

For more than the last half-century, the Dalai Lama has lived in exile. When Communist China took over Tibet, they outlawed religion, including Buddhism. Monks, nuns, and monasteries were often targets for violence and harassment by the Chinese military. The Dalai Lama remained in the country for a time, causing him to endure a prolonged period of difficulty and danger. However, when the Chinese began making more deliberate and bold attempts to assassinate him, the Dalai Lama had no choice but to flee the monastic palace in Lhasa and leave Tibet. To this day, the people of Tibet remain under the thumb of China's forced occupation and the Dalai Lama continues to live in exile.

The Beloved Goddess of China

Chinese culture eventually absorbed the figure of Avalokita into its mythology, calling him by the name Guan Yin (also spelled Kuan Yin or Kwan Yin). Originally, they retained Avalokita's male gender. By the twelfth century, however, Chinese mythology had transformed him from the son of Amida Buddha to a goddess of mercy.

While the religious leaders of Taoism and Buddhism in China seem to have argued for a time as to whether Kuan Yin was a Taoist or Buddhist deity, the masses of the country seemed to care little about where she'd come from. In almost every Chinese temple, whether of the Tao or Buddha, a representation of Guan Yin was (and, for the most part, still is) present. She is a mercy goddess for the people of China, and is said to rescue shipwrecked sailors and storm-torn vessels from the sea. She is also said to produce rain.

One of Guan Yin's most important roles is as the guardian deity of women. In most mythological descriptions, she is said to be an eternal virgin. In one myth, she is said to have abandoned the palace of her father to avoid a forced marriage and thereby keep her virginity. Despite her depiction as a virgin goddess, Guan Yin is often portrayed holding a child or infant in her arms and is considered a goddess of mothers. Embroidered slippers are often placed in front of temple statues of Guan Yin. Women who are infertile or having trouble conceiving a child will often either borrow or steal (and later return) these sandals from the temple and wear them to promote pregnancy.

The main center of Guan Yin's cult was on the island of P'u T'o. For a time, this island was governed independently by the monks of Guan Yin, free from any control from the governing body of the mainland. In its time, no females, whether human or animal, were allowed on the island at night. From sunset to sunrise, the island had to be completely cleared of all females. How this was enforced in regard to animals is unclear.

Goddess of the Eight Postures

Ofuna Kannon, or Kwannon, is the Japanese pronunciation of Guan Yin. However, this is the Japanese name for the Sanskrit name of the Bodhisattva Avalokita. As with the Chinese, the Japanese absorbed Avalokita into their mythology and originally retained his male gender. However, as time passed, Kannon became a female deity and is now recognized as Goddess of Mercy by Buddhists and Shinto followers alike. In Japanese artistic representations, she has eight specific postures in which she is portrayed.

Mercy and Plenty in the Fertile Crescent

In a land notorious for its harsh environments, vicious predators (both human and animal), and difficult agricultural issues, the gods of fertility, love, and mercy were often revered above all others. Whether they presided over the keepers of livestock, sexuality, childbirth, or music, their grace and favor was sought by all.

God of the Sheepfold (Babylonian)

Tammuz was the shepherd god of the Babylonians and Semitic Assyrians, and he was likely a counterpart or descendent of the Sumerian and Akkadian shepherd god Dumuzi, husband of the goddess Inanna. Tammuz is the god of the sheepfold, protector of herds and shepherds. As with Pan, and most other pastoral-type gods, Tammuz was also portrayed as a musician at times.

One month of the calendar was designated by the name Tammuz, and the entire month was set aside for dedications and libations in honor and worship of the god Tammuz. The Babylonians would mark the beginning of each summer, a season that brought with it terrible heat and inevitable drought, with a six-day festival. According to the myth of Tammuz, when his wife returned from the realm of the dead to find her husband was not mourning her, she sent him to the underworld in her place. However, Tammuz's sister sacrificed herself to take his place for half the year. Therefore, the fertile seasons were seen as the time when Tammuz was not in the underworld. The six-day festival that marked the onset of summer was meant to be a kind of funeral for Tammuz, who would soon have to return to the underworld.

The Merciful Dwarf (Egyptian)

Bes is a god of ancient Egyptian mythology, and was more than likely imported from the neighboring country of Nubia to the east or possibly Punt in the south. He is depicted as short, almost dwarflike in stature, covered with bushy hair, and with a lion's tail protruding from his backside. He wears a lion's skin for a garment. Sometimes he is shown cradling a serpent, or with a large phallus dangling from between his legs. On his head there are often crowns, some of which are standard while others are more bowl-shaped.

Bes is far more bestial and less dignified in his appearance when compared to the later gods of Egyptian mythology. Some believe that the existence of his artifacts is evidence that people with dwarfism were worshipped as gods or at least revered in the most ancient time of Egyptian civilization. Although entirely possible, this theory is based on speculation. Even though he is one of the oldest gods of the Egyptians, Bes did not achieve the peak of his popularity as a deity until the middle of the seventh century B.C.E.

Myth and Metaphor

In ancient times, it was not uncommon for one civilization to absorb one or more deities from the myths of neighboring civilizations. In fact, you may remember that the entire religion of the ancient Romans was taken from that of the Greeks. Gods with beneficial or agreeable qualities, such as gods of fertility and mercy, would have made happy additions to any ancient polytheistic religion.

Statues or images of Bes were considered powerful talismans for protection against the destructive forces of evil—violence, wicked spells, and even bad omens. His image was considered so valuable against evil that some people would have them in their homes. In fact, Bes appeared in more ancient Egyptian households than any other god in their religion. As far as his role as a deity is concerned, Bes is a god of protection, love, sexuality, fertility, and childbirth.

Bes shares a lot of the same traits as the Greek god Pan. First of all, both are somewhat animal-like in appearance. Also, they are both gods of music and dance. Bes is sometimes depicted playing a musical instrument and dancing joyfully, as is Pan.

In addition to their physical similarities, Bes and Pan also share a common personality trait in that both are somewhat dualistic in nature (for more on Pan, see his section earlier in this chapter). Bes is portrayed as a sexual and playful god who likes to dance and play music. He is also considered the protective deity of children, women giving birth, and mothers. However, there are times when he is also shown to be a wrathful and vengeful figure, similar to the behavior of a war god.

Myth and Metaphor _____

Bes's two-sided nature is probably a carryover from his original depictions around the time that he was absorbed as a god of Egyptian civilization. Over time, as he became increasingly popular among the people, more beneficial, fertile, and agreeable qualities probably began being attributed to him, eventually overshadowing his original warlike nature.

The Least You Need to Know

- Gods with beneficial or helpful traits such as mercy, compassion, and fertility are prone to being absorbed by neighboring cultures.

- Though a god is absorbed by a new group, he or she is often altered and modified to fit into that culture's perception of her or him.

- Gods of love and/or fertility can sometimes seem a little bipolar in personality—playful one minute and wrathful the next.

- Though gods of mercy and fertility are often kind, they can be wrathful (as most gods can) if spurned or provoked.

5

Lords of the Battlefield

In This Chapter

- ◆ War gods across the globe
- ◆ The different natures of war gods
- ◆ War gods as saviors and as destroyers
- ◆ The evolution of the war god in Norse myth from Tyr to Odin

As with death, war is somewhat inevitable in human existence. Whether fought over real estate or ideology, interspecies conflict among humans has existed since before the dawn of written language. As a result, one constant figure in the pantheons of world mythology is that of the war god. Though they are often closely related to gods of death and destruction, gods of war have their own special place on the battlefield that separates them from their kindred.

Native America

In a land of wood, stone, and bone weapons, the gods of war are fierce and fearless. The appetite of their bloodlust is often voracious and sometimes has to be staved off with the blood of human sacrifices. The peoples of the Americas knew that war, as with death, could not be stopped. It could only be delayed and/or temporarily held at bay.

The Hummingbird of War (Aztec)

Huitzilopochtli is the Aztec god of sun and war. He has two sisters. One is Malinalxochitl, a sorceress of staggering beauty. His other sister, Coyolxhauqui, is the moon. She became the moon when her brother killed her and threw her severed head into the night sky. These murderous siblings are the offspring of Coatlicue, the serpent goddess. Huitzilopochtli was the patron god of the Aztec city of Tenochtitlan. In addition to being just a basic war god, he is also the Aztec god of storms, warriors, and male youth. He also acts as somewhat of a death god, guiding the souls of dead warriors and returning them to the earth in the form of hummingbirds. In fact, his name translates as "Hummingbird of the South/Left" (the left was associated with the direction south to the Aztecs). He is often depicted as a hummingbird or with the feathers of one. He often holds a mirror in one hand and a snake in the other, symbols of his ability to cross between worlds of life and death as well as his constant battle against the forces of evil.

Warrior God of Cozumel (Mayan)

Little is known about Ah Hulneb, a Mayan god of war. It would seem that he was a regional deity, being associated with the island of Cozumel. In the island city of Tantun, Ah Hulneb is said to have commanded an army. This has led some to suspect that he was in fact a Mayan warlord who was eventually deified. Unfortunately, evidence does not exist that refutes or supports this suspicion. His name translates as "Spear Thrower."

The Land Taker (Hawaiian)

Kukailimoku, meaning "Land Taker," is the Hawaiian god of war. His face is fearsome and thick with crimson feathers. His eyes are pearly, flashing seashells. Upon his head sits a helmet. His wife is the goddess Hina (as is the wife of most Polynesian gods).

He Who Brought War (Lakota)

Though somewhat of a trickster and chaos god, similar to those portrayed in Chapter 2, Ictinike was the god of war for the Lakota tribe (he also makes appearances in the myths of the Iowa tribe). Deceitful by nature, he is often shown in the form of a giant spider. However, Lakota myth states that it was Ictinike who taught them the ways of weapons, combat, and warfare.

Twin Sons of Changing Woman (Navajo)

Changing Woman (called such for her ability to change her age and appearance) is married to the Sun, and from their union came twins, called Monster Slayer and Child Born of Water. These twins grew to adulthood in about 12 days. Shortly thereafter, they began to inquire about their father. When Changing Woman refuses to tell them about him, the brothers decide to journey to his house. Not fazed by the discouragement of their mother, the twins set off.

The journey is a difficult one, and the twins must face a number of perilous dangers. Along the way, the Dawn offers them a white prayer plume (a special feather with spiritual powers) to protect them when they enter the house of the Sun. At the final stage of their journey, the two must travel across a rainbow to gain entrance into their father's house.

The Sun, upon seeing the twins, at first refuses to acknowledge that they are his sons. He subjects them to a series of merciless trials. Luckily, however, the prayer plume they received from the Dawn protects them. In the end, they pass their father's test and the Sun embraces them as his children. Throughout their lives, the twins have many adventures and do battle with many creatures of terror and darkness.

War Gods in the Dark Lands

Kibuka and Shango are the two most well-known war gods of the African Baganda and Yoruba tribes. One a messiahlike warlord and the other a god of the storm, these two deities are the greatest war figures of Africa.

War from the Heavens (Baganda)

Kibuka is a war god, sent by the heavens to be a savior to the Baganda tribe. The Baganda king prays to the heavens for aid in battle. Kibuka arrives as an answer to those prayers. Unfortunately Kibuka, against the advice of others, has sexual relations with a female of the enemy tribe who is a prisoner. To make matters worse, he discloses to her the manner in which he can be killed. She soon escapes and tells the enemy tribesmen how to kill Kibuka.

The only way to kill Kibuka is to shoot arrows into the cloud where he hides. Soon enough, the enemy archers had thrown a wave of volleys at Kibuka's cloud. His body riddled with arrows, and knowing well that he will soon die, Kibuka flies from his cloud into the top of a mighty tree. At the site of the tree where his corpse was found, a great temple was erected.

A War God with Two Daddies (Yoruban)

Shango is the Yoruba God of War, Thunder, and Lightning. Shango is the offspring of one of the oddest unions one could ever hope to come across in all of mythology. During a journey, the god king Obatala is denied passage by Aganju, the god of fire and ferryman of the gods. Obatala goes off, hides himself, and transforms into a gorgeous maiden, then offers himself (herself) to Aganju as payment for being allowed passage. Shango is the result of this rather unusual sexual encounter.

Shango later seeks out his father/mother, who does not immediately acknowledge him as his son. It is not until Shango throws himself into a fire that Obatala recognizes him as being the result of his union with Aganju and, therefore, his true son.

War in the Old World

In Western mythology, there are numerous gods of war. Each culture in Western civilization had its own version of a war god, and some even had multiple gods that served these roles. In the Western perspective, gods of war were commonly seen as divine advisors who could lead an army to victory or fool them into defeat. Some offer merely their strength to assure victory for their favored people, while others use strategic cunning and deceit. Either way, all are revered as testaments to the valued role of warriors in the ancient Western civilizations.

The Evolution of a War God (Teutonic)

Irmin, one of the oldest Teutonic war gods, may have been replaced by Tyr at some point. Either that, or Irmin was simply another name for Tyr. No one can be certain. Though Tyr is now believed to have been an older war god than Odin, he was not perceived as such later on in Teutonic myths. In existing myths from these people, Tyr is said to be a son of Odin and Freya (or Frigga). He is a god of courage, swordsmanship, and war.

When the Roman historian Tacitus wrote of the Germanic war god, he referred to him as "Mars," but was in fact referring to Tyr. Somewhat in keeping with the nature of his alleged father Odin, Tyr was not only strong but wise. He aids his father in choosing those warriors who are to be brought to the halls of Valhalla after their deaths. Tyr also helped the Aesir gods bind the deadly wolf Fenris. When he placed his hand in the great wolf's mouth as a pledge of fealty, however, it was bitten off. When Ragnarok (Teutonic version of the apocalypse) comes, he will do battle with Hel's dreaded watchdog/hellhound, Garm. Prophecy states that during this battle Tyr and Garm will kill one another.

Odin (also spelled Woden, Wotan, or Votan), though he likely arose later than Irmin or Tyr (chronologically), became the most popular god in his pantheon rather quickly. This surge in popularity resulted in a change in the hierarchy of the Teutonic gods. Irmin (unless that name was, in fact, referring to Tyr) was likely phased out and replaced by Tyr, who was then demoted, so to speak, and made to be Odin's son. As a result, Odin came to replace Tyr as the Norse god of war and the former became a lower-level warrior-god.

Avoiding the Labyrinth

Did you know that the names we now use for the days of the week originally came from the names of Teutonic gods? For example, Friday was originally "Frigga's/Freya's Day." "Tyr's Day" became what we now call Tuesday. Thursday was once "Thor's Day." "Odin's/Woden's Day" became what we now call Wednesday.

Odin is often physically portrayed as a man of middle age (an age of great wisdom at the time, because so very few survived to see the age of 20), sitting either on his throne, *Hlidskialf*; in the great silver halls of *Valhalla*; or on his other throne in *Gladsheim*, where he conducts meetings with the other gods. Odin is said to be, in existing myths, lord of the Aesir gods. His hair is long and curly, and from his jaw hangs a mighty gray beard. His apparel is also gray, covered by a blue hooded cloak and/or an extremely long-brimmed hat that conceals much of his face. On his arm is the ring *Draupnir*, and in his hands is the powerful spear *Gungnir*, which he uses as his scepter. He is missing an eye, which he sacrificed freely so that he might have a draft from the god Mimir's Well of Knowledge. Upon drinking it, Odin spent nine days in a trancelike state, hanging from the branches of the Yggdrasil tree.

Immortal Words

Valhalla is a Teutonic heaven for brave warriors, described as a great mead hall. This realm is in the charge of Odin. For more information, see Chapter 6.

Gladsheim is the grand hall of Asgard where the Twelve Seats of the Aesir gods are housed. Odin also has a throne here, and he presides over and mediates the meetings of the Aesir gods.

Sword and Man _____

The arm-ring of Odin, *Draupnir,* was a piece of jewelry that provided endless wealth to the wearer. Forged by two dwarves, Brokkr and Sindri, it was one of three gifts they made in a bet with Loki, who said that they couldn't create better gifts than their rivals, the Sons of Ivaldi.

Odin's spear, *Gungnir,* or "Unwavering," is named as such because it will never miss its target. This spear was created by the Sons of Ivaldi, a dwarf craftsman guild.

On Odin's shoulders sit two ravens, one on each. These black birds are perhaps among Odin's greatest tools/weapons. One raven is called Hugin (Thought), the other Munin (Memory). These birds act as advisors of sorts, whispering the truth of all things into Odin's ears.

Odin is said to be the wisest of all beings, all-knowing and all-seeing (impressive considering he has only one eye). He is a god of fatherhood, death, battle, strategy, wisdom, knowledge, mead, and poetry.

Though Odin qualifies as a god of war, it's impossible to restrict him into one role or category. You have already seen him as a creator-type god in Chapter 1, and you'll see him again in Chapter 6 in his role as a god of the dead.

The Triple Goddess of War (Celtic)

Morrigan, though primarily a fertility goddess, also acts as a goddess of war and strife. Her name means "The Great Queen." She is said to be the daughter of Ernmas and the wife of Dagda, the benevolent god of Celtic mythology.

Morrigan is a single goddess. However, she is also portrayed as a triple goddess at times, made up of three separate entities. When portrayed in this way, as a trinity, she is/they are referred to as The Morrigan. In this trinity, Morrigan's name is commonly Badb. The Morrigan trinity is Badb, Macha, and Neman, who act as war goddesses in this form. Celtic warriors offered the heads of the slain to The Morrigan as dedications, and it was said that the goddesses appeared on battlefields as ravens so that they could devour the corpses of the dead.

God of Shield and Spear (Greek)

Ares (called Mars by the Romans) is god of war in the Greek/Olympian pantheon. He is also the god of courage, masculinity, and law and order. Ares is always depicted armed for battle. Even when portrayed in the nude, Ares retains his spear and helmet.

Ares is quite out of character as a Greek representation, because he is all about physical strength and prowess in combat. He is a far cry from the crafty, wise Athena. In fact, in the Trojan War written of in Homer's *The Iliad*, Athena sides with the Spartans while Ares sides with the Trojans.

Probably the most popular tale of Ares tells of his courting of Aphrodite, Goddess of Love and Beauty. Despite Ares' lust, Aphrodite loves Adonis, Prince of Kypros, and has already had a child with him. In a jealous rage, Ares assumes the shape of a monstrous boar and kills Adonis. Unfortunately, this murder bears no result for Ares. Zeus gives Aphrodite to Hephaestus, Blacksmith God of the Forge, as a wife. Hephaestus, unfortunately for Aphrodite, is quite unattractive. Soon she is happy to see the far more attractive Ares as he visits her secretly during her husband's absence. The two begin a love affair until Hephaestus is informed of it by the sun god Helios, who witnesses what's happening.

Hephaestus creates an unbreakable net that falls down onto the bed, capturing the two adulterous lovers in the act. To make matters worse, he then calls all the other Olympian gods into the room to witness them. Ares and Aphrodite are humiliated.

Twins of Terror (Greek)

The adulterous affair of Ares and Aphrodite is not a fruitless one. Soon after, Aphrodite gives birth to sons, twin boys by the names of Deimus and *Phobus*. These boys certainly take after their father, to say the least. Deimus is a terrible god of fear, terror, and dread. Phobus is a god of panic, battlefield routs, and retreat/flight. The twins act as personal charioteers for Ares, and always accompany their father into the fray of battle (much to the fret and concern of their mother). They disperse fear among the warriors of whatever side is not favored by Ares.

Immortal Words

The word for fear, "phobia," comes from the name of one of Ares' twin sons, **Phobus,** due to his role as god of panic.

Specific descriptions of Deimus are hard to find. Phobus, however, is said to have a lion's mane or a lion-like head. Agamemnon, King of Mycenae in *The Iliad*, keeps the lion-headed likeness of Phobus on his shield. Heracles/Hercules also carries the lion likeness of Phobus on his armaments.

Wise Goddess of Victory (Greek)

Greek civilization valued strategic cunning, cleverness, intelligence, and reason. This could be the result of their rivalry with numerically superior adversaries such as the Persians. King Darius led a large-scale attack on the Greeks at the Battle of Marathon. Later, his grandson Xerxes would be pushed from Greece demoralized from his encounter at the Battle of Thermopylae, where a few hundred Spartan warriors held back his great army long enough for their city to be evacuated and burned.

Athena's birth is an odd one. In some myths, it is said that Athena's mother is Metis, Zeus' first wife. Concerned that she might give birth to a son stronger than him, he swallowed the pregnant Metis (much as his father, Cronus, did to him and his earlier siblings). Inside Zeus' skull, Metis makes a helmet and garment for her daughter. The hammering of Metis forming Athena's helmet gives Zeus terrible headaches. Hephaestus smacks Zeus in the head with a hatchet, splitting the god's head open. Athena springs from the gash in Zeus' forehead (likely symbolic of her future role as a goddess of wisdom), fully grown, wearing a bronze helmet and robe. Sometimes she is depicted with a shield and/or spear.

Myth and Metaphor _____

When one considers that a number of Greek victories were won as much by strategic cunning as strength, it is no wonder that the Greeks chose Athena as their patron goddess of warfare. As with many deities of war, Athena held multiple roles as a goddess of wisdom, the arts, weaving, justice, and industriousness. Athena's most well-known tale is of the aid and guidance she provides to the hero Odysseus in Homer's *Odyssey*.

God of Seven Heads (Slavic)

Unfortunately, due to the wide use of speculation and hypothetical creativity on the part of early scholars of the ancient Slavs, confirming the validity of Slavic myths is difficult. However, among mention as a war god of Slavic mythology is Rugiviet. Little is known about Rugiviet, aside from that he is a god of war who held the center of his domain on the island of Rugen, which sits in the Baltic Sea. The name Rugiviet translates as "Lord of Rugen." He is portrayed as having seven heads and carrying a drawn sword. However, little else is known about him that can be confirmed.

War in the Land of Enlightenment

Even in a land where all life is considered sacred and the path to salvation is paved by Karma, war gods prevail. Some are deified heroes. Others are gods of old. All are bringers of justice and the bane of tyrants. The Eastern gods of war are heroes of the people, guides to warriors and protectors of the people. No matter how they are portrayed, the war gods of the East convey a very clear message—"If you threaten my people with malevolence, my wrath upon you will be swift and terrible."

The Fall of a War God (Hindu)

Indra is a warrior god of the Hindu Dharma pantheon, as well as a god of the air, weather, and rain. In the *Vedas*, his position as a powerful god was secured when he slew a dragon of drought called Vritra, allowing the rains to fall and the solar cycles to resume. Indra is a balanced god who is feared for his ability to ravage the land with storms and revered for his ability to make the land fertile with rain and sun.

Later in Hindu Dharma myths, Indra's power becomes diminished. By the time he is spoken of in the Hindu Dharma epic *Mahabharata*, Indra begins to take on a personality much as that of the Greek Ares. He tries to seduce the wife of Gautama (Gow-tah-mah). Later, when written of in *Ramayana*, the tale of the legendary warrior Prince Rama, Indra has been even further diminished. He is defeated at the hands of the Ravana, demon King of the Rakshasa demons. To secure his release, the other gods are forced to grant Ravana the boon of immortality.

Indra's gradual but steady fall from power is attributed to the political motivations of Brahman class scribes during the Brahmana period (1800 to 1400 B.C.E.). The Brahma caste began to have conflicts with the *Kshatriya* warrior caste during this time, and because Indra was a primary deity of the Kshatriyas, they chose to use their positions as myth-makers to diminish him.

Yellow Emperor's Rival (Chinese)

The Chinese war god Chi Yu existed at a time when the gods involved themselves directly within the affairs of Man. As is common with powerful supernatural beings or deities in Chinese myth, Chi Yu has bull horns. His head is steel or covered by it.

The greatest rival of Chi Yu is referred to as Yellow Emperor, against whom he wages a terrible war. During the battle, Chi Yu is said to have conjured a thick fog with his magic while invoking the aid of storm spirits, so as to confuse the forces of Yellow Emperor. However, Yellow Emperor has a cart-compass made, which leads his forces through the fog. As a result, Chi Yu is defeated.

The Warrior Who Became a God (Chinese)

Kuang Kung is God of War in Taoist mythology. Originally, when he was a man, he went by the name of Guan Yu. Guan Yu was a legendary warrior and brilliant general who lived and fought around 200 C.E. Guan Yu's greatest exploits have been immortalized in the Chinese epic *The Romance of the Three Kingdoms.* Alongside his compatriots Liu Bei and Zhang Fei, he was a powerful general in the war to stop the Yellow Turban Rebellion. This rebellion stemmed from the sudden spread of a fanatical religious cult led by Zhang Jiao, the self-proclaimed "General of Heaven."

After crushing the rebellion, their ally, the warlord Cao-Cao, turned on the three warriors in a bid for control of all three kingdoms. He captured Guan Yu and tried bribing the general to join him. During his captivity, however, Guan Yu was treated with respect by Cao-Cao. Guan Yu continually refused to join Cao-Cao, though he did serve under him as a deputy general for a short time, and was eventually released. Upon returning to the forces of friend Liu Bei, he was given the title Front General and given leadership of the now-legendary Five Tiger Generals. (For information on another Five Tiger General, see Zhang Fei in Chapter 11.)

Guan Yu's life came to an end at the hands of former ally and personal rival Sun Quan, Emperor of the Kingdom of Wu (a descendent of Sun Tzu, the great Chinese strategist who authored *The Art of War*). After being defeated and having his path of retreat cut off, both he and his son Guan Ping were executed. Guan Yu's head was sent to Cao Cao as proof of his demise.

After his death, Guan Yu was deified into the fearsome figure now know as Kuang Kung, Taoist God of War. If you have ever entered a traditional Chinese restaurant, you have probably seen a statue of him without knowing it. Red-faced and scowling, Kuang Kung is always shown holding or wielding his legendary Guandao (a halberd-like weapon) which he named Blue Dragon (some records claim that the weapon was named Green Dragon Crescent). Though just short of two millennia have passed since his death, Guan Yu is worshipped in the form of Kuang Kung by certain Chinese people to this very day.

The Eight-Banner God (Japanese)

Hachiman is the protector god of Japan and its people, as well as the Shinto God of War. Likely, Hachiman is the deified figure of fourth century C.E. Japanese ruler Emperor Ojin. Of course, he is not only a god of war, but of agriculture and fishermen as well. The name Hachiman translates as "Eight Banner God," referring to the eight heavenly banners that he carries, which are associated with the Emperor Ojin. From Shinto to Buddhism … throughout the different religions of Japan, Hachiman has endured in them all.

War Gods in the Cradle of Civilization

In the Near and Middle East, the gods of war often cross geographic boundaries. As the different cultures conquered one another, usurped leaders, and rebelled against oppressors, the balance of power between them all was in constant flux. With each new ruling culture, war gods were modified, integrated, and/or replaced.

The Evolution of Inanna (Sumerian)

Ishtar is likely a version of the Sumerian goddess Inanna (see Chapter 6) modified sometime after they were conquered by the Assyrians. The Assyrians diminished Inanna's role as Ishtar, making her an impetuous and violent war goddess. Her most well-known portrayal is seen in the Assyrian *Epic of Gilgamesh*, where she is rebuked by the hero Gilgamesh. She sends the Bull of Heaven to destroy him after he refuses to become her husband. Gilgamesh uses the death of her husband, Dumuzi, to say that Ishtar (Inanna) has a reputation for having lovers that die. She eventually succeeds in killing Gilgamesh's only intimate friend, Enkidu. However, she fails to kill Gilgamesh himself.

The Ravager (Semitic)

The war god Resheph is most likely Semitic in origin. However, variations of this god exist from Egypt to Syria. In the biblical Book of Job, there is reference to the winged sons of Resheph, leading some to conclude that he was perhaps a vulture god (or some other carrion bird). The best depictions that exist of Resheph come from Egypt, where he is depicted as having Semitic features. He wears a crown on his head and carries an assortment of weapons. Just above his forehead are either a set of horns or a hand. In the Old Testament of the Bible, the word *Raseph* (likely a late-Judaic pronunciation of the name Resheph) is often used to refer to the wrathful thunderbolts of YHVH.

To the Syrians, Resheph was a god of war as well as pestilence, death, and plague. They associated him with their war goddess Anath.

The Falcon God (Egyptian)

Menthu was the Egyptian God of War, and is among some of the most ancient Egyptian gods. There is a multitude of different spellings for his name, because hieroglyphics are difficult to transcribe into English. Menthu's name translates as "Nomad," and he was first explained to be the damaging effects of the sun god Ra. This likely led to his eventual position as a god of war. At times, it is written that he also appears in the form of a pale bull with a face of pitch black. He is often drawn with the head of either a bull or falcon.

Warrior Weaver (Egyptian)

Net (again, there is a multitude of ways to spell this name, such as Neith or Nit) is the Egyptian Goddess of War and the Hunt. Her name translates as "weaver," suggesting that she is or once was a goddess of the loom. Her symbol is a pair of crossed arrows, suggesting her role as goddess of both war and the loom. As weaver, Net creates the bandages for the mummification of fallen warriors. She is guardian deity to the four sons of Horus, son of Osiris. When depicted, she is drawn in any number of ways— as a woman with the head of a lioness, a cow, a snake, or simply as a human-looking woman with a weaving shuttle on her head.

The Least You Need to Know

- ◆ War gods are separate from gods of destruction.
- ◆ Though they often create destruction, gods of war are rarely pleased to do so and are commonly motivated by justice.
- ◆ One common theme of the male war god figure is rejection from a father figure.
- ◆ War gods are respected by their cultures, and in some civilizations their violent natures must be appeased with sacrifices (sometimes human).
- ◆ War gods are almost always portrayed holding or wielding weapons that were common to the warriors of their civilizations and time periods.

Chapter 6

The Destroyers

In This Chapter

- ◆ Gods of death and destruction
- ◆ Gods of disease and pestilence
- ◆ The paradox of life and death in connection to the goddess figure
- ◆ Gods of death and why they exist universally in the pantheons of world myths

A culture's god of death often gives valuable insight into how the people of that culture viewed death as well as their beliefs regarding what happens after death. Death is often the result of destruction, so gods of death and destruction are closely related. Sometimes, the personification of both death and destruction is represented by the same god. Whether beloved or feared, these gods represent the two constants of human existence—all life must eventually end and all that is created, no matter how strongly built, will eventually be destroyed. Whether by violence, sickness, or simply the passage of time … all that is physical must eventually turn to dust.

Enemies of the Great Spirit (Native American)

In the native mythology of the Americas, gods of death and the dead are often depicted as benevolent beings who act as soul guides to the afterlife. Gods of destruction, however, are shown to be the opposite. They are enemies to the natural order of things, taking life and exacting their wrath on the world of humankind.

Brothers of Light and Dark (Inuit/Eskimo)

In Inuit Eskimo mythology, there are two primary gods associated with death—Anguta and Aipaloovik. However, these two gods are polar opposites in nature. Anguta is seen as a benevolent creator god who comes to gather the dead and escort them to the afterlife. This is not an evil act, but one that is done in accordance with the laws of existence. Anguta does not seek to cause death, but to help those who have died in their transition from life to death.

Avoiding the Labyrinth _____

Technically, the Inuit mythological tradition does not have "gods." Though these characters have godlike qualities, characters such as Anguta and Aipaloovik were simply powerful beings known as *tuurngait*. Because the English language does not really have a proper equivalent for the true meaning of this word, the simplest choice is to refer to them as "gods."

Aipaloovik, however, is not so benevolent. He is a malevolent sea god associated with murder and destruction (including vandalism to property). His terrible storms and violent nature *cause* death, as opposed to the more soul guide–like role of Anguta, who aids humans *after* their deaths.

The Skull-Faced God (Aztec)

Mictlantecuhtle, or Mictlantecuhtli, is god of the dead and ruler of the realm of Mictlan, the lowest level of the underworld in Aztec mythology. Mictlantecuhtli is depicted as having a skull for a head, a skeletal face, or wearing a skull as a mask. He is the husband of Mictecacihuatl, who rules at his side as queen of Mictlan.

Twins of Death (Mayan)

In Mayan myth, the domain of the dead is called Xibalba. On one occasion, the Lords of Xibalba summon a pair of twins called One Hunahpu and Seven Hunahpu, challenging them to play on the ball court at Charchah, known as the Great Abyss. To reach the realm of the dead, the twins cross four rapids, called Neck Canyon, Churning Spikes, Blood River, and Pus River. They then come to the crossing of four roads (Red, Black, Yellow, and White), and choose the Black road leading to Xibalba. There they undergo a series of ordeals in a place called the Dark House, after which they must pass through four more houses, each with a trial inside: Rattling House, Jaguar House, Bat House, and Razor House.

The Lords of Xibalba give the twins two lit cigars, which they are told to return still smoking the next morning. Failing to do so, the twins are condemned to death and sacrificed by the Lords of Xibalba at the Place of the Ball Game. One Hunahpu is subsequently decapitated, and his head put into the fork of a calabash tree, which immediately bears so much fruit that the Lords of the Dead cannot find his skull. In conclusion to the myth, the skull spits into the hand of a virgin named Blood Woman, who comes to the tree and subsequently immaculately conceives and gives birth to the twins, bringing their souls back into existence. As a result of this, One Hunahpu and Seven Hunahpu are now reborn as immortal, godlike beings.

The Pig-Headed God of Death (South Pacific)

In a myth from the Malekulan people of the South Pacific, death appears as a goddess with a pig head, guarding a stone that leads into the underworld. When the dead soul arrives at the stone and encounters the goddess, she draws a labyrinth in the sand and then erases half of it. To enter the underworld, and make its way successfully through the land of the dead, the soul must fill in the blank half of the labyrinth. To do this, the soul must be able to remember the personal form of the labyrinth that it learned when initiated in life during the tribe's rituals. If it cannot remember the labyrinth, it will fall into the abyss, unable to navigate the passage through the underworld.

A Different View of Death (African)

In the mythologies of the Africa peoples, gods of death and destruction are almost nonexistent. One common thread in African myth and religion is the belief that death and destruction are caused by humans and that gods primarily create. Even gods that cause harm to humans are still kind to them. For example, the Ugandan god Ruhanga loves human beings, though he is said to be the creator of illness, disease, and death. However, such things are a part of the chain of life and therefore necessary for existence.

Destroyers of the Old World (European)

In the European perspective, the realm of death was perceived as though it were a physical place. In the Western mythological view, the realms of the gods of death lay directly beneath their own world. These gods not only ruled over the lands of the deceased, but were often viewed as terrible and malevolent bringers of death. In the Western pantheons, deities of destruction were, more often than not, goddesses. The female as an instigator of chaos and a cruel destroyer of men's lives is a common theme in European mythology.

God of Valhalla, Goddess of Death

As you saw in Chapter 2, Loki was the cause of much death and destruction due to his trickster ways. Therefore, perhaps it is only fitting that his daughter, Hel, is the Norse goddess of death, the Queen of the Underworld. Hel is portrayed as quite unattractive. Her flesh is in an eternal state of rot, such as that of a corpse. One half of her body is a putrid color of blackish green, while the other half is pale white. Hel is also thought to be the name of her domain, the lowest of the nine worlds of Norse Mythology.

 Avoiding the Labyrinth _____

> Although Hades is the name of the Greek god of the underworld, it is known for certain that this is not the name of the underworld itself. However, in the case of Hel this is not so. In some sources, Hel refers to the death goddess herself, Loki's daughter and Queen of the Underworld. In other myths, the word Hel is used to refer to the realm over which she reigns, the lowest of the nine worlds in Norse mythology. Whether this is due to mistranslation or a double meaning is uncertain.

There is another god who plays a role in the death lore of the Norse as well—Odin. Odin is perhaps the most fascinating god of the Norse pantheon in that he is quite multi-faceted in nature. He assembles and leads the dead warriors, men who have died bravely in battle, in Valhalla. Although Odin is associated with death due to this, he is not regarded as a god of death. As you will see in many chapters of this book, Odin is one god who refuses to be labeled.

From Insanity to Death (Etruscan)

Mania, goddess of insanity to the Greeks, took on a slightly different role when she was adapted into a goddess of death by the Etruscans. Later, when the Etruscans were absorbed into the Roman culture, the goddess continued to be viewed as a goddess of death. She is wife to Mantus, the Etruscan Lord of the Underworld, and said to be mother of all nocturnal spirits/demons. Mantus, Mania's husband, is associated with the Italian city of Mantua, now called Mantova.

The Golden Apple of Discord (Greek/Roman)

Eris (sometimes spelled Aris; she is called Discordia by the Romans) is not specifically referred to as the goddess of death in the pantheon to which she belongs. Technically speaking, Eris is the goddess of strife, hardship, and discord. However, the widespread death and destruction caused by this single goddess has earned her a place in this chapter, as she is undoubtedly a malevolent entity associated with countless deaths and widespread destruction.

For starters, Eris gives birth to a terrifying brood; among them are the most destructive forces of Greco-Roman mythology. Her children, as written by Hesiod in his *Theogony*, are Algea (Pain), Amphillogiai (Disputes), Androctasiai (Manslaughters), Ate (Ruin), Dysnomia (Anarchy), Horkos (Oath, who torments men who falsely swear oaths), Hysminia (Fighting), Makhai (Battles), Neikia (Disagreement), Ponos (Work and Toil), Limos (Famine), Lethe (Forgetfulness), Phonoi (Massacres/Murders), and Psuedia (Deception/Lies).

According to Homer, who credits Eris with starting the Trojan War, she is sister to Ares (called Mars by the Romans), the God of War. In her love for chaos and destruction, she sets into motion the chain of events that result in one of the bloodiest wars the world has ever seen—the Trojan War.

Since she is well known for causing trouble, Eris is shunned from the wedding celebration of Peleus and Thetis (parents of Achilles). In spite, she tosses a golden apple into the celebration, right in the middle of Aphrodite, Hera, and Athena. On the apple is inscribed the word *Kallisti* ("Most Beautiful"), implying that the apple was meant for the most beautiful of the three goddesses. Vain by nature, a quarrel breaks out between them as to which of them the apple should go. Paris, the prince of Troy, is asked to act as judge. Each goddess offers a gift if he chooses in her favor. First, Hera offers power in the political arena. Then Athena offers skill on the battlefield. Lastly, Aphrodite offers him the love of the most beautiful woman in the world (who, unfortunately, turns out to be Helen, who is already married to Menelaus, King of Sparta). Paris chooses Aphrodite and seals the terrible fate of an entire kingdom.

Having begun a war that would claim the lives of countless Trojans and Spartans, Eris truly stands out—a goddess of discord, but a prominent figure when it comes to death and destruction.

Hades and His Unwilling Bride (Greek)

Hades, quite simply, is the name of the Greek pre-Christian god of the underworld (known to the Romans as Pluto). Too often, his name is mistakenly used to refer to the realm over which he rules. He abducted his wife Persephone, daughter of the Earth Goddess Demeter, and brought her to his world. While there, she eats half the seeds of a pomegranate. When Zeus finally arrives to order Hades release her, it is too late. Having eaten these seeds, she is required to spend half the year in the underworld with her dark husband. As a result, the months when Persephone is free are spring and summer (because her mother the Earth Goddess is happy). When she is in the underworld with Hades, it is fall and winter (because Demeter is sad at the absence of her beloved daughter).

Wrath of Baba Yaga

Another remarkable image of a death goddess of sorts comes from the Russian folktale "Vasilisa the Beautiful," in which a young girl is sent into the forest by her wicked stepmother to get some light from the witch. On the way into the forest, three horses go by … red, white, and black. The witch, Baba Yaga, lives in a hut that stands on chicken legs, with fences surrounding it made from the bones of the dead whom she has devoured, whose skulls are put on sticks all around the cottage. After Vasilisa goes inside the hut, Baba Yaga comes crashing home through the forest, riding a mortar, and holding a pestle in one hand and a broomstick in the other (to sweep up her tracks).

When Vasilisa performs a series of tasks, Baba Yaga rewards her by telling her the three horses are her servants (the red horse of the dawn, the white of the day, and the black of the night), and then gives her a skull on a stick to take home with her.

Laserlike light shines through the eye sockets, guiding Vasilisa back through the forest. When she arrives home and puts the skull in the living room, the lights shining through the eyes kill Vasilisa's wicked stepmother.

The Single Eye of Death (Celtic)

Balor is a god from the pre-Christian religion of the Celts (who are the ancestors of the Irish, Scottish, Welsh, Breton, and Gaelic peoples). Balor is a one-eyed giant and the Celtic God of Death. The reason this title is given to him probably has a lot to do with that one eye. The problem with Balor's eye is that it is an eye of death, which will take the life of anyone it so much as glances at. Needless to say, Balor had to keep his homicidal eye closed most of the time.

The most popular myth surrounding Balor explains a prophecy that reaches the death god's ears. The prophecy foretells that Balor will one day die at the hands of his grandson. In an attempt to stay the hand of fate, he locks away his only daughter, Etheline, in a tower of glass (in the original myth, the tower was likely made of crystal, not glass, because glass was not yet being used by the Celts).

However, the clever god Cian is able to sneak inside by disguising himself as an old crone. This type of disguise is similar to the one used by Loki (see Chapter 2). Once they are inside, the two become intimate and soon a child is born—Lugh. Furious, Balor tosses his own grandson into the terrible sea.

Wrath from the East

Although there are a number of death-and-destruction-related gods in the East, perhaps none is more widely used across Asia than that of Yama of the Vedas. However, while he may be the most popular death god of Asia, he is not alone. The eastern parts of the world are no strangers to widespread destruction and death. Earthquakes, volcanoes, tsunami (tidal waves), hurricanes, typhoons, and (in recent years) the atomic bomb are all events that have been experienced by the peoples of Asia. When one considers this, it is no wonder that they have a wider array of such destructive and death-related gods.

Yama of the Vedas

The myth of the god Yama began in the oldest of the Hindu Vedic texts (the Vedas). This myth influenced Buddhism and would eventually spread throughout most of Asia, taking a number of forms, some of which you will see later in this section.

In the Hindu myths, Yama was the first mortal to die. He is a twin, and his sister's name is Yami. Upon dying, he witnessed the path to the celestial spheres. As a result, he was appointed as the Lord of the Dead. He has green and/or red skin and wears crimson clothing. He is often shown riding upon the back of a water buffalo. He reins with his right hand (although sometimes he is depicted as holding an iron rod in that hand) and holds a looped rope (some myths refer to it as a noose) which he uses somewhat as a lasso to pull souls from dead bodies.

Yama is aided by an odd scribe by the name of Chitragupta who, similar to a macabre Santa Claus, keeps an accurate record (sort of a "naughty list") of the Karma, whether positive or negative, accumulated by the actions of every individual on the planet. Chitragupta's meticulous record keeping is of great use to Yama, as it ensures that all people are judged appropriately for their actions. The Brahmans are sent on to the celestial plane. Those who are not yet ready are sent to the harsh realm of Naraka and purified of the negative Karma they collected during their most recent life. This process can at times take thousands of years. Naraka is not exactly "hell," and a more detailed explanation is provided in the following section. Since Yama is considered King of Naraka, he is often called Yamaraja (Raja = King).

Yama is also thought of as Lord of Justice (or *dharma*, a word which is layered with integrated meanings, and which can be translated as the law of existence, destiny/fate, and/or acceptance of the will of Brahma). Although he is the appointed judge and lord of the departed, Yama should in no way be thought of as the giver or taker of life or death. In fact, he is more of a servant to Vishnu and Shiva, the sustainer and destroyer of the Hindu Dharma *Trimurti* (three-member Godhead). In a later Hindu text called the *Katha Upanishad*, Yama is portrayed as a teacher and the wisest of the devas (a lower echelon race of divine beings to which Yama belongs).

Immortal Words

In Hindu Dharma myth, the **Trimurti** refers to the three entities that are the natures of the unknowable god that govern physical existence. The first member is Brahma, the Creator and most revered of the three. The second is Vishnu, the Sustainer who sleeps through each existence from its creation until its destruction. His dreams create the illusion of the physical reality in which we live (an idea that heavily influenced the Wachowkski Brothers when developing *The Matrix* films). The third and (quite literally) final member of the Trimurti is Shiva, God of Destruction.

Understanding Naraka

The Sanskrit term *Naraka* is often mistranslated into English as the Hindu equivalent of the Christian "hell" or Catholic "purgatory." However, this misunderstanding is likely a result of there being no exact word in English equal to *Naraka*. Naraka is not a place of eternal damnation, as is the hell of Western Christian theology. It is also not a place of forced purification where souls must remain until some final Judgment Day, as is the Catholic purgatory. Instead, Naraka is a place of purification where the spirits of the deceased come to be cleansed through suffering over a span of time (the length of which depends on how much negative karma the spirit accumulated during life). Damnation by a god is not what sends a person to Naraka, but rather their own negative and immoral actions during life.

Yama of Buddhism

Yama, as already stated, was an influential figure in the mythology surrounding Buddhism in Asian culture. In Chinese, Yama is called Yanluo. Unlike the Yama of Hinduism, Yanluo is both Lord of the Dead as well as their judge. In Tibetan Buddhism, he is referred to as Yamantaka. In Buddhist myths, Yami is often spoken of as Yama's consort, not his sister.

Enma-Dai-O: Japanese Yama

Another example of the Yama figure can be found in Japanese mythology, in that of the death god Enma-Dai-O. He is portrayed as a gigantic figure with a red face, adorned with a long beard and always grimacing. His eyes are large and bulging. In Japanese culture, Enma-Dai-O is also used as a type of *boogie man*, and stories about him are told to children to encourage good behavior. For example, children are told that if they tell lies one day, Enma-Dai-O will come and take out their tongues.

Dancers of Death, Lovers of Destruction

Kali is known as "the black one," and she is perhaps the most terrifying goddess figure in all mythology. She is often shown with black skin. From her terrible mouth of bloody fangs falls a lolling, blood-red tongue. Around her neck hangs a necklace of human skulls. Her symbols are darkness and blood, and from her likenesses rivers of blood are often shown to flow. She is said to live at the top of Mount Vindhya in India. At deaths, when humans lament and mourn, Kali dances with joy. In some myths it is said that she was originally the victim of infanticide. The first mortal baby to be murdered, she ascended into Heaven as a wrathful goddess of death, sickness, and destruction.

Kali, though a harbinger of death, has a role in the cycle of creation, destruction, and rebirth. She is a consort of Shiva (sometimes, she is said to be his wife) and in some myths it is said that she was tamed of her reckless and destructive behavior by him. One of the most famous images of the Hindu Lord of Death is of the dancing Shiva, known as Shiva Nataraja. However, it is interesting to note that in one of Kali's common depictions she is shown standing or dancing over the corpse of a dead Shiva. The ruled female becomes the ruler.

Shiva (also spelled Siva) is the Hindu Dharma God of Destruction, so it is only fitting that Kali is close to him. The goddess most commonly referred to as Shiva's true wife, however, is Shakti (also said Sati).

One image shows Shiva dancing beneath a halo of fire, with four arms: one hand points downward in the posture of release, another is uplifted in the posture known as "fear not." Shiva's third right hand holds a drum, and his fourth left hand a flame. The right hand signifies birth, and the left death, so that the god embraces the opposites of the beginning and the end (of the individual, and of all the worlds of the universe). Because the dancing Shiva is shown standing on a dwarf whose name is Ignorance, death becomes a positive thing, releasing our souls from the illusions of the physical world (which the Hindus called Maya).

Gods of the Fall (Middle and Near Eastern)

From Babylon to Egypt, the concept of death was an enigma that the mythologies of the Near and Middle East attempted to unravel. Death was a passageway from the harsh world of humanity into the wondrous realm of the gods. To cross the threshold was a finite act, one from which few would ever return. Those who did return, however, were granted immortality and power over life and death.

Inanna's Horrible Sister

Ereshkigal is the Sumerian goddess of the underworld. She is probably best known for her role in the *Descent of Inanna* myth. Inanna is sister to Ereshkigal and, unlike her dark sibling, is a very complex goddess figure, one that is far more difficult to label. Whereas Ereshkigal is the Goddess of the Underworld, Inanna's roles as a goddess are multi-faceted. She is a mother goddess, Queen of Heaven and Earth, a bird-snake goddess, and more. Also, judging from the most well-known myth in which she plays a part, it would appear that Ereshkigal is full of homicidal jealous rage for her sister.

When Inanna travels into Ereshkigal's realm, her sister sets upon her the "eye of death." Inanna, obviously, dies. Adding insult to injury, Ereshkigal hangs Inanna's corpse on the wall. Three days later, however, Inanna's advisor and companion Ninshubar appeals to her friend's patriarchal gods. All but one—Enki—refuses to help Inanna. Enki fashions two androgynous beings from the mud under his fingernails. He breathes on them and they are brought to life. These beings, one of which is called a *kurgarra* and the other a *galatur*, go to the underworld. Using the "water of life" and "food of life," they are able to resurrect Inanna. Ereshkigal orders that, because none who enter her realm can be allowed to return to life, Inanna must find someone to take her place. After searching through her mournful relatives, she condemns her quite unremorseful husband, Dumuzi, to take her place.

The Jackal-Headed Guardian (Egyptian)

Anubis is actually a Greek spelling of the name of the Egyptian god of the dead, Anpu or Yenipu. For the sake of familiarity, the name Anubis will be used here. Anubis has the body of a man and the head of a jackal. He is the patron deity of embalming and the protector of tombs.

Anubis also acts as a guide for the souls of the dead, taking them from this world to the judgment hall of Amenti. Once there, the heart of the deceased is placed on one side of a scale. On the other side Amenti places a feather that represents truth and righteousness. The balance of this scale decides one's fate in the afterlife. If one's heart outweighs Amenti's feather, the outcome will be grim.

Anubis is the son of Osiris and Isis (or Nephthys). When Osiris was killed by treachery, Egyptian myth tells that Anubis embalmed him until the goddess Isis could resurrect him. In other versions, Anubis' body acts as a sarcophagus of sorts, and he swallows his father's corpse to preserve it until resurrection.

Enemy of the Sun (Egyptian)

Apep may have at one time actually been an Egyptian sun god. However, his role as a solar deity seems to have been usurped at some point, probably when Attum-Ra (later just Re or Ra) was adopted as a chief god by the rulers of Egypt. In the surviving myths, he is portrayed as more of a demon than a god. He is evil incarnate, the absolute personification of darkness and malice.

As the sun god Ra rides his chariot into the western sunset, he enters the dark realms. He must ride successfully through this dangerous land every night, doing battle from his chariot with the evil serpentine Apep, who is called "the enemy of the sun" for this reason. Every morning, however, Ra arises triumphantly on the eastern horizon in the form of the sunrise.

The Least You Need to Know

- Death gods aren't always portrayed as evil, because death is seen by some cultures as a part of the life cycle.

- Underworld is an umbrella term meant to refer to the worlds of the dead or afterlife.

- Underworld does not necessarily mean hell, in the way this word is used today.

- Gods of the dead are rarely seen as responsible for *causing* death.

Part

Heroes

Since man's first steps into the great unknown, which was then no further than the horizon, heroes have walked among us. Their perilous journeys, violent battles, and courageous deeds have granted them immortality in legends of valor and songs of glory. They are the models of men, displaying amazing amounts of courage, honor, and skill, at levels which others may never reach but continue to strive for.

Whether the half-divine sons of gods or simply human warriors of uncommon valor, they stand as a testament to the potential of Man. They represent the hope of a man that, when it matters most, he will prove to be greater than he appears, braver than he feels, and stronger than he ever thought possible.

Chapter 7

Journeying with Heroes

In This Chapter

- ◆ Understanding The Hero's Journey
- ◆ Identifying Jungian archetypes
- ◆ Learning the work of Joseph Campbell
- ◆ Journeying into the underworld

At the heart of many myths exists a fascinating cycle of separation, initiation, and return. We now refer to this cycle as "The Hero's Journey." This journey is not restricted to myths of the ancient past. In fact, its use continues to prevail to this day. The Hero's Journey of today manifests in movies, fiction, urban legends, and even comic books. This acts as a universal metaphor for the human experience, and understanding how the structure of this journey works is an essential part of having a working understanding of mythology.

Reflections of the Psyche in Myth: Jung's Archetypes

Carl Gustav Jung, born in 1875, was a Swiss psychiatrist and a student of Sigmund Freud. Later in life he began to question the theories of his mentor, leading him to develop his own theory of psychoanalysis, which he called *analytical psychology*. Jung's analytical theory sought to positively influence the deep-seated drives of the human psyche by connecting the psychology of individuals to universal cultural patterns and symbols, which Jung called *archetypes*.

Immortal Words _____

Libido is psychic and/or emotional energy stemming from primitive physical urges, usually focused on the attainment of some goal.

Jung agreed with Freud's idea that the *libido* and the unconscious played key roles in the development of personalities. However, the two disagreed about the exact natures of these roles. Freud believed that the libido was just a sex drive, the impulses from which were the basic motivators of all human behavior. Jung, however, saw the libido as the energy of life; therefore, sexual impulse was only one of many manifestations.

Perhaps one of the most revolutionary of all Jung's early concepts came about when he separated the unconscious into two parts—the *personal unconscious* and the *collective unconscious*. Jung's separation of the unconscious mind contrasted dramatically with the more physiologically centered ideas of Freud, as well as a large majority of other psychiatrists. Many viewed Jung's theory as too philosophical, even metaphysical, to be used for psychoanalysis. Jung did not deny his belief in the existence of a world beyond that of the senses. In fact, he seems to have embraced the mystical aspects of his theory, and is quoted as saying, "I simply believe that part of the human Self or Soul is not subject to the laws of space and time." During a 1959 BBC interview, when asked if he believed in the existence of God, Jung replied "I don't believe—I *know*."

Immortal Words _____

An **archetype** in Jungian psychology is an inherited idea or mode of thought stemming from the experiences of the human race and present in the unconscious of individuals.

The personal unconscious, according to Jung, is the part of the human psyche within which repressed experiential material is stored. The collective unconscious, however, connects all humans as a race. This part of the psyche contains the racial memory of humankind, and it contains the cumulative experience of all human generations. These cumulative experiences manifest in the form of *archetypes*.

In his work as a psychiatrist, Jung began to observe that a large number of his patients, while conveying dreams to him, often reported seeing images in their dreams that were not a part of their actual experience. This led him to start searching for the source of these images. Throughout the 1920s, Jung traveled frequently to places such as America, India, and Africa. During these trips, he found that a number of symbols, themes, and character-types existed in all cultures, despite being separated from one another—culturally, linguistically, and geographically. These common elements, these archetypes, were found in religions, myths, artwork, and folklore.

As a result of his findings, Jung concluded that the human knowledge of these archetypes is not learned but already present in the collective unconscious of the individual. The presence of archetypal images in the collective unconscious allows humans to sense them intuitively. Archetypes often include mythic figures, the most common of which is the Hero. There exists a multitude, however, such as the Wild Man of the Woods, the Wanderer, the Serpent, and lastly a dark and terrible figure that Jung referred to as the shadow. The shadow represents the primal, lustful, bestial, and savage side of human nature. The shadow cannot be shed, only held back or repressed, as it is a part of the human Self.

Jung organized the human Self into parts, the most essential being the *shadow, persona, anima,* and *animus.* The *persona* (or mask) is one's outward self, the person that you show to others on social levels. The *anima, shadow,* and *animus* are quite opposite. These parts of the self represent the unconscious contrast of the public persona. These parts represent the traits that people even hide from themselves, primarily because they do not match with their personas. The *anima* and *animus* are especially hard to accept, because they represent the opposite-sex qualities of humans. For males, the *anima* represents their "inner female," and is often based on one or more maternal figures. For females, there is the *animus,* which represents their "inner masculinity." In turn, the *animus* is often based on one or more paternal figures.

Immortal Words

Anima/animus are the opposite-sex traits that contrast with the public persona. For men, the *anima* is the inner feminine. For women, the *animus* is the inner masculine.

Jung died in 1961 in Zurich, Switzerland. However, even after death, his work has continued to influence scholars in a number of fields—mythology, the humanities, psychology, and even human resources, to name just some.

Depth Psychology

Perhaps the most prevalent example of Jung's legacy is evidenced by the birth of *Depth Psychology*. Depth Psychology is closely linked to the study of myth due to its use of archetypes to explain the deeper meanings behind human experiences and behaviors.

Immortal Words

Depth Psychology refers to any psychological approach that examines the depth (meaning hidden or deeper parts) of human experience.

Depth Psychology, as it exists today, is actually a methodology of psychoanalysis that is an integration of the theories of Sigmund Freud (psychoanalytical), Alfred Adler (Individual Psychology), Carl Jung (analytical psychology), and James Hillman (archetypal psychology).

Depth Psychology states that the human psyche is both conscious and unconscious. The unconscious in turn contains repressed experiences and other personal-level issues in its "upper" layers, and "transpersonal" (collective and/or archetypal) forces in its depths. The psyche spontaneously generates mythical/religious symbols and is therefore not just instinctive in nature but spiritual as well. If this is true, then Depth Psychology implies that a person's choice to have a spiritual life does not and cannot exist. Instead, the question posed by Depth Psychology is how people deal with that spirituality. In short, what do/should people do with it?

All minds, all lives, according to this school of psychoanalysis, are ultimately involved in some sort of myth-making. Mythology is not a series of old explanations for occurrences that ancient science or technology could not explain. Myth, in Depth Psychology, is viewed as the collective wisdom of humanity being expressed by symbolic storytelling.

The largest school of Depth Psychology in the United States is the Pacifica Graduate Institute in Carpinteria, California. Go to www.pacifica.edu for more information.

During the last few decades, Depth Psychology has also begun to adopt the teachings of another myth scholar—Joseph Campbell.

Behind the Mask of Myth: Joseph Campbell

Joseph John Campbell was born in 1904 in White Plains, New York. He became interested in Native American culture at an early age, which he attributed to trips that he took with his father to the American Museum of Natural History in New

York, which displayed exhibits of Native American artifacts. As a child, he immersed himself in the myths of Native Americans. This led to Campbell's lifelong passion for myth and to his examinations of common mythological threads that existed between separated human cultures.

Campbell began his academic career at Dartmouth College, where he originally studied biology and mathematics. However, he found these fields of study unfulfilling and abandoned them for the humanities.

After completing his Master's degree, Campbell received a fellowship from Columbia to study and carry out research in Europe. Campbell studied Old French at the University of Paris in France, and *Sanskrit* at the University of Munich in Germany. He proved to be a gifted linguist, learning to read and speak both French and German fluently after only a few months of study. He would remain fluent in both languages throughout the rest of his life.

During his time in Europe, Campbell was introduced to the works of several significant writers. The ideas presented by the writings of these men would be the catalyst for his life's work. These men, who would have such an impact on Campbell's future work, were James Joyce, author of numerous classics such as *Finnegans Wake;* Thomas Mann, a German novelist and social critic;

Immortal Words

Sanskrit is a written language that was taught to the people of India in ancient times by migratory tribes that are referred to today as the Indo-Europeans or Aryans.

and a Swiss psychiatrist by the name of Carl Gustav Jung. He also developed a close friendship with Jiddu Krishnamurti, a well-known writer, scholar, and public speaker from India who addressed such subjects as human relationships, meditation, and how to spark positive changes to a global society.

Avoiding the Labyrinth

The Aryan people of the Indo-Europeans should not be confused with those mentioned in the ideologies of hate groups such as Nazism or White Supremacy. To the contrary of what these groups believe, there is no evidence to support that the Aryan or Indo-European tribes were entirely Caucasian. Also, there are no Vedic, Sanskrit, or Old Persian texts that make any mention of such things as "master races" or "racial purity." In fact, it would appear by how far they would eventually spread—from India to Iran to Greece to Germany (and beyond)—that these tribes were quite racially tolerant.

In 1929, when Campbell returned to Columbia from his travels, he insisted that he be allowed to study Sanskrit and Art in addition to Medieval Literature. When the university did not allow this, Campbell decided not to continue the Ph.D. program at Columbia. He left the university, and would never again pursue a traditional doctorate. Weeks after leaving Columbia, the stock market crashed and the Great Depression began.

During the Great Depression, Campbell spent five years reading in near seclusion. He has been quoted as saying "I would get nine hours of sheer reading done a day. This went on for five years straight." During this time, Campbell amassed an impressive mental arsenal by immersing himself in and completely absorbing a vast array of myths, legends, religious texts, academic journals, and other types of literature. Toward the end of this five-year period, Campbell began a project that would become a massive four-volume work on myth, *The Masks of God*.

The volumes of the collection are organized as follows:

- Primitive Mythology

- Oriental Mythology

- Occidental Mythology

- Creative Mythology

Based primarily on anthropological and historical information, the previous series would differ greatly from Campbell's other works. For example, in his work *The Hero with a Thousand Faces*, Campbell discusses the *monomyth* as it applies specifically to The Hero's Journey cycle. This book would also greatly influence George Lucas in his creation of the *Star Wars* epic.

Immortal Words

Monomyth refers to parallel structures and patterns that are experienced by particular character archetypes in different tales, myths, and legends from all across the globe. The term has also been used as an alternative way to refer to The Hero's Journey cycle.

The Hero's Journey

Campbell's Hero's Journey theorizes and illustrates how a multitude of myths from all across the globe, having survived for several millennia, all have the same fundamental structures in common. Although the basic makeup of The Hero's Journey is often briefly summed up as separation, initiation, and return, it is not quite that simple.

Campbell's Hero's Journey structure has a number of stages:

1. **Call to adventure**—The hero must accept or decline the call to adventure. However, to refuse the call often results in negative consequences. For example, in the original movie *Star Wars*, Luke Skywalker refuses to follow Obi Wan Kenobi to rescue Princess Leia because of his commitment to helping his uncle work. However, when the pair arrives at Luke's home, they find his uncle and aunt murdered. Their murders free him so that he may answer the call to adventure.

2. **Road of trials**—The hero is tested in some way, and either succeeds or fails. For example, again from *Star Wars*, Luke Skywalker succeeds in rescuing Princess Leia. However, he fails many tests put before him by Yoda.

3. **Complete the mission/boon**—By completing the task set before him or her, the hero often obtains important self-knowledge and/or some object or skill which will save/improve his or her world. For example, by facing his father and the evil emperor in *Return of the Jedi*, Luke Skywalker rescues the galaxy from oppression and saves the soul of his father from the Dark Side. Also, his trials with Kenobi and Yoda teach him to wield a light saber and to "use the force."

4. **Return to point of origin**—Simply put, the hero must voyage back from whence he came, as Luke Skywalker does when he returns to Tatooine, his home planet, to save his friend Han Solo from Jabba the Hutt in *Return of the Jedi*.

5. **Apply the learned skill/acquired boon**—The knowledge, skill, weapon, or item that the hero has gained from his journey is now used to save/improve the world. When Luke returns to Tatooine, he uses the force as well as his light saber (a skill and a boon collected in his journey) to save himself and rescue his friends from being executed.

In *The Hero with a Thousand Faces*, Campbell wrote, "A hero ventures forth from the world … into a region of supernatural wonder; fabulous forces are there encountered and a decisive victory is won. The hero comes back … with the power to bestow boons on his fellow man."

To Hell and Back: The Nekyia

One of Joseph Campbell's students was a man by the name of Dr. Evans Lansing Smith, who acted as a contributor and consultant for this book. In continuing the evolution that began with Jung and continued with Campbell, Dr. Smith turned his focus toward one very specific and common theme of mythology—the descent into the underworld. Smith refers to this theme as the *nekyia*.

Immortal Words _____

> Derived from Greek for "dead," *necro*, **nekyia** was a word used by the Greeks to refer to the eleventh book of Homer's *Odyssey*, in which Odysseus travels into Hades to consult the spirit of the blind prophet, Tiresias, so that he might find out how to get back home. Here, it is used to refer to the theory of Dr. Evans Lansing Smith for universal structures and collective archetypes that make up all heroic journeys/descents to the underworld.
>
> **Necrotype** is an integration of the Greek word *necro* (dead/death) with the word "archetype" (see earlier section on Jung). This word refers to universal symbols of the human imagination (i.e., archetypes) catalyzed by the journey to the underworld (*nekyia*).

The nekyia cycle is parallel with Campbell's Hero's Journey—separation, initiation, and return. However, the environment is quite different. For example, while the hero of archetype must answer a call to adventure, the hero of nekyia must answer a call to death. The separation is not just from the hero's home, but the entire world of the living.

The *necrotypal* hero must journey into a world from which no one returns—the *necropolis*. The difference between ordinary heroes and necrotypal heroes is that heroes of nekyia journeys *do*, in fact, return from realms of death and darkness to the lands of light and life. Not all nekyia myths are literal journeys into an *afterlife*, but are symbolic journeys into low and dark places, where the hero is tested and/or faced with death. Archetypal heroes may fail their tasks and be able to physically survive. For the necrotypal hero, however, survival in failure is not an option—failure will result in an eternity of death and darkness (and, sometimes, a fate worse than death).

Take the myth of Persephone, for example, daughter of the earth goddess who was kidnapped by Hades and held captive in the underworld. While there, she could not eat the food of that world as to do so would trap her there forever. However, Persephone fails her test and eats half the seeds of a pomegranate while in the underworld.

Torn by grief at her daughter's kidnapping, the earth goddess begins failing in her duties. Plants begin dying, clouds fill the sky, and cold covers the face of the earth. Seeing the state of things on Earth, Zeus demands that Hades return Persephone to her mother. However, though Hades follows Zeus' commands, the God of Thunder and Lightning cannot save Persephone entirely. Since she faltered and ate half the seeds of the pomegranate, she will forever be required to spend half the year in the underworld. As a result, when Persephone is free and with her mother, the earth has spring and summer. When Persephone returns to Hades in the underworld, the earth has fall and winter.

From ancient Babylonian/Sumerian myths to American Indian to modern-day Christianity, the nekyia is a universal occurrence in mythology.

Avoiding the Labyrinth

Calling the underworld of Greco-Roman myths Hades is probably one of the most common mistakes in mythology. Hades is not the name of the underworld, but of the god who presides over it. Necropolis comes from the Greek words *necro-* (dead/death) and *-polis* (city), so it translates as "City of Death" or "City of the Dead." In modern times, this term is often used to refer to the concept of the underworld in general.

For specific examples of the nekyia, please refer to the Index and look up the myths to any of the following heroes:

- Inanna
- Odysseus
- Jesus' Harrowing of Hell
- Beowulf
- Hercules/Heracles
- Scathach
- Persephone

Although this brief list identifies a handful of necrotypal heroes who complete nekyia journeys, it should in no way be considered complete. This list should only be seen as a guide so that you may begin to understand the nekyia and learn to identify necrotypes for yourself.

Finally, the underworld itself will mean different things in different versions of the myth. It is like a mansion with four chambers, which we can call the Inferno, the Crypt, the Cornucopia, and the Temenos.

As the Inferno, the underworld into which the hero journeys is a place of torment and suffering, where sinners are punished for misdeeds and crimes committed during life. As a Crypt, the underworld is an ancestral vault, a place where the hero/heroine encounters the familial dead. Typically, the ancestor provides crucial information about the hero's destiny, as when Odysseus is warned by his dead mother and by Agamemnon about the suitors waiting to kill him when he returns home to Ithaca.

The ancestor may also reveal the hidden mysteries of the soul and the universe, mysteries that may be symbolized by archetypal images, or necrotypes. These images may be seen as the seed forms of all things that exist. Hence, the underworld is a Cornucopia, brimming with the fruits of the earth.

Such encounters with the ancestral dead, and the revelations they provide, lead to a dramatic transformation of consciousness, and to the birth of a new sense of identity. In this sense, the underworld is a *Temenos*, a Greek word referring to a sacred space of revelation and transformation.

All four of these chambers of the underworld may be applicable to any particular version of the nekyia, although different conceptions of the underworld may emphasize one or more of the chambers.

Finally, the descent to and return from the underworld (the nekyia) may be best understood as a kind of allegory, a symbolic image of the journeys we all go through in life, right here and now, day after day, year after year. Perhaps D.H. Lawrence said it best: "Every great conquest of life requires a Harrowing of Hell." The nekyia is a myth to live by, as well as a myth to die by.

From Womb to Tomb

From the moment an individual is born, he or she emerges from the mother's womb innocent, helpless, and vulnerable, and the way humans are at the moments of their births bears similarities to our feelings when it comes to death. Humans wish to die without heavy sins upon their consciences—to die innocent (though this, of course, is impossible). Also, human beings are helpless to stop death's inevitable occurrence. Lastly, death comes upon us when we are vulnerable—to disease, hunger, weather, or some extreme physical trauma.

Oddly, just as we arise from the enclosure of the womb in birth, we are enclosed into a tomb or coffin after our deaths. This is referred to as the concept of "From womb to tomb." In the nekyia, the journey into the underworld is very much a metaphor for one's desire to return to the womb, a place of nourishment and beneficence, only to find one is in fact face-to-face with the tomb, a place of wisdom, fear, corruption, frailty, and the reality of death.

The Least You Need to Know

- The Hero's Journey begins with the call to adventure.

- The Hero's Journey cycle includes separation, initiation, and return.

- One manifestation of The Hero's Journey, called the nekyia, is a descent into the underworld.

- There is a close archetypal relationship between the womb and the tomb.

Chapter 8

Tragic Heroes

In This Chapter

- ◆ The fatal flaw of the tragic hero
- ◆ The sorrowful journey walked by heroes of tragedy
- ◆ The paradox of tragedy—free will versus fate
- ◆ The lesson of the tragic hero–character archetype

The downfall of the hero is often the result of his own actions, the tragic consequences of some fatal flaw in his character or physical makeup. The Greeks give us the term now used for this genre of hero—tragedy. The once grand and adventurous lives of these heroes come crashing down into ruin, leaving them traumatized, insane, maimed, and/or destitute before the sweet release of death finally brings an end to their suffering.

The High Flyer (Greek)

Ikarus (also spelled Icarus) is the son of Daedalus. Father and son are imprisoned in a tower of the labyrinth by the King of Crete for Daedalus' involvement in the birth of the Minotaur (see Chapter 9). Soon, Daedalus uses his ingenuity to devise an escape plan that consists of making wings for the both of them by taking bird feathers and sealing them together with wax.

After completing the first phase of their plan, Daedalus and Ikarus bind the wings to their backs and take a running leap from the tower. Daedalus warns Ikarus that they must be careful of one factor that could destroy their plan—the sun. Since the wings are primarily held together by wax, Daedalus explains to his son that they must not fly too close to the sun or the heat will melt their wings. Ikarus, unfortunately, behaves as if he has ADD and in the exhilaration of flight completely forgets about his father's warning.

Ikarus soars higher and higher, eventually coming too close to the sun. His wings melt away and Ikarus plummets to his doom into the sea—which came to be called the Icarian Sea as a result of this myth. In some myths, he is saved at the last minute by the goddess Pallas Athena, who transforms him into a bird (usually, a partridge). In other myths, Ikarus' body later washes ashore to be found by the legendary demigod hero Herakles, who gives the fallen son of Daedalus a proper burial.

Avoiding the Labyrinth

In most myths, Daedalus and Ikarus are portrayed as being father and son. However, there are other versions of this myth that portray the two men as uncle and nephew. The truth is of no consequence, however, as the chain of events in the Ikarus myth is always nearly identical no matter which of these relationships the different versions claim.

Oedipus the King (Greek)

Oedipus is probably the most widely known hero of tragic mythology. Oedipus, unfortunately for him, is doomed to a tragic life from the day he is born. You see, he is born into a lineage of Theban rulers who were doomed by the Curse of the House of Pelops.

One of Oedipus' ancestors, Pelops, had to compete in a deadly chariot race against King Oenomaus in order to win the hand of beautiful Hippodameia. To ensure his victory, he bribed Oenamaus' charioteer, Myrtilus, to sabotage his opponent's chariot. In exchange for doing this, Pelops promised Myrtilus that he could have sex with Hippodameia on their first night. Myrtilus replaced the wheel pins with wax, which melted and sent the king crashing to his death. Before dying, Oenamaus cursed Myrtilus that he would die at the hand of Pelops.

Curse of the House of Pelops

After the race, as Pelops, Hippodameia, and Myrtilus are returning to the House of Pelops in Pelops' winged chariot, Hippodameia asks for a drink of water. He stops at an island and goes to fetch water for his bride. When he returns, he finds

Hippodameia in tears. She tells him that while he was gone Myrtilus had tried to rape her. Pelops confronts his saboteur, who reminds him of their previous agreement that he would have first sexual rights to her. The three get back in the chariot and continue their journey.

As they fly on, Pelops pulls a hard turn with his chariot and kicks Myrtilus. The traitorous saboteur falls out to a watery death. However, before fulfilling the curse placed on him by Oenamaus, Myrtilus screams out his own curse upon Pelops. Myrtilus curses Pelops and all the descendents of his house to lives of ruin and tragedy. This curse is blamed for the hard and tragic lives that plague those of Pelops' bloodline, including Oedipus.

A Fatal Prophecy

Oedipus is the son of King Laius and Jocasta (in the versions written by Homer, her name is Epicasta). In some versions of the Oedipus myth, King Laius receives an ominous warning from an oracle, telling him that he will be murdered by the hands of his own son. Other myths account his knowledge of this to the Curse of the House of Pelops.

When Jocasta becomes pregnant, Laius takes measures to save himself from fate after the child turns out to be male. Knowing of the prophecy, Laius has a spike driven through the infant's feet before having him taken far away and abandoned. However, a shepherd of King Polybus of Corinth finds the injured child and brings him to the palace. Polybus and his wife Periboea (in other versions, her name is Merope or Medusa) raise the boy as their own son, naming him Oedipus, which means "swelled foot," because of the injury with which he was found.

A Search for the Awful Truth

As Oedipus grows older, he becomes increasingly inquisitive about his origins. King Polybus and Queen Periboea avoid answering his questions and/or give him conflicting fabrications. The one thing that no one *ever* reveals to Oedipus, however, is the fact that he is not truly the son of Polybus and Periboea. Eventually, Oedipus decides that he will never be able to find the answers he seeks in Corinth.

Oedipus decides that his best chance of finding the truth about his identity is at the Apollonian Oracle of Delphi (for more information, see Chapter 3). The oracle conveys the same prophecy to Oedipus that it had given to his true father, King Laius, telling him that he is doomed to murder his father as well as marry his mother.

A Tragic Confrontation

As with King Laius, Oedipus now takes measures that he hopes will avoid the fulfillment of his fate. Believing that he is the son of Polybus and Periboea, Oedipus decides not to return home to Corinth. His reasoning is that if he is not near the man he believes to be his father, he will not be able to harm him. Unfortunately, it is the actions of Oedipus' attempt to avoid fate that speed his fulfillment of the prophecy. Of all the places he could go to avoid Corinth, Oedipus chooses Thebes, the kingdom of King Laius, his true father.

As Oedipus travels, he comes along a narrow path and is confronted by a man he does not know. Unfortunately, the man is King Laius. As a result of the trail being so narrow, neither man can pass unless the other gives up the right of way. However, both men are stubborn and arrogant because of their strength. Soon, a quarrel breaks out between them and Oedipus strikes Laius down with his sword, killing the Theban king. Although he is not aware of it, Oedipus has just fulfilled the first part of the Delphi Oracle's prophecy by killing his true father.

The Mystery of the Sphinx

When Oedipus arrives in Thebes, he finds a kingdom in turmoil. The king is missing, and a terrible creature called the Sphinx is wreaking havoc throughout the land and making travel in and near the city nearly impossible. In true heroic fashion, Oedipus' intelligence defeats this terrible monster. The Sphinx is fond of a specific riddle, and anyone it comes upon is presented with the choice of solving the riddle or being eaten alive. Most people, needless to say, make a point of avoiding the Sphinx. Oedipus, however, hero that he is, actually goes looking for this thing.

The Sphinx presents Oedipus with its riddle: What goes on four legs in the morning, two legs in the day, and three legs at night? Oedipus is solves the riddle and presents the Sphinx with the answer: man, because he crawls as an infant, walks during manhood, and uses a cane in old age. Some say that the explanation he gives is that a man crawls to get out of bed in the morning, walks on two feet during the day, and makes love to a woman at night with his "third leg." Opinions on which explanation is the most valid vary.

Her riddle solved (most agree that the Sphinx was a female), the Sphinx dies. Some myths say Oedipus slays her. Other myths claim the Sphinx actually kills herself. One thing that all versions of the myth do agree upon, however, is that the Sphinx dies.

The Oracle's Words Fulfilled

After his amazing defeat of the Sphinx, Oedipus was hailed as a champion hero by the people of Thebes and presented to Queen Jocasta. By this time, it has been learned that the missing king is in fact dead. Her late husband's kingdom is in need of a new ruler, one who is strong, so Jocasta marries Oedipus and therefore makes him King of Thebes. Having married Jocasta, Oedipus has now fulfilled the remaining part of the prophecy by marrying his own mother.

Avoiding the Labyrinth

Due to the popularity of Oedipus as a character, there exist a multitude of myths about him, not all of which are in agreement on certain details. For example, Jocasta's suicide and Oedipus' blinding and exile occur close together in some versions while in others there is a gap of several years between the events. Also, all myths agree that Oedipus had four children: Eteocles, Polynices, Ismene, and Antigone. However, the specific mothers of these four children are confused by the various contradicting versions.

Years pass before the truth of Oedipus' identity is revealed by the gods. The most popular version of the myth states that when a famine strikes Thebes, an oracle is consulted and the truth is revealed—that Oedipus' unintentional sins are the cause of the famine. Jocasta, upon learning the horrifying truth of her own incestuous relationship, hangs herself. Oedipus goes mad, stabbing out his own eyes. In some versions, the loyalists of King Laius put them out.

The Knight of the Cart

Sir Lancelot of King Arthur's knights was a later addition to the Arthurian legend. Lancelot is one of the most talented knights in Arthur's court. Sadly, his love of Arthur's wife, Queen Guinevere, was the catalyst that brought the majesty of Camelot crashing down.

In a quest to rescue the kidnapped Queen Guinevere, Lancelot falls deeply in love with her. Both are married. Although in the legends it is rare that any actual sex takes place between the two, their affair is still scandalous. When the truth of their affair is revealed, Lancelot's wife commits suicide in some versions, while in others she simply dies of sorrow or a broken heart.

Myth and Metaphor _____

> The story of Lancelot and Guinevere is quite similar to another tragic romance from Celtic legends, that of *Tristan and Isolde*. Although French writers added Lancelot to the knights of Arthurian legend, they may have done so due to myths added by English writers of a Sir Drustanus, which was a phonetic modification of the name Tristan. Though chronologically the tales did not fit, the Celtic hero Tristan as Sir Drustanus was, as with Lancelot, a late addition to the roll of the Knights of the Round Table.

When the affair is revealed to Arthur, he is confronted by the harsh laws of his time and must condemn Guinevere to death for the crime of treason to the crown. However, in one of the most daring rescues of romantic myth, Lancelot shows up at the last minute to save her from death. He single-handedly rides in, takes on the whole of Camelot's royal guard, grabs the condemned queen, and makes a break for it. Sadly, to avoid being viewed as weak in the eyes of the nobles, Arthur must pursue them and he soon lays siege to Lancelot's castle. This battle allows the evil, illegitimate son of Arthur, Mordred, to begin his attempt to usurp the throne and kill the king (see Chapter 10).

The Sons of North Briton

The Sons of North Briton is a tragic ballad that comes from Nova Scotia, which tells the story of two young boys who are abandoned by their parents and left in Scotland. Seven years later, the two boys have grown into strong young men and able warriors. One day, as the brothers are out in the woods either hunting or traveling, they encounter a man they do not know. Soon, a quarrel breaks out between the stranger and the two brothers. Though the ballad does not specify exactly *what* the source of the argument is, one thing is made perfectly clear—the fight is started over some ridiculously trivial matter.

Words soon turn to blows, and weapons are drawn. The brothers cross blades with the stranger in a vicious battle that ends in both of their deaths. Before they take their last breaths, however, the man tells the brothers his story, and why he must live. The stranger, you see, has come to Scotland in search of his two lost sons, whom he became separated from exactly seven years before. As you may have already guessed, as the stranger continues to tell his story the boys begin to realize that they are the lost sons he is looking for. Before dying, they both tell the man their born names. Hearing this, the stranger realizes what tragedy he has brought upon himself, discovering that the two men he has just killed are, in fact, the same two sons that he has come to Scotland to find.

Tragedy of Cu Chulainn and Ferdiad (Celtic)

Another story of tragedy is that of Setanta, also called *Cu Chulainn*. Of his companions, one of Setanta's most beloved friends was a warrior named Ferdiad. Ferdiad was strong and skilled, a champion among a famed group of Iberian warriors called the Men of Domnu, and the two were near equals on the battlefield. When Setanta attended Scathach's school of the warrior arts, Ferdiad was one of his fellow pupils. In the later years of Setanta's life, however, a clash between the two warrior friends would change Setanta's life into one of sorrow and guilt.

In a conflict known as the War for the Brown Bull, Setanta stood alone against the army of the evil Queen Medb. The evil queen was a sorceress, and Setanta seemed to have been the only warrior in his land immune to her magic. Setanta let her warriors come and killed them by the hundreds with each passing day. Seeing her forces dwindling, and knowing that such heavy losses could endanger her campaign, Medb made a deal with Setanta. Each day, Setanta would fight only one of her warriors. While they fought, her army would be allowed to advance. When and if that warrior was defeated by Setanta, however, her army would be required to stop and could travel no further that day.

Immortal Words

Cu Chulainn (often seen with a number of alternate arrangements and spellings, such as Cuchulainn and Cucullan) is the nickname/title that was given to the boy-warrior Setanta, meaning "The Hound of Chulainn." For details on how Setanta received this unusual title, see the *Scathach and Aoife* section of Chapter 14.

An Offer He Can't Refuse

Queen Medb eventually became frustrated with the slow advancement and called Ferdiad to the front. Sadly, Ferdiad's clan had allied with Medb in their bid to obtain the Brown Bull. Until this point, however, Ferdiad had managed to stay away from the front lines, allowing him to avoid crossing swords with his good friend. Now he found himself before Queen Medb, being ordered to fight a man that he loved as a brother.

At first, Ferdiad refused to fight Setanta. However, in the warrior clans of the ancient Celts, a man's reputation was among his most valuable assets. Medb threatened to have her bards, writers, poets, and satirists compose nothing but songs that spoke of his cowardice unless he did as she told him. She also offered him a reward of such vast riches that it is said to have exceeded a king's ransom. Having to choose between either the defamation of his name and honor or wealth and glory, Ferdiad had no choice but to accept Medb's offer.

A Battle of Four Days

Setanta recognized his old friend Ferdiad approaching and went out to greet him. Ferdiad was honest and told Setanta why he had come—to do battle. Setanta begged his friend not to force them to cross blades, but to no avail. So the two warrior friends engaged one another in mortal combat, fighting the entire day. As the sun set in the west, neither man had gained the upper hand. Exhausted, and realizing they were at a stalemate for the moment, the two men kissed and returned to their camps.

Setanta, concerned for the welfare of his friend, sent half his healing herbs to Ferdiad. In turn, Ferdiad sent half his meal to Setanta. As a symbol of their continuing friendship in the face of hard but unavoidable circumstances, the horses of both warriors were kept and fed in the same stable.

The second day's battle turned out to be the same as the first's, raging from sunrise to sunset with neither man taking the advantage. The third day also ends with no victor. However, at the end of this day the two men parted ways in sadness, knowing full well that one of them would likely fall on the next day, as they were both exhausted and injured from the constant fighting. That night, Setanta's and Ferdiad's horses were kept in different stables.

On the fourth day, Ferdiad fell in combat on the mighty spear Setanta called *gae bolg*. When Setanta saw his friend dead on the field, all of his famous battle fury faded from his heart. With tear-drenched cheeks, he picked up his fallen comrade and carried him across the river from Ireland to Ulster, so that Ferdiad would be buried among his own people.

Setanta's Sorrow

The guilt that Setanta felt at having killed such a close friend weighed heavily on him for the rest of his short and painful life. The death of Ferdiad marks a shift in Setanta's battle against the army of Queen Medb. His greatly feared battle fury and his formerly unbreakable will to fight abandoned him at a time when he needed them most, and with each passing day his wounds became more and more numerous.

Soon, Setanta's skin was so riddled with battle wounds that he had to stuff grass under his clothes and armor, as wearing them would otherwise be too painful. The myth of Setanta in the War for the Brown Bull says that there was not a space on his body the size of a needlepoint that was not affected by some painful wound. Even Setanta's healing herbs were not enough to keep him well. Despite all the pain and injuries, Setanta never stopped protecting his homeland, never gave up. Bruised and bleeding, he continued to defend the borders of his homeland.

Setanta's Final Order

Word of Setanta's weakened state soon reached the ears of Sualtam (who is said by some to be Setanta's true father). Sualtam rode out to the battlefield in search of Setanta, worried for the boy-warrior's life. When he arrived, he found Setanta lying on the field of battle, exhausted, bleeding, and close to death. Setanta told Sualtam not to weep for him, nor to avenge him. Instead, the boy-warrior told him to ride like the wind to King Conchobar and tell him that Setanta could no longer defend the land against the four clans united under the dark queen, and to warn him that Medb's forces would be on their way soon.

Avoiding the Labyrinth

When reading the tales of Setanta/Cu Chulainn, it is easy to forget that he was only a boy (most take place when he's between 8 and 15 years old). What makes Setanta so impressive is that he was not only so strong and brave, but he was also just a boy. In fact, one story about Setanta tells of a battle in which he challenged an *adult* warrior to single combat. The man refused, proclaiming loudly that he wouldn't fight one unable to grow his own beard. Clever as he was brave, Setanta created the appearance of a beard by staining his lower jaw before he rode out the next morning. When all warriors across the field saw what appeared to be a beard on Setanta's chin, the adult warrior ran out of excuses and rode out to fight Setanta. He was quickly defeated by the boy-warrior.

Sualtam did as Setanta ordered, leaving Setanta there on the battlefield, presumably to die. When King Conchobar's army arrived to push back Medb's forces, Setanta was still lying where Sualtam had left him. When he heard the sounds of battle, the "Hound of Chulainn" rose up and joined the ranks of his fellow warriors on the field, despite his countless wounds.

Hagbard and Signe

The original legend of Hagbard (also spelled Hagbart) and Signe comes from a larger epic that is now lost to the passage of time. The most common version of the myth that still exists is in the form of a Danish ballad. The actual legend can also be found in both verse and prose forms in the *Saxo Grammaticus.*

In this tragic tale, Hagbard and Signe love one another more than life itself and are betrothed. Sadly, their dreams of marriage are shattered when Hagbard's cruel father, King Sigar, has him hanged. What's worse, he has this done right in front of Signe. Alone and overcome by grief, Signe runs to her bower room, bars the door, and sets the place aflame. In this way, the two are reunited in death.

This is a tale of terrible injustice. In the end, however, justice finds its way to King Sigar. The story tells of how Haki, King of the Vikings and brother of Hagbard, disgusted by his father's evil act, bursts forth from the sea. In a homicidal rage, Haki cuts King Sigar down and avenges the execution of Hagbard and suicide of Signe.

> **Myth and Metaphor**
>
> The tale of Hagbard and Signe has often been referred to as the "Romeo and Juliet" of Northern Europe. This is said due to the obvious parallels between the two stories, such as familial conflict, ideal love, and a woman who voluntarily follows her deceased lover into death.

The Longhaired Strong Man (Semitic)

Samson is a character from the biblical Old Testament, taken from the Hebrew text, *Tanakh.* His name is also spelled Shama'un in Arabic and Shimshon in Hebrew. In the *Tanakh,* Samson is one of the 12 Judges of Israel. Samson was to keep his hair long as part of a contract with YHVH. As long as his hair remained uncut, YHVH would make Samson strong, nearly invulnerable. Samson was a very mighty man, with a reputation for killing Philistines. By some accounts, he killed thousands of them in his lifetime.

> **Myth and Metaphor**
>
> Samson has been referred to as the "Biblical Hercules," primarily because these two characters have a number of similarities. There are two primary parallels between the myths of Samson and Hercules/Herakles: both killed a lion with their bare hands and both met their downfall as a result of a wife. Also, Samson, similar to Hercules, had quite a short temper for the majority of his life.

After one such Philistine-killing fiasco, which took place at his own wedding party, Samson left his new wife behind and returned home without her. After a *long* time, Samson went back for her only to learn that his father-in-law had given her to one of the long-haired warrior's own friends. The father refused to give the original daughter back to Samson, and offered the girl's younger sister as a replacement wife.

The Philistine Killer

In a rage at his father-in-law's refusal to return his wife, the myth states that Samson attached 300 torches to the tails of foxes and turned the panicked creatures loose on the lands of the Philistines. Crops, homes, and entire towns were reduced to ashes as a result. When the other Philistine tribesmen learned of why Samson had done this, they burned his abandoned wife and reluctant father-in-law alive. Samson, not one to be one-upped by the Philistines when it came to violence, went on a killing rampage. He cleaved an unspecified number of Philistine men in their hips and thighs.

Needless to say, the Philistines were about fed up with Samson, who had by now fled to Etam, the land of Judah. Soon, an army of 3,000 Philistines showed up outside Etam and demanded that Judah's tribe hand Samson over. Samson tricked everyone, however, by telling the men of Etam that he could only be held by using two new ropes. They pounced upon him with a pair of new ropes, and Samson pretended to be unable to escape. As he was led out to the Philistines, Samson broke free and pulled out a donkey's jawbone. This might lead one to ask whether he was already carrying around the jawbone (and if so, why?) or if he simply tore it from the mouth of the nearest donkey. Regardless of when or how he acquired the jawbone of a donkey, the long-haired strongman now used it as a weapon and went on yet another Philistine-killing spree.

Samson's Love, Delilah's Betrayal

Samson had for years been protected by his pact with YHVH. Not until he met a certain woman by the name of Delilah did he run into any problems. Samson easily fell head over heels in love with Delilah (who is said to have been exceedingly beautiful), and the Philistines finally smelled an opportunity to exact their revenge. They bribed Delilah with silver (1,100 silver coins by some accounts) to discover and reveal to them the weakness of Samson.

Delilah, after many failed attempts, eventually learned of her husband's weakness. If Samson's long hair were ever to be cut, she learned, it would violate his contract with YHVH and he would become as vulnerable and weak as the next man. That night, while the strongman slept, Delilah had a servant shave Samson's long hair. His covenant with YHVH now violated, Samson was weakened and vulnerable. The Philistines immediately pounced at this chance for some payback.

Avoiding the Labyrinth

Although the myth of Samson and Delilah clearly states that Delilah had one of her *servants* shave her husband's head, many artistic depictions of the scene show Delilah cutting Samson's hair herself. Such depictions may have been done in this way in order to effectively illustrate both the method and result of Delilah's betrayal of Samson without bringing any additional figures into the painting that would take away from the focus of the couple.

In the Hands of the Philistines

With Samson, a man who had killed so many of their tribesmen, now in their custody, the Philistines pulled no punches. They did not kill him, however. Instead, they tortured, beat, and humiliated the fallen hero. They started with burning out Samson's eyes by holding a hot piece of metal near them. To be completely fair, the Philistines *had* promised Delilah they would not touch Samson, so she may have thought that he would not be harmed. However, by using an instrument of hot metal, they were able to blind and torture Samson without violating that agreement. After burning out his eyes, the Philistines dragged Samson to Gaza, where he was imprisoned and turned into a slave.

Myth and Metaphor

You may wonder why Delilah is not mentioned in Chapter 12 on the wrathful female. Simply put, the wrathful female in myth is one who is in some way provoked. Delilah, however, has not been wronged in any way by Samson, nor is she motivated by a need for personal vengeance. Delilah's reason for betraying Samson is simple—greed. For her, Samson's destruction is not about justice or righting a personal wrong, but about furthering her own wealth and status.

To celebrate having Samson in their custody, the Philistine leaders held a celebration in honor of their god, Dagon. As they ate and became drunk, they decided to have the blinded and humiliated Samson brought before them for their entertainment. The hall quickly filled with Philistines who desired to take a "free shot" at their most hated enemy. When the hall had filled up, and no more people could fit inside, the remaining Philistines gathered on the roof to witness what they anticipated to be a beating of epic proportions. What they failed to realize, however, was that much of Samson's hair had grown back and, apparently, his strength had returned with it.

Samson had only one thing left to do before he died, and it was the one thing he seemed to do more than any other—kill some more Philistines. After being led into the hall, Samson asked one of the attendants to place him near the central pillars, so that he might lean on them in his weakened condition (which, of course, he was faking). Once there, he reached out with his massive arms and, in one powerful motion, brought the pillars crashing down. Seeing as how those pillars were holding the place up, the entire structure collapsed as well, killing every Philistine inside … and Samson.

Judas Iscariot

Over the last 2,000 years, Judas Iscariot has been called a lot of things and few of them have been good—the Betrayer, and The Great Traitor, among others. You may be wondering why Judas Iscariot is included in a chapter dealing with tragedy. It is true that there are many of the Western Christian tradition who view Judas Iscariot as an evil, greedy betrayer who sent Jesus Christ to a fate of torture and death for a bounty of 30 silver pieces. That's not a very big reward, especially when you consider that the Philistines gave Delilah 1,100 pieces of silver to hand over Samson.

The tragedy of Judas Iscariot's tale is not as obvious as that of, say, Lancelot or Oedipus. One must examine the myth closely to understand how Judas may be seen as a tragic figure. In truth, had Judas Iscariot *not* betrayed Christ, then the final pieces of the prophecies about the messiah would never have been fulfilled. Therefore, perhaps it is wrong to view him as the damned soul that many believe him to be.

Sword and Man _____

The Judas Tree is an actual genus of tree, *Cercis siliquastrum*, found in Europe. These trees sprout reddish-purple flowers. The common name of the tree comes from the belief that Judas hung himself from one of these trees after the death of Christ. This tradition is also associated with similar tales about different tree species that were once straight, but became dwarfed, gnarled, or stunted because they allowed their wood to be used to make the cross upon which Christ was crucified. These stories usually include Judas, saying that he hung himself from the same type of tree that was used to make Christ's cross. Such stories are known to be attached to the following trees, among others: the ash, the dogwood, the dwarf birch, the elder, and the fig tree.

There are two commonly used explanations that attempt to explain how Judas' actions were not done out of malice or greed. The first states that Judas did what he did in order to place Christ in a position where his true identity as the messiah would be undeniable. The second explanation, also the more frequently used of the two, especially by the church, is that Judas was under the influence of Satan. This version usually states that Satan deceived Judas and provoked his anger at Mary Magdalene's washing of Jesus' feet with expensive oils to such a degree that he betrayed Christ for 30 pieces of silver. There is, too, another version (which is purely a popular fabrication based on no textual, mythical, or historical references) that Judas joined Jesus' disciples because he was already serving as a spy for Pontius Pilate. The 30 pieces of silver, according to this explanation, were not a bounty for Christ's head, but Judas' payment for services rendered as a Roman spy.

Nearly every story regarding Judas' death states that he met with a bad end. In Catholicism, there is a popular belief that he hung himself after Christ's crucifixion. According to Acts 1:18–19, Judas used the silver he received for handing Christ over to the Romans to buy Aceldama, the potter's field. When he set foot on the newly bought land, however, he fell to the ground and burst open. Another Biblical myth states that he gave the money to the temple, and that the holy men there used the money to buy the burial land for Jesus' tomb. Some stories say that Judas died later in life, run over buy a speeding chariot.

Majnun Layla (Arabic)

Majnun Layla is the title of an Arabic story of *Bedouin* origin, which means "driven mad by Layla" or "the madman of Layla." The story tells of a young man named Qays who falls in love with a beautiful maiden named Layla. In some versions, the two have known each other since childhood. In other versions, Qays sees Layla's beauty and is immediately love struck.

Immortal Words

Bedouin is an Arabic term that literally means "desert people." This term is used for the nomadic tribal peoples of the Arabic world, who traveled on horseback and had a rather warlike nature. The Bedouin warriors were famous throughout the Near and Middle East for their incredible skills of combat and horsemanship.

The story goes that Qays had the heart of a poet, and produced a number of beautiful works, the subject of which being his love for Layla. However, when he went to Layla's father to ask for her hand in marriage, her father refused. In most versions of the tale, the father's refusal to allow the marriage is said to have been the result of some social taboo in Arabic law. Soon after this, Layla was given in marriage to another man. Qays became known as Majnun Layla because he was driven mad from seeing the woman he loved being given to another man in marriage. He left his tribe's camp and is said to have spent the rest of his days wandering the desert as a madman.

The Least You Need to Know

- The tragic hero is commonly flawed, and the ill fortune that befalls him is often of his own making.

- For the tragic hero, the sins of the past are never forgotten and will always return to destroy him.

- At times, tragedy falls on a hero as a result of unavoidable circumstances and not from a "fatal flaw."

- Tragic heroes are not so much to be pitied as remembered, and many serve as powerful examples of what one should *not* do.

- The tragic hero often serves as a reminder to us that darkness can strike our lives during even the brightest of times.

Chapter 9

Plight of the Demigods

In This Chapter

- The demigod heroes
- The tragic lives of the sons of gods and mortals
- The demigod's quest for discovery
- The tormented demigod's quest for redemption

Originally, the Greek words "hero" and "demigod" were terms used to refer to men who were the sons of a mortal and a god/goddess. However, in modern times the meaning of the word hero has come to be used for those who act with bravery, integrity, and/or nobility. Demigod has come to refer to more than just half-gods, but to lower-level gods of mythology as well. However, the word demigod will be used with its intended Greek meaning of one who is the offspring of a god/goddess and a mortal. The half-gods are not in themselves divine, and often their lives are difficult, cursed, and/or tragic. For example, Nanave is stoned from his home village and Hercules is tormented throughout his life by the goddess Hera.

Nanave, Son of Shark King (Hawaiian)

Nanave is the part-god son of the Hawaiian Shark King Nanaue, who returned to his ocean kingdom before his son was born (see Chapter 3).

When Nanave was old enough, he began to swim in the waterfall pool beside his mother's home. Sometimes, she would become concerned about how long her son had been underwater and attempt to catch a glimpse of him. However, the only thing she ever saw was a shark swimming in the water.

Nanave had become a regular figure among the local fisherman, who just thought him to be a curious young man. Every day he would stand near the pool as the men set out to fish. He was always seen wearing the feathered cloak that his father had left for him. Before the village fishermen left, Nanave would ask them where they were going to be fishing for the day. The fishermen, seeing no harm in telling the boy, always revealed their intended fishing spot to Nanave. After all the fishermen had left, Nanave would dive into the pool and swim away. Much to his mother's concern, he would be gone for hours on end.

Nanave Revealed

After a while of this, the fishermen begin catching fewer fish with each passing day. The people of their village begin to grow hungry as the amount of food available continues to diminish. The village chief, suspicious, demands that every person in the village assemble inside the temple. The chief informs his people that a problematic god must be among them, taking their fish. He then sets up a trap to find out the identity of the perpetrator. The chief sets out a long bed of leaves and instructs all the males of the village to walk across them. If a person was truly a human, then his feet would leave marks and depressions on the leaves. However, if the person were a god in disguise, then his feet would leave no mark.

Avoiding the Labyrinth

Nanave is unique among the other demigods in that he is not provided with a special teacher to guide him during the absence of his father. This may explain why he was willing to do something as foolhardy as jeopardize the village's fishing and risk being discovered.

Nanave's mother starts to panic, knowing full well that her son is the child of the Shark King. She is certain that he will be killed if the villagers discover this. When the time comes for Nanave to walk across the leaves, he sprints over them with too much speed and loses his footing. As he falls, one of the village men tries to catch him. Instead, he accidentally catches hold of Nanave's magical and protective feathered cape. The cape is yanked from Nanave's shoulders, revealing the shark's mouth on his back.

The Shark Prince Escapes

The people immediately chase Nanave from the village. However, before the mob catches him, he escapes by diving into the pool and assuming his true shape as a shark. The villagers throw large rocks into the water. They continue to do so until the pool is filled with stones.

The villagers depart, believing that they have killed Nanave. However, Nanaue the Shark King had cut out a special place for his son at the bottom of the pool, a secret passage that led to the ocean. Nanave swims out to join his father, King of Sharks, in his sea kingdom and is never seen again. From this time forward, the fishermen of the village refuse to tell anyone where they are going to fish ever again. They do this out of a belief that the sharks could hear their plans and eat the fish or chase them away.

Myth and Metaphor

In the case of islander demigods, the half-god's discovery and/or journey to the magical/hidden land of his lost father is common. You will see this again in the myth of Maui of Taranga's Topknot.

Maui of Taranga's Topknot (Pacific Islander)

Pacific region myths state that Maui is a half-god hero. When he is still unborn, his mother has a miscarriage. She ties the miscarried fetus into a lock of her hair and casts Maui into the sea. However, Maui is resurrected and nurtured by the supernatural spirits of the sea.

Maui one day finds his way back to his mother and four brothers at the royal House of Assembly. Taranga counts her sons (all of whom are named Maui) that day and is shocked to find that there are five heads instead of four. She counts out the first four again and when she comes to the fifth he introduces himself to her as Maui-tiki-tiki-a-Taranga (the Maui that was formed in the topknot of Taranga).

Myth and Metaphor

Demigods are often rescued, resurrected, or aided by divine or supernatural entities. In some cases, the door swings both ways, so to speak, and the demigod may be tormented by similar divine beings, as in the case of Herakles/Hercules.

The Lost Son Returns

Overjoyed at the discovery of a son she'd given up for dead, Taranga invites the boy to sleep next to her at night. Thrilled to be back in the arms of his mother, Maui happily accepts. However, Maui is soon perplexed when he discovers that his mother is sneaking away from the room each day at dawn.

Curious to know the truth of what she is doing, wanting to know where she is going, and suspecting that she might lead him to where his father lives, Maui devises a plan. One night, he hides away his mother's clothing and covers up any gaps in the walls of their room that might let in the light of dawn that awakens her each morning.

Maui's Discovery

The next morning, Taranga awakens and realizes that it is past dawn. In a panic, she bolts from the room. Maui follows and sees her pull up a clump of reeds before entering a hidden cave. He transforms himself into a pigeon and follows her into the cave. This leads him to the domain of his father, and he discovers the underworld village where his mother is able to reside with his father. Perched in a tree above his parents, he begins to drop berries from above. Annoyed by this, the people start to lob stones at him. Not realizing that the pigeon is in fact his son in disguise, Makea-tu-tara, Maui's father, also begins to throw stones. Maui returns to his true form and the stone throwing ceases.

So that Maui might be allowed to remain in the underworld village, Makea-tu-tara performs certain baptismal ceremonies. Unfortunately, Makea-tu-tara inadvertently forgets to recite a portion of the prayers and because of this Maui leads a somewhat cursed life. Regardless of this, the half-god son of Makea-tu-tara and Taranga becomes legendary by achieving great feats, often with the aid of the magical jawbone of his powerful ancestress, Muri-ranga-whenua. Unfortunately, the curse placed upon him as a young man will one day turn out to be the end of him.

Alexander the Great

Legendary conqueror Alexander the Great, or Alexander III, lived from 356 to 323 B.C.E. He was said to have been the half-god son of Zeus-Ammon and Olympias (see Chapter 3), a myth likely started by his mother. Alexander's tutor was the famous Greek thinker Aristotle. Before Alexander's mysterious death at the age of 33, he had conquered most of the known world from the Nile River in the West to the Indus River in the East.

As with many conquerors and warrior-kings of legend, Alexander the Great has become the subject of many myths and events that are absolutely void of historical facts. One story of a young Alexander tells of the origin of the conqueror's famed black horse, Bucephalus.

The Taming of Bucephalus

Alexander was viewing his father King Phillip II's horses, one of which was quite untamed. The horse bucked and bit at his handlers. Alexander begged his father to give him the horse as a gift. Fearing that the horse might kill the boy, his most likely heir, Phillip initially refused. However, Alexander persisted and eventually made a wager with his father that if he could ride the horse then he would be allowed to keep it. Phillip agreed to the wager, feeling very confident that the young prince would not be able to ride Bucephalus, and Alexander approached the wild and violent horse.

The young prince took hold of Bucephalus' reins and calmly turned the horse's head in the direction of the sun. The animal immediately calmed down. Alexander, wise from his education under Aristotle, had noticed that the horse was startled to violent panic by the sight of its own shadow. The young man then mounted the horse and took off in a gallop, much to the fret of his father and the royal advisors.

The Gordian Knot

Another myth surrounding Alexander is that of the Gordian Knot. When Alexander's army reached the border of Asia, they came across an enormous and complicated knot. Tangled inside of the giant knot was a small, two-wheeled cart. The myths of the time stated that the knot was left by Gordius, father of King Midas, and there was a well-known local prophecy that stated whoever could untie it would become ruler of all Asia.

Alexander had every intention of conquering Asia, along with the rest of the world, and he wasn't about to let the Gordian Knot stand in his way. He realized that if he could solve the enigma of the knot, it would mean that he was the ruler of which the prophecy spoke. He approached the knot, inspected it for a few moments, drew his sword, and cut the entire mess asunder. With this simple but clever action, Alexander the Great was able to lay claim to the prophecy and thus to all of Asia, where the story of what he had done soon spread like wildfire across the continent.

Herakles

Herakles (most commonly known by his Latin name, Hercules), son of Zeus and Alcmene (see Chapter 3), is perhaps the most well-known Greek hero in the modern world. As a result of being an illegitimate child of Zeus, Hera (Zeus' wife) hated Herakles and was a constant tormentor to him throughout his life.

Myth and Metaphor

The snake is a common archetype companion for wrathful females or goddesses. Often associated with feminine violence, the snake would be a most appropriate weapon for Hera to use in her assassination attempt of the infant Herakles.

As a baby, Hera sent two snakes to Herakles' cradle in an attempt to kill him. However, already possessed with superhuman strength from his father, the infant Herakles snatched up the serpents and strangled them in the iron grip of his little bare hands. In some versions of the myth, Herakles is in the cradle with his half-brother Eurystheus. In this version, it is Amphitryon, Alcmene's legal husband, who sends the snakes to discover which baby is of his bloodline and which is the demigod son of Zeus.

The Education of a Demigod

As Herakles grows up, Zeus and Amphitryon provide the best of instructors for the young demigod's education. Herakles is taught wrestling by Autolycus (son of Hermes who had the power to become invisible), archery by Eurytus (a famous archer who would one day challenge the god Apollo in archery, at the cost of his life), swordsmanship and fighting by Polydeuces (a fellow son of Zeus renowned for his fighting skills, once killing King Amycus of the Berbryces in a pugilism/boxing match), and music by Linus (a famous Greek composer as well as a genius). Unfortunately,

Myth and Metaphor

Half-god heroes are often trained and educated by legendary warriors, wise men, or gods. In the absence of their true fathers, these teachers make it possible for the sons to live up to the standard of their godly bloodlines.

Herakles' power seems to have made him an arrogant young man. When his music teacher, Linus, tries to punish the young demigod, Herakles kills him by bashing him with his own lyre. As a result of this act of violence, Herakles is sent to be a guardian of Amphitryon's cattle herds. At the age of 18 (some versions claim that he was several years younger, likely to give the story a more shocking effect), while serving his punishment as a shepherd, Herakles is said to have killed a man-eating lion with his bare hands.

After gaining favor with Creon, King of Thebes, Herakles is given the hand of Megara (Creon's daughter) in marriage. The early years of Herakles' marriage to Megara are truly happy ones. The son of Zeus truly loves Megara and the couple has three sons. However, the wrathful Hera does not allow Herakles' happiness to last long. Tragically, the angry goddess strikes Herakles with a fit of homicidal madness. In his rage, he kills Megara, all three of his sons, and two children of his friend Iphicles. Heartbroken and distraught after regaining control of his senses, Herakles voluntarily exiles himself and travels to the Apollonian Oracle at Delphi for guidance. The oracle tells Herakles that he must serve the King Eurystheus, the demigod's disdainful half-brother, for 12 years as penance for the lives he has taken. He presents himself before Eurystheus and so begins the *athloi*, also known as the Twelve Labors of Herakles.

Immortal Words

Athloi is a Greek word meaning contests, prizes, and/or labors.

The Twelve Labors

Eurystheus, seeing Herakles before him, offering 12 years of absolute servitude, sees a perfect opportunity to rid himself of his demigod half-brother. Herakles' first labor is to kill the Lion of Nemea, a terrible beast said to be a sibling of the Sphinx (the half-lion oracle) and the last is to capture Cerberus (a monster hound that guards the gates of the underworld). Hercules succeeds, strangling the lion to death with his bare hands.

Next, Herakles is sent to kill the Hydra, a serpent with many heads. At first, every time Herakles cuts off one of the creature's heads, another grows in its place. With the help of Iolaos, he defeats the creature by having Iolaos sear the necks with a hot iron after the heads are severed, preventing them from regenerating. The rest of Herakles' labors are as follows:

- Captured the Keryneian hind
- Captured the boar of Mount Erymanthos
- Cleaned the stables of Augeas
- Killed the birds of Stymphalos
- Captured the bull of Crete
- Captured the mares of Diomedes

♦ Stole and brought to Eurystheus the belt of Hippolyte, Queen of the Amazons

♦ Stole the cattle of Geryon

♦ Acquired and brought to Eurystheus the Golden Apples of Hesperides

♦ Brought Cerberus from the underworld and presented the beast to Eurystheus

When the Centaur Nessus tries to rape Herakles' second wife, Deianira, he slays the creature with an arrow tipped with the poisonous blood of the Hydra. However, Nessus has told Deianira that his bloody toga will work as a love charm (of course, this is a ruse). She takes the blood-soaked piece of clothing and later places it across Herakles' shoulders in hopes of curbing his rampant infidelity. The venom-soaked blood of the Centaur, however, drives Herakles mad with pain instead.

Avoiding the Labyrinth

There has been some minor debate as to whether the Hercules of Roman legend is the same hero as the Greek Herakles. The argument is that Herakles was likely based on some historical Greek warrior while the Roman myth is pure fiction. Regardless of this, the Roman myths of Hercules were undoubtedly based on those of Herakles.

In some myths, this poisoned blood of Nessus is enough to kill Herakles. In other versions, the hero survives for a short time, living in excruciating pain that eventually leads him to voluntarily stand upon a funeral pyre, begging for someone to light the flame. In both versions, when Herakles is burned on his funeral pyre his mortal body is burned and his godly body ascends to Olympus. In Homer's *Odyssey*, Herakles is depicted as a guardian in the underworld realm of Hades, dividing his time between Olympus and the land of the dead.

Lord of the Labyrinth

Minos, son of Zeus and Europa, was king of Crete. He married Pasiphae, the daughter of Helios, the sun god. When the validity of Minos's kingship comes into question, he appeals to the god of the sea, Poseidon, for a sign. From the waves of the sea emerged a bull of the purest white. The bull is provided to be used as a sacrifice to Poseidon. However, Minos's greed overtakes his good sense and he keeps the white bull for himself. He replaces the intended sacrifice with one of his other bulls, thus incurring the wrath of Poseidon.

The sea god strikes Queen Pasiphae with an uncontrollable lust for the bull. She is so overcome with sexual desire for the beast that she wishes to have intercourse with it. She has Daedalus, the great Minoan engineer, construct a wooden cow in which she is able to hide, and has it presented to the white bull. The bull mounts the wooden cow and has sex with Pasiphae. The queen is impregnated by the encounter, and the result is a hideous half-beast, half-man called the Minotaur.

King Minos, wanting to banish the Minotaur from his sight forever, enlists Daedalus to construct a mighty labyrinth. When completed, the Minotaur is thrown in. Later, when Minos defeats the Athenians, he begins forcing them to sacrifice seven of their young girls and men to the Minotaur each year.

When Minos eventually learns of Daedalus's involvement in his wife's beastly pregnancy, he has the engineer and his son Icarus locked in a tower of the labyrinth. Father and son later escape from the tower by making wings out of feathers and wax and flying away (see Chapter 8).

Avoiding the Labyrinth

Although it is doubtful that there was ever truly a half-man, half-bull creature called the Minotaur, there actually *was* a real labyrinth on the island of Crete. The Minoans were a bull-worshipping people, and the so-called Minotaur was likely just a large bull. However, the remains of an immense labyrinth have been found in the ruins of the Minoan culture.

Warrior Son of Ninsun (Babylonian/Assyrian)

Gilgamesh is the warrior-demigod of *The Epic of Gilgamesh*. He is the part-god son of the goddess Ninsun and King Lugulbanda of Uruk. (Technically, Gilgamesh is $\frac{2}{3}$ god and $\frac{1}{3}$ human because his father was also a part-god.) As a man, Gilgamesh takes over kingship of Uruk. However, due to his half-god nature, he becomes quite a terror to his people. He wrestles with young men and often harms, cripples, or kills them (though it is not certain if he hurts them intentionally) due to his great strength. He takes his pleasures with any woman who catches his fancy. The people put up appeals to the gods for help.

The goddess Aruru, heeding the requests of the people, washes her hands and takes up a piece of clay, which she tosses into the wilds below. From this lump of clay is made the hero Enkidu, intended to be a match for the reckless Gilgamesh. Created in the wild, Enkidu at first looks much like an animal, his entire body covered with thick fur. For a short time, Enkidu remains in the woods, living amongst the animals.

Myth and Metaphor

In Ancient Mesopotamian mythology, it was very common to read of a god creating new beings out of mud or clay. For this culture, such incidents of creation were not restricted solely to primal myths.

The Corruption of Enkidu

Soon Enkidu becomes a problem for a local trapper, filling in pits and sabotaging traps. The trapper goes to Gilgamesh for help. The King of Uruk sends a woman called Shamhat the harlot back to the woods with the trapper. She reveals her nude form to Enkidu, and the animal-like hero takes his pleasure with her for seven straight days. Having now lain with a human woman, the animals abandon him.

Shamhat takes Enkidu from the forests, clothes him, and has his hairy body trimmed and groomed. No longer an animal, Enkidu takes on the appearance of a warrior and takes up a weapon into his hand. He set his sights on Uruk, desiring very much to test his strength against the mighty Gilgamesh.

A Clash of Warriors

When Enkidu arrives in Uruk, the people are overjoyed to see one of such a similar build to Gilgamesh. They believe that he is a champion sent to save them from the violent king. Gilgamesh, who is about to enter a wedding house and have his way with the bride, finds his way blocked by Enkidu. The two heroes clash, trading blow after blow, and in the end neither is able to gain the advantage. Exhausted and respectful of each other's strength, the two form a brotherly friendship.

Gilgamesh, overjoyed to at last have a "playmate" he won't so easily break, insists that the two of them go on a journey so that they might make their names legendary and become immortal. The pair agree to travel to the Forest of Cedar and slay the monster Humbaba.

The Battle with Humbaba

After consulting the elders, who advise the two heroes against fighting Humbaba, they go to visit Gilgamesh's mother, the Wild Cow Goddess Ninsun. To aid them in their journey and protect them in battle, Ninsun enlists the aid of Shamash, the sun god, and his wife Aya. Ninsun, seeing how mighty Enkidu is and how happy her son is to have his friendship, adopts the new hero as her own son. Having thus prepared themselves, the two warriors set off for the Forest of Cedar.

When they arrive at their destination, the heroes are confronted by the terrifying Humbaba. A vicious battle ensues. Near the end, both Gilgamesh and Enkidu seem to be weakening. Luckily, the sun god Shamash steps in and uses the 13 Winds to blind Humbaba, who is then defeated by Gilgamesh.

Avoiding the Labyrinth _____

There are large gaps in the clay tablets that *The Epic of Gilgamesh* was found written on. One such gap is during the battle with Humbaba. At first the heroes have the upper hand, and then there is a missing piece. When the gap ends, the heroes are weakening and Humbaba seems to have turned the tables on them. Unfortunately, because of the gap in the tablets it is unknown what transpired during the moments in between.

Snubbing of Ishtar

Upon returning victorious to Uruk, Gilgamesh catches the eyes of Ishtar, Goddess of War. She offers herself to him in marriage. Gilgamesh, however, refuses her offer and insults the goddess. He points out that her lovers have a tendency to be killed. Very angry, Ishtar returns to the heavens and goes crying to her father Anu. She begs him to allow her to send the Bull of Heaven after Gilgamesh to kill him for his insult. Anu agrees and the Bull of Heaven is unleashed upon the land of Uruk. The beast tears through the city until Gilgamesh and Enkidu are able to find its weak spot and thereby kill it. To add further insult to the spiteful goddess, Gilgamesh severs one of the bull's haunches and sends it hurtling in Ishtar's face.

However, a goddess cannot be treated in such a disrespectful manner without there being at least some repercussions, no matter who Gilgamesh's parents are. Not wanting to harm Gilgamesh, since he is the child of Ninsun, the gods decree that death should fall upon Enkidu. The former wild man soon has a dream vision of this, and prophesies his own death to Gilgamesh. Soon thereafter, he falls ill and dies. Once again, the mighty Gilgamesh is left without a friend.

The Least You Need to Know

- ◆ Half-gods and part-gods are the offspring of a god and a mortal. Sometimes, as in the case of Gilgamesh, they may be the offspring of a god and a part-god.

- ◆ The lives of demigods are often difficult and rarely end happily.

- ◆ Though they are strong and hard to hurt or kill, demigods are not immortal or indestructible.

- ◆ Though they are often responsible for terrible deeds, demigods often seek out ways in which to redeem themselves for their past transgressions.

Chapter 10

Heirs to the Throne

In This Chapter

- ◆ The myth of the lost heir's return
- ◆ The messianic lore of King Arthur
- ◆ The fratricidal founders of Rome
- ◆ The myths of rightful heirs who avenge their usurped fathers
- ◆ The journey, education, and training of the lost heir/returned king hero

The return of the lost heir is a common motif in mythology. Often these myths have a similar structure (aside from that of Romulus and Remus). First, the son is separated from the father as a boy/infant as a result of the father's death or an evil usurper. The exiled heir is usually educated and/or trained by a special teacher. The rightful heir then returns to rescue the oppressed people from the tyranny of the current usurper or illegitimate ruler. However, these types of characters often suffer from having traitorous offspring.

Return of the Lost Son

The tale of Cormac is written about in the Irish story *Geineamain Cormac* (or *The Birth of Cormac*). Cormac's father was the King of Tara, named Art, Son of Conn-of-The-Hundred Battles. The night before Art is to fight in the battle of *Mag Mucrama*, he has sex with a maiden named Etain, the daughter of a blacksmith. Somehow knowing that their union would result in a son, Art, Son of Conn, told Etain that she would give birth to the future king of Ireland. Worried what might happen if he were to die on the battlefield, he instructed Etain to take his son to the warrior Lugna Fer Tri. Lugna was to act as foster father to Cormac, and would know of the child's birth, as it would be announced to him by a clap of thunder.

The Road to Lugna

Etain sets off for the home of Lugna near the end of her pregnancy, wanting her son to be born in the home of his foster father. However, she goes into labor before reaching her destination and gives birth to Cormac in a bed of ferns. At the moment of Cormac's birth, a large clap of thunder cracks the sky at the home of Lugna Fer Tri. Knowing that this is a sign that the son of his close friend has been born, the warrior sets out to find him.

Myth and Metaphor

The special teacher is a common thread in the "return of the lost heir" myth. Because the fathers of these exiled future kings are usually absent, the presence of a special teacher is necessary to validate that the returning heir has been properly trained and educated for the position of ruler, even though he did not have a father (who was then responsible for such things). Cormac is taught by Lugna, Arthur by Merlin, Jason by Chiron, and Arjuna is taught by Indra (though, of course, Indra *is*, technically, his father).

Myth and Metaphor

The she-wolf is a common element in the future king myth. Aside from the tale of Cormac, a she-wolf also suckles the infant brothers Romulus and Remus, mythical founders of the great city of Rome.

On the night of Cormac's birth, Etain rests as her handmaiden keeps watch. Unfortunately, the handmaiden soon falls asleep, and a she-wolf steals away the infant. When Lugna arrives, he finds the women hysterical and weeping. They tell him that the baby is gone but are completely ignorant as to how the baby has disappeared.

A man of the forest later brings news to Lugna that he has witnessed a human infant at the mouth of a she-wolf's cave, playing amongst the cubs. Lugna soon finds and retrieves Cormac, bringing the newborn future king (as well as the wolf cubs) to his home and raising him alongside his own sons.

Mac Con's Crooked Judgment

When Cormac is old enough, Lugna brings him to Tara and introduces him to King Mac Con, successor of his father King Art, Son of Conn. They witness a situation where a woman's sheep, which had eaten some of the king's crops, are being confiscated by Mac Con. Cormac, showing the wisdom of a true king, asserts that this is an unjust decision. He demands that only the wool of the sheep be taken because, as with Mac Con's crops, it will grow again with time. When Cormac says this, the side of the house on which King Mac Con had made this crooked decision collapses. Local legends state that this event is signified by the Crooked Mound of Tara.

The people are inspired to know that the rightful king, Cormac, is now back in Tara. When the tale of his wise and just decision spreads among them, they know that Cormac would be a competent ruler. Inspired by Cormac and disdainful of Mac Con, the people rise up and forcibly remove Mac Con from the throne. For the duration of Cormac's reign, his kingdom prospers and the people are happy.

Sons of Rome

Said to be the sons of Mars and Rhea Silvia, a *Vestal Virgin*, Romulus and Remus are twin brothers who founded the great city of Rome. As infants, the boys were set adrift in a small vessel when the Tiber flooded. However, they later washed ashore and were guarded and nourished by a great she-wolf until they were old enough to fend for themselves.

Immortal Words

A **Vestal Virgin** is a priestess of Vesta/Hestia, goddess of the hearth. Vesta was worshipped in every great house with a small, ever-burning flame that was tended to by at least six Vestal Virgins. These Vestal Virgins were selected at the age of six to ensure that they were, in fact, virgins. The selected girls were required to serve five years in service to the Vestal flames at some point in their lives. Service as a Vestal Virgin was often carried out during the girls' early adolescence to late-teen years. If at any time during her term of service a Vestal Virgin lost her virginity, she faced execution by being buried alive.

When they grew up, Romulus and Remus took to building what would become the great city of Rome. After Romulus built the city's mighty walls, Remus jumped over them in jest. Feeling that Remus was being disrespectful, Romulus attacked his brother. A quarrel broke out between the two, and in the fight that ensued Romulus killed Remus.

The Once and Future King

The myths surrounding the life of King Arthur are probably based on a real-life warrior chieftain of the Britons who lived sometime between the late fifth and early sixth centuries. Little is known of the real Arthur, aside from the fact that he was a warrior chieftain who led the Britons against the invading Saxon hordes when the island was invaded around 500 C.E. Since then, a multitude of myths and legends about his life and exploits have arisen. The story of King Arthur is probably one of the most widely written legends in the last thousand years. As a result, there are a multitude of versions regarding how he came to power. However, it is important to note that not all these versions are compatible.

In the original Arthur legend, which is probably the most historically compatible, it states that he was born in Cornwall at Tintagel castle. As chieftain, he resided in the Welsh region of Caerleon with his wife Guanhuvara (later called Guinevere). Most of these original legends deal with Arthur slaying beasts that terrorize the people, such as the Demon Cat of Losanne and the wild boar called Twrch Trwyth.

Lost Son of Uther

Arthur's father is Uther Pendragon. Merlin the Sorcerer uses his skills of magic to allow Uther to shape-shift into the form of the husband of a woman he covets. Later, also with Merlin's help, Uther manages to make her his wife. To secure the service of Merlin, however, Uther must agree to hand over the firstborn son of their union, as well as his sword, as compensation to the powerful sorcerer.

When Arthur is born, Merlin comes to receive what he has been promised. Bound by honor, Uther Pendragon reluctantly hands over his son and the sword (after he makes a few failed attempts to renegotiate a different type of payment). Merlin takes the sword to an anvil that rests upon a stone and, with a spell, plunges the blade through both. The spell doesn't allow anyone but Arthur to free the sword from its resting place. Merlin then informs the nobility of the stone's purpose and/or has it etched into the stone that only the rightful king of the Britons could remove the sword. He then takes the child to be raised in the house of a knight who is of poor to modest means.

The Sword in the Stone

Uther Pendragon later dies without an heir, throwing the land into anarchy. Without a king, the nobility begin fighting for supremacy while unjust lords take to robbing and exploiting the people. Divided by internal warfare, the Britons become easy targets for tyranny.

Later, when Arthur is barely an adolescent, the knight he serves brings his older son, Kay, to a special tournament. Because no one has yet to free the sword from the stone, it has been decided that the winner of this tournament will be crowned King of the Britons (though this is only in some versions of the myth). Neither Arthur nor the knight in whose charge Merlin placed him is aware of the entire truth behind the boy's lineage.

When Arthur, acting as squire to Kay, forgets to bring the young knight's sword and is unable to get back into the inn, he sees the sword in the stone and removes it, believing it to be some kind of war memorial. When he gives the sword to Kay, he and his father take Arthur back to the stone and return the sword to its place. After several men try and fail to pull it out, Arthur again removes the sword with ease and is recognized as the true heir to the British throne.

Sword and Man

The sword as a symbol of legitimate kingship is a common archetypal occurrence in ancient and medieval myth.

Arthur's reign will be one of reformation, prosperity, and a return to order. Arthur creates a new capital city, Camelot, unlike any seen before. Also, he has a large round table constructed where he meets with his men, the Knights of the Round Table. This table symbolizes how all the men who sit at it are equal.

The King of Avalon

Later on during Arthur's reign, he receives the magical sword, Excalibur, from the Lady of the Lake. The sword's scabbard, however, may be what is most precious. When strapped to the side, it protects the wearer from harm. When Arthur unknowingly goes into battle against the usurping Mordred with a fake scabbard, he is fatally wounded.

The conflict between Arthur and Mordred is in fact one of father versus son. Before his marriage to Queen Guinevere, Arthur was enchanted and seduced by his sorceress half-sister Morgan La Fay. The result of their union is an illegitimate son, Mordred, who is raised by his mother to take control of the throne.

Sword and Man

The use of a special or magical sword/weapon by the warrior-hero is a common element of many combat-centered myths. For example, Arthur has Excalibur, Siegfried (see Chapter 11) has Balmung and Gram, and Parasurama has the axe of Shiva (see Chapter 3).

Mordred dies on the sword of his father. However, as death closes in on Arthur, he hands Excalibur over to one of his knights, ordering that he return it to the Lady of the Lake. Before Arthur dies, legend says that a magical vessel from the mystical island of Avalon appears. Aboard are three enchantresses who take Arthur to Avalon to be healed of his wounds. Despite the many different variations of the Arthur myth, one common thread is that Arthur will one day return as a messiah when Britain is in dire need of him.

Protector of the People

The original epic poem, *Beowulf,* was probably composed sometime around 700 C.E. The currently used version comes from a manuscript of the poem, which had until then been transferred through oral tradition, that was written sometime near the beginning of the eleventh century C.E. By the time the story was written down, 300 years after its composition, it had already been heavily influenced by the adoption of the Christian religion in the Western world. As a result, the written text had likely been altered from what had been originally recited during pre-Christian times.

Immortal Words

Mead is an alcoholic beverage of the Western and Northern European peoples, made from the fermentation of honey.

Beowulf is the name of a legendary Geat warrior who comes from across the sea to aid the neighboring Danes when the people and lands are being decimated by the terrible, man-eating monster called Grendel. King Hrothgar is ruler of the Danes and a kinsman of Beowulf. Seeing the suffering that the beast is causing, and the bodies of his warriors piling up in the *mead* hall, he is happy to accept Beowulf's help.

Battle with Grendel

In an amazing feat of physical strength, Beowulf faces Grendel alone and unarmed. He uses himself and his band of fellow warriors as bait, the lot of them pretending to be asleep in the mead hall where so many of Hrothgar's warriors had met their deaths while facing the creature. When Grendel comes crashing into the mead hall, expecting another meal of human flesh, he gets far more than he bargained for.

Beowulf engages Grendel in hand-to-hand combat and tears off one of the creature's arms, ripping it from the shoulder socket. The monster escapes (minus one arm, of course), fleeing to the arms of his wretched sea-witch mother. Shortly thereafter, Grendel dies of the wound inflicted on him by Beowulf.

Grendel's Dame

The death of Grendel causes his mother (often referred to as Grendel's Dame) to hit the warpath. She goes on a bloody killing spree, and for the Danes the old horror is now replaced by a new one. Even though Beowulf could easily leave the Danes at this point without tarnishing his reputation or honor, he chooses to stay and fight. Were he to leave, he would not be a true hero of legend.

Beowulf makes the perilous journey to the cave of Grendel's Dame at the bottom of the sea. After a furious battle, Beowulf cleaves her head from her shoulders with a sword. Victorious, Beowulf returns to his homeland where he will eventually become a great king.

The Brave King Stands Alone

Many years later, Beowulf meets his death with noble bravery while fighting a fierce dragon that is terrorizing the people of his kingdom. One of Beowulf's warrior retainers had stumbled upon the dragon's cave, which he saw was full of treasure. Unable to control his greed, he stole a golden goblet from the cave. When the dragon awoke to find that someone had stolen from its gold horde, the beast goes homicidal and begins attacking the land with its sharp talons and fiery breath.

Beowulf, though far older now, gathers together a band of his warriors and sets out to slay the troublesome beast. This will be the last adventure of the warrior king's amazing life. Sadly, during the violent battle with the fire-breathing monster, Beowulf is abandoned by his own warrior retainers, who flee in terror at the sight of the ferocious dragon. Though Beowulf loses his life, he does not let his people down. The warrior king succeeds in killing the dragon before his wounds force him to take his final breath. In the end, Beowulf becomes a warrior-messiah, giving his life for his people.

Leader of the Argonauts (Greek)

Jason is the son of King Aeson and the rightful heir to the throne of Iolcus. However, Pelias, the stepbrother of Aeson, usurped the throne while Jason was only a child.

Jason's mother saved him from the power-hungry Pelias by sending him away to Chiron the Centaur to be educated. Around this time, a seer prophesied to Pelias that he would one day be killed by someone of his and Aeson's bloodline, and that when this man appeared, he would be wearing only one sandal.

Grown strong and skilled from his years of tutelage with Chiron, Jason later returns to the land of his birth. Along the way, he loses one of his sandals while helping an old woman across a river. After he brings her safely across, the old woman turns out to actually be the goddess Hera in disguise. For his kindness, Hera (as well as Athena) comes to his aid later on in his adventures.

Man with One Leather Sandal

When Pelias sees the one-sandaled Jason, he panics, remembering the prophecy about his doom. Wanting to rid himself of Jason as quickly as possible, and by any means, Pelias convinces the usurped prince to seek out the Golden Fleece that was stolen away from Iolcus and taken to Colchis by Phrixus. Jason soon assembles a band of legendary warriors and seamen to join him on his quest. To facilitate their travels, Jason has a special 50-oared boat constructed, which is named the *Argo* (hence the group's name, the *Argo*nauts). Some versions of the myth claim the boat is named for the man who created it.

Jason and the Argonauts make it to Colchis. Medea, the traitorous daughter of King Aetes of Colchis, falls in love with Jason and betrays her father by helping him obtain the Golden Fleece. The fleece is protected by a giant, coiled serpent, which Medea enchants into a deep slumber with her knowledge of poison and the magical arts.

A Hero's Ruin

The Golden Fleece in his possession, Jason returns home. He takes Medea with him, lest she be executed by her father for her betrayal. When they arrive in Iolcus, Jason learns that Pelias has had his father Aeson killed. Medea, at Jason's urging, avenges Aeson's death in a most gruesome fashion (see Chapter 12). As a result of this, she and Jason are forcibly exiled. They soon settle in the kingdom of Corinth.

Even though Jason is remembered as a mighty hero who survived perilous dangers and fought many adversaries, it would be his own actions that would later bring him low. When he later turns his back on Medea, he will incur the very worst of her murderous wrath. In the end, Jason's life will be reduced to ruins at the hands of the one woman who ever truly loved him ... Medea (see Chapter 12).

Archer Prince of the Pandavas (Indian)

In the Hindu epic *Mahabharata*, Arjuna is the third and most wise and heroic of the five Pandava princes. He is also a son of Indra (for more information on Indra, see Chapter 5). In the *Mahabharata*, Arjuna is a courageous warrior renowned throughout the land for his skill as an archer.

Arjuna makes a pilgrimage to the Himalayas to obtain divine weaponry from the gods that can be used in battle against the Kauravas, the enemy clan of the Pandavas. From there he travels to the city of his father Indra, Amaravati, where he practices with the weapons he received from the gods and improves his skills in combat. After Arjuna has been trained, Indra sends his son into battle against the Daityas, the sons of Kashyapa (a grandson of Brahma). Arjuna defeats the Daityas and returns to his fellow Paravas to face the Kauravas in an epic battle.

During the struggle against the Kauravas, Arjuna's charioteer, Krishna, reveals his divinity to the prince and offers him a revelation about existence and the nature of the godhead (for more information on Krishna, see Chapter 3). This scene of *Mahabharata* is called the *Bhagavad-Gita*. Interestingly, even though Arjuna was a key character of the *Mahabharata*, it is the Vishnu avatar Krishna who has been given the most importance in the modern Hindu Dharma faith. For more information on the Krishna avatar, see Chapter 3.

The Giant Slayer (Hebrew)

Historically, David was a real King of Israel sometime around 1000 B.C.E. In Jewish and Christian texts, David was the son of Jesse and Nazbat and the youngest among his brothers. Though he was a legitimate son of Jesse, upon his birth his mother made it appear as though he were the son of a slave girl that Jesse favored.

David was very devout and served as one of Jesse's shepherds. However, contrary to some modern beliefs, David used more than just a sling and stones to protect his flock. In fact, David was quite strong, killing three bears and four lions with his bare hands.

When David was 28 years old, the prophet Samuel appeared and anointed him in secret as the legitimate successor of Saul, the current King of the Israelites. After this, David's mother revealed that he was, in fact, *not* the son of a slave girl. When Saul heard this, he found it laughable to think that this young shepherd would be able to succeed him as king. In fact, he constantly made jokes at David's expense.

Goliath of Gath

Saul's empire, however, soon came under threat from the Philistines. The Philistine army had with them a terrible giant from Gath by the name of Goliath. Myth stated that Goliath was 6 cubits and a span in height. That's about *10 feet tall!* Seeing this behemoth of a man, Saul's army began to lose nerve. Arrogantly, the Philistines issued the challenge that if any warrior could defeat their champion Goliath, they would concede defeat. However, not one of Saul's soldiers had the strength or bravery to face the giant Philistine champion.

David, bringing food to his brothers, arrived on the battlefield and insisted that he could defeat Goliath in single combat. Although everyone thought he was completely mad, the sad truth is that there was no one else willing to be sent out to fight the mountain of a man. David was relentlessly insistent that the god YHVH would protect and aid him in smiting the Philistine champion, because the giant wore the emblazoned likeness of the non-Hebrew god Dagon on his chest plate.

David went to look for stones for his sling. As he searched, five stones spoke to him and when he put them together in his sling they fused into a single perfect missile for the weapon. With this one stone, he struck Goliath with a fatal blow to the head and the giant fell dead on his face. In the Jewish tradition, Goliath falling forward was a sign that the Philistine god Dagon, whose image was on the giant warrior's chest plate, was inferior to the Jewish god YHVH.

Courting Bathsheba

A Hittite named Uriah helped David remove Goliath's armor. In return, David promised Uriah that he would have a Hebrew wife. This, however, interfered with the will of YHVH because Bathsheba was David's intended wife. However, as a result of David's promise, he had to marry Bathsheba to Uriah.

The will of YHVH, however, was not something that could go ignored or unfulfilled. David had to marry Bathsheba, as she was the bride YHVH had chosen for him. Later, the King of Israel had no choice but to send Uriah to his death so that he could marry Bathsheba and fulfill the will of YHVH.

Sons of David

David and Bathsheba gave birth to two sons. The first son, Solomon, would become one of the most wise and legendary kings in all of ancient history. When YHVH offered Solomon a choice between infinite wisdom and untold riches, Solomon chose wisdom. As a result of this wise choice, Solomon lived a blessed and prosperous existence.

The second son of David, Absalom, was very different from his brother. Although David loved Absalom beyond measure, the ungrateful prince betrayed his father by leading a rebellion against the throne. Much to David's sorrow, Absalom was killed in battle when his attempted uprising failed. This event led to "David's Lament," one of the most touching ancient speeches ever written.

The Death of Israel's King

David was told that he would die on a Sabbath day. The King of Israel, however, truly did not want to die on a Sabbath. Because the Sabbath is a day of rest, it was the law that the body of anyone who died on the Sabbath was to be left rotting for the day and not dealt with until the following morning. As a result, dying on the Sabbath was something that no Jew would have desired.

Knowing that Azrael, the Angel of Death, would not come for him while he was studying the Law of God, David spent every Sabbath day engrossed in the study of holy texts. However, when the day came that David's time was up, Azrael created the sound of a commotion in the garden. Hearing this, David left his Book of God's Law so that he could investigate.

When David reached the garden steps, unfortunately, Azrael caused them to collapse, and David plummeted to his death. The King of Israel's corpse, sadly, had landed in a spot that exposed it to the rays of the sun. Luckily, David's wise son Solomon used his skills of the mystical arts to summon a multitude of giant eagles that shaded and fanned the corpse until the Sabbath had ended and it could be moved and given proper rites.

The Least You Need to Know

- ◆ The return of the lost heir motif is commonly used in ancient to medieval myths.

- ◆ Most of these hero types are separated from their royal fathers as boys or infants.

- ◆ While in exile, the lost heir is often educated and trained by a special teacher.

- ◆ The return of the lost heir often marks a period of peace, prosperity, and order for a kingdom.

Chapter 11

Legendary Warriors

In This Chapter

- ◆ Immortalizing fearless warriors, men of deeds and action, in myth and legend
- ◆ Setting the wrong things right—the path of the legendary warrior-hero
- ◆ Learning the journey of the warrior-hero
- ◆ Discovering the downfall of the warrior-hero—treachery, betrayal, and sorrow

There is a saying that immortality will come to such as are fit for it, and these fearless and skilled men of the battlefield are no exception. Sometimes wild and reckless, sometimes calm and strategic, all these mythical characters have achieved immortality through their hazardous deeds and courageous actions. Some fight for salvation, some against a corrupt system. There are those who battle for glory, those who wish to test their skills, and still others are driven by revenge.

The Warriors of the Rainbow (Cree Tribe)

The Warriors of the Rainbow story is actually a prophecy from the Cree tribe. Legend says this prophecy was made by an elderly woman named

Fire Eyes. The prophecy states that the earth will one day no longer be able to sustain the voracious greed of the Yonegis (White Men). As a result, there will come a day when the waters will turn black, killing all the fish; the sky will be as smoke, causing dead birds to fall from it; and the trees will vanish, leaving nothing more than a barren wasteland.

However, in these dark days a band of warrior saviors will arise, called the "Warriors of the Rainbow." These warriors will bring with them the old myths and ways of life. People will flock to them to learn of the ways of the Great Spirit. The Warriors of the Rainbow will become the protectors of those who remain in what will be the darkest hour of the human race. After these armies of the willing have been assembled, the Warriors of the Rainbow will lead them in a fight against the forces of evil, the disciples of bigotry, avarice, and hatred. The prophecy leaves no doubt that the forces of evil do not stand a chance.

> **Myth and Metaphor**
>
> In certain Native American cultures, the rainbow in myth is depicted as a bridge between Earth and the heavens. Considering this, the title of Warriors of the Rainbow may mean to suggest that these warriors are either sent by, or are the personified wrath of, the Great Spirit.

The people will remember how to pray to the Great Spirit. In groups, they will be taught how to once again hold civil counsels for the benefit of all. Humans will remember how to love one another, putting an end to the destructive evils of greed, anger, pride, and jealousy, which will become traits to be shunned. Most of all, however, humans will be reminded of what it is to live in harmony with nature. Above all, this is said to be the one lesson the Warriors of the Rainbow will bring that will save mankind from itself.

Hero of the Fenian Cycle (Celtic)

The majority of Finn Mac Cumhail's (also said Finn MacCool) adventures are written of in a series of tales referred to as *The Fenian Cycle*. He was the son of Cumhail, uncle of the famous Celtic king Conn-of-the-Hundred-Battles. Yes, Finn Mac Cumhail was a cousin of Cormac Mac Airt (for more information on Cormac, see Chapter 10). His tales bear striking similarities to those of Cormac, as well as King Arthur. In fact, it is argued by many that the myths of King Arthur are in fact the story of Finn Mac Cumhail. However, Finn was more of a warrior chieftain than a king.

Avoiding the Labyrinth _____

There is a multitude of different English spellings for the name of Finn Mac Cumhail. Mac, meaning "son of," is always spelled the same though it is sometimes connected to the father's name to form one name. It is also shortened sometimes into "Mc." Some alternative spellings of the name Finn are Fiann, Fionn, and Fenn. His lineage name, Mac Cumhail, has also been given a number of alternative spellings, such as MacCumal, MacCumhal, and MacCool (the most common alternative spelling). Any of these spellings could be used to refer to the same legendary Celtic warrior-hero.

Before Finn's birth, his father was killed in battle by Goll, a rival chieftain from the Morna clan. After Cumhail's death, Muirne-of-the-White-Neck gave birth to a fair-haired baby and gave him a false name, Demne, so as not to raise suspicions that could provoke retaliation from the Morna clan that had killed the boy's father. After Finn was born, Muirne sent him away to be raised by the druidess Bodhmall and the warrior-woman Liath. Under the tutelage and training of these fierce foster mothers, Finn/Demne grew up a wise and skilled warrior. In his years of tutelage under the druid priestess Bodhmall, he also learned how to use the arts of magic.

The Boy Warrior's Training

Finn's/Demne's training and education under Bodhmall and Liath made him uncommonly strong and wise. Even as a young boy, he achieved deeds that exceeded his age. In one tale of his amazing boyhood deeds, Finn/Demne threw a large stone into the air from one side of a house. He then sprinted through the house in a flash, beating the hurling stone to the other side and catching it on one finger.

Eventually, Muirne remarried to a lower king who was powerful enough to discourage any further violence from Goll Mac Morna toward her or her son. The threat now held back for the time, she returned to retrieve her son. Later, Finn/Demne was sent to serve in the house of the great and wise druid Finneces (also spelled Finnegas) so that he might further his education. In the house of the wise druid, the boy, who had until now been known as Demne, received a new name from his foster lord Finneces—Finn.

In the service of Finneces, Finn's intelligence increased immensely. This came from Finn accidentally consuming small portions of salmon that had been fed hazelnuts from the Nine Hazels of Wisdom. While preparing the fish for Finneces, Finn burned his thumb on the fish from time to time, then stuck the thumb in his mouth.

As a result, Finn received a rather odd ability to see into the truth and wisdom of matters by putting his thumb in his mouth.

Son of Cumhail, Enemy of the Morna

Unfortunately, since the death of Finn's father, Goll Mac Morna's power as a chieftain had only increased. As a result, no kings or chieftains would employ him under their service in fear of retaliation from Goll. Unable to secure a position under any of the lords, Finn went to the one person that even Goll must bow to, one of the strongest kings of Ireland, Fiachadh (or Art, see Chapter 10).

Under the service of Fiachadh, Finn made a name for himself on the battlefield. At one point, he even saved the life of his cousin, the High King of Ireland, Cormac Mac Airt. Soon after, King Fiachadh re-formed the elite band of warriors made up of his best men, which he called the *Fianna*. In recognition of Finn's deeds, he placed the son of Cumhail in charge. Goll Mac Morna, who had been the leader of the Fianna until now, was not pleased with being replaced by Finn.

Rise of the Fianna

Now a powerful chieftain and leader of the greatest fighting force in Ireland, Finn sought to avenge his father and put an end to the life of the troublesome Chieftain Goll Mac Morna. He gathered his best 150 Fianna and rode out to do battle with the Morna clan. After a bloody battle lasting several days, Goll met his death on the blade of Finn.

However, in some stories the two men reconciled. In one version of the Finn myths, for example, Finn used magical weapons inherited from his late father to kill the fairy Aileen who, every year at Samhain, burned down the palace of Fiachadh after using his magical music to put the men to sleep. Seeing this amazing deed of Finn, which no other Fianna had been able to accomplish, Goll became a willing and devoted ally of the son of Cumhail.

The Fall of Finn Mac Cumhail

Under the wise leadership of Finn, the Fianna became the most legendary fighting force in all of Ireland. However, as with many heroes, a woman turned out to be his downfall. In recognition of Finn's amazing service and leadership of the Fianna, King Cormac Mac Airt promised his daughter Grainne to him in marriage. Unfortunately,

Grainne had already fallen in love with another of the Fianna, a friend of Finn's named Diarmuid. When he let Diarmuid die from wounds on a boar hunt, he was later killed for the deed.

There are many contradicting versions of the death of Finn Mac Cumhail. Some say he was betrayed by Goll Mac Morna. Others say that he never died, that he (very similar to Arthur in Avalon) left this world and resides in a distant magical realm. One day, when Ireland is in terrible need, he will return to save the land and its people from certain doom.

The Slayer of Fafnir (Teutonic)

Siegfried is the hero of the German epic *Nibelungenlied*, and is also closely associated in myth with Sigmund, hero of the Icelandic epic the *Volsunga Saga*. Many of the deeds accomplished and events experienced by these two heroes are similar if not identical. Considering the close relationship between these two cultures, it is no wonder that the myths would influence one another.

Siegfried is the son of Siegmund, King of the Netherlands, and his queen, Sieglinde. One of his earliest and greatest feats was the slaying of the dragon Fafnir. After killing the dragon, Siegfried bathed in its blood to become invulnerable. A leaf stuck to the back of his shoulder, however, caused him to have a weak spot.

By killing the Nibelungen Hoard possessors, Siegfried became the Nibelung ruler. When the Danes and Saxons attacked the royal court of Burgundy, Siegfried came to their aid and was instrumental in defeating the invaders.

 Avoiding the Labyrinth _____

The Nibelungen Hoard was a vast treasure of enormous wealth. Unfortunately, it was also very, very cursed. Any who possessed the treasure were doomed to tragedy, suffering, and death. Some say that Nibelung was a dwarf king who asked Siegfried to help him divide the wealth between his three sons. The term is now applied to those who possessed the treasure and/or those who were under the influence of its curse.

Again, however, Siegfried's end is the result of female wrath. To help his friend Günter win the hand of Brunhild, Queen of Isslund (Iceland), Siegfried donned a cloak of invisibility and with it helped Günter appear to complete the tasks that Brunhild required of a suitor. These tasks were near-impossible feats of strength and, without the help of Siegfried, Günter would never have been able to complete them. In return for his help, Siegfried was given the hand of Günter's sister, Kriemhild, in marriage.

Unfortunately, when both queens learned of this they were quite enraged. They became jealous of one another's husbands. Brunhild, knowing that it was Siegfried and not Günter who passed her trials, desired Kriemhild's husband. Kriemhild was angry that her husband was forced on her as a reward for trickery. Kriemhild revealed her husband's weak spot to Brunhild. Brunhild then convinced Hagen, uncle of Günter, to kill Siegfried, and thus a heroic life was ended by treachery.

A Warrior of Many Wives (Teutonic)

Ragnar Lodbrok was a legendary Viking warrior in the latter half of the eighth century. At the age of 15, he inherited the throne of Denmark from his father, Sigurd Ring. Later, he would actually invade England. Aside from his great deeds, Ragnar Lodbrok was also known for having a multitude of different wives throughout his lifetime.

First he married Lodgerda, a warrior queen who ruled over a small region of Norway. Ragnar lived in Lodgerda's kingdom for three years. However, he eventually had no choice but to return to his own kingdom without her because she refused to leave, and in his absence, his warriors and subjects began taking their allegiances and loyalties elsewhere.

After that, he married Princess Thora, daughter of King Herodd of East Gothland, after slaying a dragon that had hatched from the egg of a swan. The dragon grew quickly into a gigantic dragon that encircled the castle of King Herodd. When Ragnar slew the serpent, he was given Thora's hand in marriage. In fact, Ragnar's name is a reference to the oxhide armor he wore as he fought the dragon. Thora had a thing for snakes, and raised a nest of adders that Ragnar eventually had to kill. In one myth, Thora kept a pet snake in a treasure chest full of gold. As the snake grew, so did the amount of gold. During his marriage to Thora, it is said that Ragnar gave up raiding.

Later, after Thora died, Ragnar took up raiding once more. During this time he encountered the beautiful foster daughter of a peasant couple, Aslaug. He married Aslaug and they had five sons. However, when the warriors and subjects of his kingdom expressed their displeasure with having a queen of lowly birth, Ragnar considered seeking out a new bride in the daughter of the King of Sweden, Eystein. Luckily, however, it was discovered that Aslaug was in fact the daughter of Sigurd and

Brynhild (or Siegfried and Brunhild in German) and he was able to keep his wife. As a result, he sent his sons to court the daughter of Eystein.

Ragnar died a terrible but noble death. Ella, King of Northumberland (on the isle of Anglo-land, or England), captured Ragnar and removed the magic shirt that he wore, which kept the warrior from harm. Ella then had Ragnar thrown into a pit of poisonous snakes. It was in this pit that Ragnar cried out his dying words, "Laughing I die!" This proclamation of joy in the face of death is typical of Viking warrior-heroes.

Hero of the Two Swords (Japanese)

Miyamoto Musashi (in Japanese, last names are written and spoken first, so his first name would be Musashi) was an actual person, considered a *Kensei* and perhaps one of the greatest swordsmen in the history of Japan. He is credited with creating and developing the *Niten-Ichi Ryu* (Two-are-One School) style of swordsmanship. This school is also sometimes referred to as *Nito-Ryu* (Two-Sword School). In Japan at the time, this was a revolutionary sword form which required the wielding of two swords simultaneously. Between the ages of 13 and 39, Musashi tested his skills and developed his philosophy of the sword as he fought in more than 60 death matches. He never lost a single match … and died at the age of 62 from natural causes.

Although Musashi was a real person, as well as a legendary duelist and warrior, there are a number of stories surrounding his life that have taken on mythical proportions. The most well-known of these stories is the "Duel at *Gan-ryu* Island," as it is now called.

Immortal Words

Kensei is a Japanese word meaning "Sword Saint," and a title given to legendary Japanese swordsman Miyamoto Musashi, creator of the two-sword technique known as *Niten-Ichi Ryu*.

Ryu means "School" or "Style," and often refers to a school or style of classical Japanese martial arts. So, **Gan-ryu**, which was the school and sword style founded by Sasaki Kojiro, could be translated as either "School of the Flowing Rock," and/or "School of the Cliff Dragon."

Clash of Rival Swordsmen

Gan-ryu was, in fact, not the name of the island but of the school of swordsmanship created by Musashi's greatest rival, a young but powerful swordsman by the name of

Sasaki Kojiro (again, Kojiro would be the man's first name). Sasaki was quite proficient at the use of a deadly technique called the *Tsubame-Gaeshi*, meaning "Swallow Cut," which employed the use of the *Tachi* or *No-Dachi* sword. The *Tachi* and *No-Dachi* are both elongated versions of the more commonly used *Katana*. The *No-Dachi*, however, has a straighter blade than most *Nihonto* (Japanese swords) of the time. The technique involved slashing upward and immediately curving around to slash downward in one fluid, fast, and very powerful stroke. In fact, Kojiro had never been defeated with this technique … until he stood against Musashi.

Immortal Words

The word **Nihonto** does not simply refer to a sword of Japanese style. In order for a sword to classify as a *Nihonto,* it must have been created with the traditional Japanese methods of sword making, perhaps one of the most closely guarded secrets in that country's tradition. A *Nihonto* swordsmith spends decades learning the art and a lifetime perfecting it. Often, a true *Nihonto* maker must pass a rigorous certification process before being allowed to work on his own. In modern times, a true *Nihonto* katana costs anywhere between $2,000 and $40,000 dollars. There are uncertified sword makers, of course, who sell *Nihonto*-styled katana that are less costly, often priced between $150 and $2,000.

The story goes that both swordsmen were at the house of a *daimyo*, Musashi as a guest and Kojiro as a warrior retainer. The two men, well-known rivals, exchanged words until the daimyo intervened and declared that the two men should finish their quarrel properly in a duel the next morning at a sandbar just off the coast.

Musashi's Wooden Oar

The night previous to his duel with Kojiro, the story goes that Musashi entertained a friend in his lodging and, as a result, overslept the next morning. Without bothering to fix his topknot, Musashi hurried out to get a boatman to row him to the sandbar, leaving a towel (commonly worn by samurai to protect their topknots while sleeping) wrapped around his head. On the way, he fell asleep only to wake up halfway to the sandbar, realizing that he did not have his sword. He borrowed an extra oar from the boatman and began to whittle out a makeshift *bokken*, or wooden sword.

When Musashi finally arrived at the sandbar, Sasaki Kojiro was waiting for him. Having been made to wait for at least three hours for his opponent's late arrival, Kojiro was fuming with indignant anger. When he saw the disheveled state of

Musashi's appearance, the towel on his head, and the hastily carved wooden sword in his hand, Kojiro began to make fun of his rival in front of those present, most of whom were his students. Musashi, however, seemed unaffected by Kojiro's insults. In fact, in one version of the story, Musashi simply smiled at his opponent, angering Kojiro even further.

The Duel with Gan-Ryu

Musashi fashioned the towel on his head into a suitable headband as Kojiro drew his long sword. Kojiro then threw his scabbard into the ocean as a symbol that he planned to either defeat Musashi or die.

"You must not be very confident," Musashi said to Kojiro upon seeing this, "throwing away that scabbard as though you won't be using it ever again."

Musashi then raised his wooden sword and pointed it at Kojiro's throat … the duel began. There are different accounts of what happens next. The most common is that, as the flustered and angry Kojiro attempted to use the Swallow Cut, Musashi rushed in with his long oar and struck. He then withdrew. As the two swordsmen stood apart from each other, none of the witnesses could tell what had happened. Musashi's headband fell off. The wind blew the cloth from his head, revealing a bloody gash.

Avoiding the Labyrinth

There is debate as to what exactly took place at "Gan-ryu Duel." Why did Kojiro's daimyo choose a remote sandbar as the location of the duel? Many believe that, because Kojiro had a rather large number of students with him at the sandbar, the idea was that they were to kill Musashi if and when Kojiro was defeated. If that happened, they didn't want any unnecessary witnesses to muck up their story. Luckily, Musashi arrived with the incoming tide. This made it possible for him to make a speedy exit. Similarly, this lucky coincidence has led some to believe that Musashi's tardiness wasn't so accidental, after all. Some speculate that he'd purposely timed his arrival with the tide change so that he could escape the wrath of Kojiro's disciples. Also, because the oar was longer than Musashi's usual katana, some speculate he'd also "forgotten" his sword on purpose so that he could create a bokken that was long enough to counter the length of Kojiro's extremely long *No-Dachi*. It is likely Musashi was well aware of the dimensions of the oar and knew that having a longer sword made in time would have been both impossible and hypocritical (since he often ridiculed schools that stressed the use of a longer katana).

At first, everyone is overjoyed, believing that Kojiro has won (most of those present, of course, are Kojiro's students). Their joy at seeing the gash on Musashi's forehead, however, was quickly doused when their *Sensei* (teacher) suddenly fell to the ground. Upon closer inspection, they found that his skull had been crushed. When they turned to look for Musashi, he had already made his way back to his boat, shoved off, and was being rowed back to the main island. This would be the last fatal "death match" duel that Miyamoto Musashi would ever fight for the rest of his days. Some have speculated that Musashi had not intended to *kill* Kojiro, which is why he used a wooden sword to begin with. Failing to spare his opponent's life, proponents theorize, Musashi chose to walk away from death-match dueling so that he might avoid having any more blood on his hands or spots on his karma. However, as with many things surrounding Musashi, most of these ideas are based on speculation.

The Slayer of the Oni (Japanese)

Minamoto Yorimitsu was a legendary Japanese hero of the Heian period (tenth century). He is known as the slayer of the *Oni*, which are demonic, horned, tusked monsters that are entirely covered with dark fur. Myth says that a gang of *Oni* who were followers of the demonic Shuten Doji resided on the mountain *Oe-yama* (pronounced Oh-ay-ya-ma). The Shuten Doji followers conducted murderous raids of Kyoto for years until the emperor ordered Yorimitsu, whose skill with a sword had already made him a living legend, to bring an end to the bloodshed. Believe it or not, there is actually a certified historical Japanese report of these orders and the events that transpired, which date the battle between Yorimitsu and the *Oni* Shuten Doji as taking place on January 25, 990 C.E.

Immortal Words

Yama is a Japanese word meaning "mountain." Therefore, *Oe-yama* means Oe Mountain.

According to some legends, Shuten Doji was once human. He was a murderer and robber, but human. However, when he had killed a staggering number of people, the *Kami* (Shinto gods) punished him by transforming him and his followers into hideous *Oni*. Yorimitsu assembled his band of warriors, four men known as the *Shitennou*. Before they set out for the mountain, the warriors all disguised themselves as mountain-dwelling Buddhist monks (*yamabuse*). As the *Shitennou* warriors traveled, they encountered three curious old men who bestowed upon Yorimitsu a magic helmet and an enchanted elixir called *Shinbenkidokushu*. These old men were actually *Kami* in disguise, specifically three local Shinto deities named Sumiyoshi, Iwashimizu, and Kumano.

Still in their monk disguises, Yorimitsu and his warriors paid a visit to the palace fortress of Shuten Doji, pretending to be evil fallen priests. They were invited inside and served a feast of human flesh. Not wanting to blow their cover, the warriors had no choice but to eat the dishes. As they ate, Yorimitsu poured the enchanted elixir *Shinbenkidokushu* into Shuten Doji's goblet. When the evil *Oni* leader drank the elixir, it caused him to fall fast asleep.

Avoiding the Labyrinth

Minamoto Yorimitsu should not be confused with another hero of the Heian period by the name of Minamoto Yoshitsune, whose tragic yet heroic exploits took place during the twelfth century. The Heian period of Japanese history had a multitude of legendary heroes, and an entire book could be written to document them all. Other Japanese heroes of the Heian period are Musashibo Benkei (legendary warrior for the *Naginata* halberd), Kamakura Yoritomo (warrior turned Shogun and ally of Minamoto Yoshitsune), and Abe Seimei (a legendary sorcerer who is credited with defeating some of Japan's worst monsters).

Their target thus incapacitated, Yorimitsu and his warriors saw their chance. They drew their weapons and violently attacked the sleeping Shuten Doji. As Yorimitsu slashed at the head, his warriors stabbed at the body with their spears. Even though drugged, Shuten Doji was able to put up a fight. After Yorimitsu cut the *Oni*'s head from his body, the severed head flew at him. Yorimitsu's head was bitten down on by the jaws of the monstrous head. Luckily, the magic helmet he had received from the disguised *Kami* protected him from the attack. Any normal helmet would have been crushed as easily as if it were made of tin foil. Protected by the helmet (which was referred to from then on as "The Helmet of Yorimitsu"), the swordsman and his warriors were able to defeat Shuten Doji and save the region of Kyoto from his reign of terror.

Lu Bu: The Flying General (Chinese)

Historically, the man named Lu Bu was a Chinese general and later a warlord during the latter half of the second century, a period of transitional chaos known as the Era of the Three Kingdoms, when control of the country changed from the longstanding leadership of the Han Dynasty to that of the kingdoms of Wu, Shu, and Wei. According to history, the real Lu Bu appears to have been a better warrior and battlefield general than he was a warlord. His skills in archery, combat, and horsemanship are said to have been without equal. His valuable aptitude for warfare gave Lu Bu the uncanny ability to charge through enemy forces on horseback without receiving so much as a scratch. This caused people to begin calling him "The Flying General," because he could ride through the enemy unharmed, as though he had flown over them.

Avoiding the Labyrinth

There are two primary texts that deal with the Era of the Three Kingdoms, one historical and the other fictional. When researching this period, it is important not to get the two works confused, as one will not know whether one is citing historical fact or romantic fiction. The historical facts and events of this period may be found in a text called *The Records of the Three Kingdoms,* which was compiled and written by historian Chen Shou (sometimes spelled Shen Zhou) sometime in the mid-third century. More than a thousand years later, these events were sensationalized and romanticized by author Luo Guanzhong in his work *The Romance of the Three Kingdoms,* which quickly became (and very much remains) one of the most popular novels of the Asian world.

In the Chinese epic *The Romance of the Three Kingdoms,* Lu Bu is portrayed as both handsome and fierce. He would often fight battles in which he is greatly outnumbered, riding his legendary horse Red Hare and wielding his enormous halberd, which was called "That Which Scorches the Heavens," often shortened in English translations as "Heaven Scorcher," or something of similar effect. In all actuality, Lu Bu's fictional portrayal does not appear to be all that different from his historical self. However, in myth he is portrayed as nearly superhuman in strength and war ability, often achieving impossible combative feats such as taking on entire armies all by himself.

Lu Bu the Betrayer

Whether in history or mythology, one thing is very clear when it comes to the warrior Lu Bu—he was only ever loyal to one person: himself. Lu Bu is infamous for his betrayals, having turned traitor on every single man he ever served. From officials of the Han Dynasty to self-serving warlords, Lu Bu seems to have been willing to stab just about anyone in the back. The thing that made Lu Bu's betrayals all the more despicable is that most of his lords treated him extremely well while he was in their services. Even worse, *both* of the warlords (these being first Dong Zhuo, followed later by Yuan Shao) whom Lu Bu served had even gone so far as to make him their adopted son.

Sword and Man

The legendary horse Red Hare was coveted by many heroes and warlords of the *Three Kingdoms* novel. Originally, this amazing steed belonged to the incredible warrior Guan Yu, who was deified into a war god after his death (see Chapter 5). Dong Zhuo, however, had the horse stolen and used it as a bribe to convince Lu Bu to serve under him as his general. Lu Bu, a wild card who was loath to serve any master, agreed to serve Dong Zhuo as a result and this is how he came to be the rider of the legendary warhorse called Red Hare. Later, however, he would come to covet something—the beautiful maiden Diao Chan—more than a great horse, leading him to turn on his lord.

The most well-known story about one of Lu Bu's betrayals, or at least the most popular one in Chinese folklore, tells of how he turned against the warlord Dong Zhuo as a result of his love for a woman. This story was greatly romanticized in Luo's *The Romance of the Three Kingdoms*. According to this fictional account of what happened, Lu Bu fell in love with a beautiful maiden named Diao Chan while he was serving as a high-ranking general under Lord Dong Zhuo.

Myth and Metaphor

There are two main views on the character Lu Bu of the *Three Kingdoms* novel, and most who read it stand on one side or the other. The first view of Lu Bu is as a wild, arrogant, ungrateful, deceitful, back-stabbing murderer who cares only for himself. The other opinion of Lu Bu, however, sees him as a "fallen hero" character type. The novel does offer more than enough points of evidence to support both sides of the debate. Lu Bu is all the terrible things that he is seen to be by those of the first opinion. However, the story also seems to go to great lengths to provoke feelings of pity for Lu Bu from the reader. According to the legend, Lu Bu spent the days of his later years drunk and depressed. The historical Lu Bu, however, did not have any "later years" in which he could wallow in his own self-pity.

Over time, Diao Chan is able to convince the mighty warrior to slay his longtime master. At the time, Dong Zhuo had kidnapped the young Han Emperor, Han Xian, holding him as a hostage and using this as a powerful piece of political leverage. Diao Chan, being the devoted adopted daughter of an extreme Han loyalist named Wang Yun, aggressively manipulates Lu Bu by showing romantic interest in him until she manages to snare the warrior into killing Dong Zhuo and returning Han Xian to the capital.

There is some debate as to whether or not Diao Chan's expressions of affection toward Lu Bu were genuine or simply clever devices that she used to gain temporary control over his actions. According to the romanticized tale of Luo's novel, Diao Chan *did* eventually agree to marry Lu Bu. Some parts of the novel even hint that the actual cause of Lu Bu's betrayal was the knowledge that Diao Chan was going to be betrothed to Dong Zhuo. No matter what opinion one chooses, the character Diao Chan sharply drops out of the storyline as soon as Lu Bu has betrayed and murdered Dong Zhuo, an act that makes him a debatably tragic or "fallen hero"—the great warrior of legend who betrayed his own lord all for the love of a beautiful maiden who stole his heart. Of course, the historical truth paints nowhere near as pretty a picture of Lu Bu's betrayal of Dong Zhuo.

The Ugly Truth

According to historic record, Lu Bu and Dong Zhuo met during a conflict commonly referred to as "The Uprising of the Ten Eunuchs." That's right … eunuchs. I know what you are thinking, and it's a long story. However, to answer the question that most likely just popped into your head—*yes*, this conflict was *exactly* what it sounds like, an uprising led by and comprised of *eunuchs*, as in a group of effeminate, castrated male house servants. At this time, Lu Bu was serving as a warrior retainer under a regional governor of the Han Dynasty by the name of Ding Yuan. Believe it or not, the eunuchs actually turned out to be a lot tougher then they sounded or acted, because it appears that the local magistrate and nearby military contingent failed miserably in their efforts at getting things back under control. Soon, the eunuch army had the entire capital city of Luoyang in a complete state of pandemonium. Under Ding Yuan's orders, Lu Bu was sent with his unit to support General He Jin, leader of the besieged Han forces at Luoyang, whom he found had already been overrun and executed by the eunuchs before his arrival.

Only one warlord proved himself capable of retaking Luoyang, restoring order, and putting down the rebellion of eunuchs—Dong Zhuo. Likely attracted to the idea of serving a powerful warlord as opposed to the meager salary that came with serving a public official, Lu Bu agreed to serve Dong Zhuo. As a condition, however, Lu Bu was required to bring his new warlord the head of his former employer, Governor Ding Yuan. He did so without hesitation. For many years from this day, Lu Bu and Dong Zhuo appear to have been attached at the hip. It was often said that a person never saw one of the two men without the other standing right beside him. Most likely, Lu Bu's incredible combat skills made Dong Zhuo (a man with quite a few powerful enemies) feel protected when he was nearby, so the warlord kept the man close and used him as a personal bodyguard while giving him the title of "Knights' General" in order to keep up appearances.

Myth and Metaphor

Many myths, as you've likely realized by this point, were created around or based upon an actual person or historical event. Often, after an exceptional warrior dies, stories of his or her abilities begin to be blown way out of proportion in fireside stories and folktales. However, since the man in question is now dead, the truth of what feats he was actually capable of achieving can't be verified, making such tall tales easier to believe at the time they are told. A modern example of this can be seen in the slew of outlandish stories that sprang up in the mid- to late-'70s about actor and legendary martial artist Bruce Lee shortly after he died in 1973. For example, one such legend purported that the man who died in a Hong Kong hotel room in 1973 wasn't Bruce Lee at all, but a student/stunt double/look-alike of Lee's whom he'd asked to impersonate him due to death threats. According to this tall tale, the real Bruce Lee was alive and on the run from a secret society of Kung Fu assassins angered by Lee's teaching of Eastern secrets to Westerners. Obviously, this is a little hard to swallow.

However, tensions between Lu Bu and Dong Zhuo existed and increased with time. Dong Zhuo, for example, had a nasty habit of lashing out with lethal violence, suddenly and without warning, when he would lose his temper (and, unfortunately, he had a very short fuse). Since Lu Bu was the person most frequently near Dong Zhuo, he often found himself the target of these sudden outbursts of violence. Sometimes, Dong Zhuo is said to have recklessly thrown weapons at people (we're talking about *swords* and *halberds*), namely Lu Bu, during these temper tantrums. Lu Bu, luckily, was rather quick and wily, allowing him to dodge the airborne weapons and avoid serious injury/death.

Avoiding the Labyrinth

Dong Zhuo making the offering of Ding Yuan's head a condition of Lu Bu's defection may seem rather cruel. However, aside from being a regional governor for the Han, Ding Yuan was also a minor warlord and rival of Don Zhuo. Ding Yuan, you see, was a loyalist of the Han Dynasty while Dong Zhuo sought to either bring the Han down or to usurp the throne for himself. As a result, having Lu Bu murder a man who stood between him and his goal was (strategically) a wise move, though rather ruthless.

Historically, Diao Chan is not mentioned as being involved in Lu Bu's betrayal of Dong Zhuo. Wang Yun, however, written as Diao Chan's Han loyalist father in the fictional account of the period, *was* actually involved. In actuality, Lu Bu's love affair was not with the daughter of Wang Yun, Diao Chan, but with one of Dong Zhuo's concubines (her name is not known). Eventually, all of the above issues accumulated to a breaking point, and when Wang Yun (actually the Han Imperial Minister of the Interior) suggested that Dong Zhuo should be killed because he threatened the safety of the Han Dynasty, Lu Bu made a decision to act when his lord returned (Dong Zhuo was away at the time of Wang Yun's visit).

Apparently, most of Dong Zhuo's officers were more loyal to Lu Bu than they were to him. This is probably due to the fact that they had shed blood beside the Knights' General on the field of battle while Dong Zhuo had hung back in relative safety (apparently he was not really a "lead from the front" kind of guy). So, Lu Bu gathered 12 of his most trusted fellow officers and put together a plan. When Dong Zhuo returned, Lu Bu and his fellow officers met him at the castle gate and surrounded him. Though it is not believed that Lu Bu was the first to strike, it is believed that he was the one who delivered the killing stroke to Dang Zhuo.

Making More Enemies Than Friends

Near the close of the second century, Lu Bu's legendary immortality was put to the test. Unfortunately for Lu Bu, this was a test that he failed. After betraying Dong Zhuo, it didn't take long for the conspiring officers to begin turning on one another. Soon, a handful of them staged a betrayal of Lu Bu and he had to flee the territory. He went to seek a position under one of Dong's rival warlords, Yuan Shao, who immediately gave him a small contingent of troops and tasked the warrior with crushing an army of bandits, led by Bandit Chief Zhang Yan, who were terrorizing and robbing the locals. Lu Bu made quick work of the bandits, thereby securing a position for himself under Yuan Shao. Unfortunately, the knowledge that Lu Bu had betrayed his last lord made him a hard man to trust and soon Yuan Shao began to view the warrior as more of a threat than an asset. Sensing this, Lu Bu fled the territory that night, under cover of darkness, just in time to avoid the incredible number of trained assassins that Yuan Shao had hired to kill the general.

Lu Bu was now a free agent, a wild card with nothing to lose. He managed to rally a small unit of warriors to his side and led a siege upon the city of Yangzhou in the region that came to be known as Wei, a territory under the rule of a very powerful warlord and self-appointed prime minister by the name of Cao Cao (pronounced "Cow Cow"). The soldiers of Yangzhou, frightened by Lu Bu's reputation, gave up the city without much of a fight. At the time, Cao Cao was away from his home territory, laying siege to Xuzhou, a stronghold held by his longtime rival Liu Bei, the sworn brother-in-arms of legendary warriors Guan Yu (see Chapter 5) and Zhang Fei (see the following section) as well as the warlord in whom the legendary Five Tiger Generals (see the following section) placed their allegiance. When news reached Cao Cao that Yangzhou had fallen, he decided to abandon his siege and retake the city held by Lu Bu.

Lu Bu may have been a bit *too* fearless, but he wasn't delusional either. After more than 100 days of being besieged, with their food and supplies nearly gone, Lu Bu realized that his small collection of troops would soon be crushed if they continued their stand against Cao Cao's vast army. Lu Bu led his forces in a daring escape, fighting their way past the enemy army, and fleeing to Xia-pi to make an alliance with Liu Bei, who would later become ruler of the Kingdom of Shu (called Han Shu), and had returned to his home there after Cao Cao had abandoned his siege. Liu Bei agreed to ally with Lu Bu, giving him a home and post in the nearby city of Xiaopei, only to have the disloyal warrior stab him in the back by sacking Xia-pi and forcing the Shu ruler to flee his home territory and seek aid from Cao Cao.

From this moment, Lu Bu makes a multitude of complicated and unstable alliances and stages just as many elaborate and shameless betrayals. It doesn't take long for him to find that he and his army are isolated, outmanned, and hurting for support. Seeing that he was in such a weakened position, Lu Bu's most powerful enemies pounced.

The Flying General Falls

By now, Lu Bu had made far too many enemies and lost far too many friends. Cao Cao and Liu Bei, who were fierce rivals, had even agreed to a truce and joined forces to deal with the out-of-control warrior. Lu Bu made a shaky alliance with the warlord Yuan Shu (not to be confused with Yuan Shao) and fortified his position at Xia-pi in anticipation of the coming siege by the Cao Cao-Liu Bei alliance. Soon, Cao Cao had personally marched his army to the walls of Xia-pi. After three months of a bloody siege, Lu Bu's men betrayed him in what can only be referred to as karmic payback. There is some debate in the records about how this transpired, apparently. Some records indicate that his men simply defected and he had no choice but to surrender. The other, slightly more interesting, version states that they attacked Lu Bu in his sleep and restrained him, then dragged him outside the city and delivered him to Cao Cao.

Avoiding the Labyrinth _____

It is important to note that, in this period of Chinese history, execution by way of hanging or strangulation was a punishment reserved exclusively for women (presumably because this would cut off the windpipe, not allowing them to beg for their lives, which they believed only women and cowards would do). Therefore, Cao Cao's decision to have Lu Bu executed by hanging was more than just a punishment, it was an insult and way to crush the war-god-like image of Lu Bu that existed in the minds of a majority of his troops. What kind of a war god is killed in a manner reserved for women? Having Lu Bu hanged told those present that Cao Cao saw him as the kind of coward who would have begged for his life had he been given the chance. This was a wise move, in a twisted sort of way, but failed to completely destroy the legend of Lu Bu, "The Flying General."

Now that Lu Bu had been captured, Cao Cao considers enlisting him as a general. However, under Liu Bei's advisement (a man who, ironically, is often seen as being more merciful than his rival, Cao Cao), he has Lu Bu strung up and executed by hanging. Historical documents estimate Lu Bu's execution as having taken place sometime in February of 199 C.E.

The Truth and Legend of Zhang Fei (Chinese)

Historically, Zhang Fei was a warrior general who lived during late second- and early third-century China, and was another crucial player in the time known as the Era of the Three Kingdoms. Zhang Fei was also the sworn brother of Guan Yu (see Chapter 5) and Liu Bei (see mention in previous section). Unlike Lu Bu, the Zhang Fei of history differs greatly from the one depicted in Luo's *The Romance of the Three Kingdoms*.

One day, the daughter of enemy officer Xiahou Yuan was out collecting firewood when she was spotted by the troops of Zhang Fei. They quickly captured her and brought the girl before him. Though she was Zhang Fei's captive, the two began to grow rather close. Eventually, the two were married and would have two daughters, one of whom would one day become the wife of the future ruler of the Han Shu empire.

Historically, Zhang Fei does not appear to have been a very likeable fellow. In fact, he met his end at the hands of his own troops. Apparently, the heroic general of myth was a bit of a jerk in real life, treating his superior officers with courtesy while treating his own subordinates like dirt. As a result, two of his lower-ranking officers conspired to kill Zhang Fei as he staged the unit for an assault on the Kingdom of

Wu, ruled by Sun Quan (a descendent of Sun Tzu, legendary strategist and author of the well-known text on warfare and leadership called *The Art of War*). The attack was meant to exact revenge upon Wu for the execution of Zhang Fei's sworn brother Guan Yu, which the Sun family and its forces had carried out. After killing Zhang Fei, the two officers (named Zhang Da and Fan Jiang), along with a large majority of his troops, defected to Wu.

In the Chinese epic *The Romance of the Three Kingdoms*, Zhang Fei is depicted rather differently from his historical self. In the story, Zhang is originally a ruthless killer. However, when his travels cause him to cross paths with the noble warrior Guan Yu and Han Dynasty loyalist Liu Bei, he sees the light and reforms his cruel ways (at least, he changes them a little bit). This encounter sparked a chain of events that would lead to Zhang Fei becoming one of the Legendary Five Tiger Generals, idealistically natured warriors of vision who swore fierce loyalty to the original cause of Liu Bei, which was for the restoration of the crumbling Han Dynasty (this was a dream that would never be realized, however).

Another addition to Zhang Fei in Luo's fictional account is in his portrayal of the general as a brawler and a drunkard. While such inventive alterations make Zhang Fei a more colorful and interesting character, there is little historical evidence to support it. There is nothing wrong with this, of course, from a mythological point of view, because sometimes the facts do not make for a very good story, and what an amazing story is that of Luo Guanzhong's literary Zhang Fei.

Zhang Fei and the Five Tiger Generals

The Five Tiger Generals are perhaps the most beloved collection of heroes in all of Chinese folklore, perhaps even more popular in China than hero groups such as the Argonauts are in the West. The Five Tigers each had his own special reasons for fighting on the side of Liu Bei, and each had a unique and rich character in his own right. The Five Tiger generals were given this title for their roles in the establishment of the Han Shu Empire under Lord Liu Bei, and they are as follows:

◆ **Guan Yu**   A legendary warrior, competent general, and skilled strategist who saw in Liu Bei a man who he believed could, with the help of likeminded men, lead the country out of chaos. Sadly, Guan Yu was the first of the three Peach Garden Oath brothers to die.

◆ **Zhang Fei**   A reformed murderer and bandit who saw the error of his ways when he encountered Liu Bei and Guan Yu, who were fighting an insurgency of religious fanatics known as the Yellow Turbans. After helping them quell the Yellow Turban Rebellion, Zhang Fei swore an oath of brotherhood with the two men in what came to be called "The Peach Garden Oath." Zhang Fei was the second of the Peach Garden Brothers to die.

- ◆ **Ma Chao**   Ma Chao "The Splendid" harbored a deep hatred for Cao Cao of Wei, against whom he'd fought a number of campaigns before ever joining Liu Bei. After receiving a rather sincere letter from Liu Bei requesting aid, Ma Chao mobilized his renowned cavalry immediately. Ma Chao and his troops met up with Liu Bei's forces just in time to aid them during a battle known as The Siege of Cheng Du. His reinforcement of Liu Bei's troops ended the siege in no more than ten days. One of Ma Chao's most well-known titles was that of *General of the Agile Cavalry.*

- ◆ **Zhao Yun**   Little is known about the historical life of Zhao Yun. It appears, however, that he made an impression on the Peach Garden Brothers when he rushed to the aid of Liu Bei's family when they were mistakenly left behind as Liu's forces fled the field at the Battle of Chang Ban. He charged his way through the Wei army alone, retrieved Liu Bei's family, fought back the enemy, and brought them all safely to the Shu camp (for more on the rescue at Chang Ban, see the next section). For this brave act, Liu Bei gave Zhao Yun the title *General of the Standard.*

- ◆ **Huang Zhong**   Commonly, Huang Zhong is known as the oldest of the Five Tigers, a man of middle age. He was said to have been called "Master of the Bow of Giant Strength." After being on the losing end of a battle against Liu Bei's army, during which he lost a duel with Guan Yu, Huang Zhong asked to be allowed to join them. Of the Five Tigers, he is the only one whose appointment to the group was ever disputed. Guan Yu felt Huang didn't belong since he'd originally served with an enemy. Despite this, Liu Bei had come to view Huang as a valuable general and capable warrior.

Zhang Fei's Stand at the Bridge of Chang Ban

Though this event is often referred to as the "Battle of Chang Ban," the most impressive moment in this part of the story has to do with a famous stand made by Zhang Fei. Zhang Fei, while crossing the bridge in the retreat from Chang Ban, saw fellow Five Tiger General Zhao Yun escorting Liu Bei's family back to safety. In the exhausted warrior's arms was the infant Liu Shan (son of Liu Bei and future ruler of the Han Shu Empire). Without time to muster a force to aid Zhao Yun, Zhang Fei turned around and rode at full gallop back across the Chang Ban Bridge. He did not stop until he had successfully placed himself between Zhao Yun and the pursuing enemy troops.

As the brave Zhao Yun carried the baby Liu Shan to safety across the Chang Ban Bridge, all the warriors pursuing him stopped dead in their tracks at the frightening sight of Zhang Fei upon his horse, swinging his halberd. Knowing that he was now in a dangerous situation, Zhang Fei had to think fast. So, he likely did the first thing that came to his mind.

Myth and Metaphor

Events such as that of the Bridge Chang Ban are common in stories of the fictional character of Zhang Fei. For example, one such tale claims that Zhang Fei once fooled Cao Cao into delaying the advance of his army by ordering his cavalry troops to drag logs behind their horses. The great cloud of dust they created, when seen from a distance, appeared as though a large ambush was being staged up ahead. When Cao Cao saw this, he called for a temporary halt on the advance of his troops, believing that a surprise attack from a large number of enemy troops must be waiting for them.

Alone and relatively isolated from the main unit, Zhang Fei stood up high in the stirrups of his saddle, pointed his halberd at the enemy troops, and snarled as he growled out: "My name is Zhang Fei of Yan! Let any man who is daring enough come forth and fight me to the death in combat!" According to the story, in both the historical and fictional accounts, not so much as one of the 10,000 soldiers present took Zhang Fei up on his challenge. According to the fictional account, it is said that the frightening sight and bold words of Zhang Fei were enough to scare the enemy officer, Xiahou Jie, to death (literally). After a few moments, seeing that he'd managed to temporarily shock the enemy troops into a collective stupor, Zhang Fei turned around, calmly trotted his horse back across the bridge, and set the Chang Ban Bridge on fire. With the only bridge allowing passage in that direction now in flames, Cao Cao's Wei army had no choice but to give up their pursuit.

A Brother's Loyalty

One of Zhang Fei's most fierce attributes in *The Romance of the Three Kingdoms* is his fanatical loyalty to Liu Bei. When his sworn brother Guan Yu returns to Liu Bei's forces after being forced to serve under Cao Cao (Liu Bei's sworn enemy) while being held captive, Zhang Fei accuses him of having defected to the enemy. As a result, these two powerful warriors engage in one-on-one combat.

Throughout the fight Guan Yu holds back as best he can, not wanting to harm his somewhat simpleminded friend, while trying to convince Zhang Fei that he is wrong in his assumptions. The warriors fight three fierce and exhausting rounds. Finally, however, Zhang Fei sees the truth of things and the misunderstanding is resolved. Luckily, neither fighter is seriously injured or killed during their duel.

The Tiger Slayer (Chinese)

Wu Song was known as the "Tiger Slayer," primarily because, well, he once slew a tiger. His heroic exploits are recorded in the Chinese classic titled *The Water Margin*. Another Chinese work, *Jin Ping Mei*, which is based on the classical piece, also tells of his adventures. The story from which the hero gets his title tells of how, as Wu Song was coming home, he encountered a ferocious man-eating tiger. As the beast pounced, Wu Song caught it in his iron grip and killed the beast with his bare hands. As a result, he was offered a position as the local constable.

Myth and Metaphor

The theme of a strongman who secures a position of high rank after killing a man-eating tiger with his bare hands is rather universal in mythology. This story could be compared to that of Herakles or Samson in this way.

Wu Song's life took a turn for the worse when his brother, Wu Dalang, brought him to his house to introduce his new wife. It is well known that Wu Dalang was not the most handsome of men. In fact, he was considered fairly ugly. His wife Pan, however, was extremely beautiful. She did her best to seduce Wu Song, but the hero would not be charmed. When the opportunity arose for Wu Song to take a new job protecting gold caravans to the capital city, the hero jumped at the chance. At least now he would be able to escape the sexual advances of his sister-in-law.

Unfortunately, during Wu Song's absence Pan took a lover and the pair murdered his brother with poison. By the time Wu Song returned, his murderous sister-in-law had already had his brother's body cremated, thus destroying the evidence. However, Pan's lover had bribed the local judge and the law took no action … so Wu Song did. He confronted Pan and her lover and killed them. As a result, he was exiled and had to flee to the region of Megzhou.

Myth and Metaphor _____

The theme of the bandit hero is very common in world myths. In this way Wu Song's close relationship to the people, robbing of the corrupt, and refusal to acknowledge the power of the authoritative body makes him comparable to the well-known figure of Western myth, Robin Hood.

After his exile, Wu Song became a bandit-hero, giving justice to those who had been wronged when the corrupt officials would not. As a result, he was very much a hero of the people, and they often hid him from the authorities. In one case, he was disguised by the owners of a restaurant that he had helped by removing a local bully who had taken the establishment from them by force. They dressed him up as a priest, therefore causing Wu Song to receive yet another title: "The Priest."

The Least You Need to Know

- The warrior-hero is not always law-abiding.

- Most often, when the warrior becomes a hero of the people, he fights against a corrupt system.

- The warrior-hero is often based on a real person whose legend is transmitted orally, becoming more incredible with each telling.

- The warrior-hero sometimes wishes for nothing more than to become immortal in the minds of others. Through myth, his wishes are granted.

Part  3

Heroines:
Women of Myth

Who said that a woman's place is in the home? Whoever it was, he must never have met these ladies of adventure. These brave women of the shield and spear walk the paths of warriors, heroes, and men, very often bringing even the gods to their knees in submission. From the legendary warrior-women of the Amazon to the wrathful and defiant Lilith, the first wife of Adam, these women prove that their place is most certainly not in the home, but on the roads to glory and immortality.

Chapter 12

Ladies of Wrath

In This Chapter

- ◆ The wrath of a woman scorned
- ◆ The manipulating female figure in myth
- ◆ The power of the dark feminine
- ◆ The murderous wives and homicidal daughters

You know what they say, "Hell hath no fury like a woman scorned." The wrathful fury of wronged females in mythology is perhaps one of the most terrifying powers it portrays. These female characters are notorious for bringing death, misery, and ruin to the likes of heroes, kings, and even gods who have wronged them. Whether he is a father, brother, lover, or husband, no man is safe after the furious wrath of these raging women is evoked upon him. These kinds of dark women or wrathful female characters are representative of what may be one of the greatest fears of the male psyche—to be deceived, manipulated, dominated, or murdered by a female close to him.

Revenge of the One-Handed Girl (African)

The myth of One-Handed Girl comes from African tribal tales of a brother and sister with elderly parents. Knowing that he is soon to die, the father asks his children if they would rather have his property or his blessing. His selfish son asks for property. His daughter asks for his blessing. Soon after, their mother also sees her death drawing near. She also asks if they would rather have her property or her blessing. Again, the son takes the property and the daughter takes the blessing.

Both parents now dead, the brother tells his sister to put all of the family property outside so that he might take it away. She does so, and spends days hungry, alone, and sorrowful. The brother leaves her with no food or tools, only a cooking pot and a mortar to grind corn into flour. However, as a result of her parents' gifts, she is soon blessed with an abundance of food. All the women in the village find their pots have cracked and mortars have broken. The lonely girl now has the only working pot and mortar in the village. As a result, every woman in the village borrows the girl's pot and, in return, gives her a portion of their meals and ground corn. She also finds a pumpkin seed and plants it. The seed grows and provides her an entire patch of plump pumpkins.

Not long after leaving, one of the young men of the village passes by the hut of the girl's brother. The brother asks how his sister is doing and learns that she has grown prosperous and well fed, despite him taking all the family property with him and leaving her with nothing but a pot.

Hearing of this, the brother grows enraged with envy, having already squandered the property he inherited. In the night, he sneaks into his sister's hut with a large sack and steals away with her cooking pot and mortar. When the girl awakes, she finds it gone and realizes she has been robbed.

A Spiteful Sister-in-Law

With no mortar to grind corn for her breakfast, the girl goes to her pumpkin patch and is pleased to find it overflowing with ripe, large, plump pumpkins. She eats her fill and takes the extra to the village for sale. The women in the village, finding these to be the tastiest pumpkins they've ever eaten, pay well and buy all that she is willing to sell. She continues to sell her pumpkins every day, earning more than enough money to support herself. She is soon able to collect enough money to buy a brand-new cooking pot and mortar. In a short time, the girl has grown quite rich.

One day, her brother's wife sends one of her slaves with a sack of grain to buy a pumpkin from the girl. When the girl learns that the slave comes from her brother's house, she hands him a pumpkin and, though she has but a few left, tells him to present it to her brother's wife as a gift and that she need not worry about paying with the grain.

The wife is happy to receive the pumpkin, but selfish. She soon tells her slave to go tell her husband's sister that she wants another pumpkin. When the slave arrives, the girl has no pumpkins left, and tells him that she has none to give. The wife throws a fit when she is told of this. When her husband comes home a couple of days later, she tells him that his sister refuses to sell her a pumpkin even though the girl sells them to others in the village.

The brother is angered by what his wife has told him. He takes a machete and goes to his sister. He demands to know why she refuses to sell his wife a pumpkin. She explains that she *gave* her one, but that when she came to ask for a second, there were none ripe enough to give, as there are now. The brother does not believe her and goes to the patch with his machete. The girl sticks her arm out to block him from chopping one of the unripe pumpkins from the vine, telling him that if he chops the pumpkin he will have to take her hand with it. Without hesitation, her brother brings the blade down on the vine, severing the pumpkin … as well as his sister's hand.

He then breaks his way into his sister's home, removes everything of value, forces her out, and sells the home to one of the villagers. As though her hand and the pumpkin are not enough, he takes everything she has and leaves her homeless and destitute. With only one hand, the poor girl can't even work to earn her food.

The One-Handed Princess

Seven days the girl wanders, starving and heartbroken. She climbs a tree and weeps. Later, a prince sits under the tree and her tears fall upon him. When he sees her, his heart is captured. He feels horrible to see this lovely girl weep so. However, she refuses to come down. So he goes away with his attendants and hides, waiting for her to come down. Thinking they have left, the girl climbs down and succumbs to fatigue. As she sleeps, the prince has her injured body loaded onto a stretcher and taken to the palace.

As he nurses her to health, the prince falls deeply in love. His parents, the king and queen, agree to the marriage. Though they wish he'd chosen a wife with two hands and more wealth, they cannot deny him a wife that brought him such happiness. In fact, the girl proves to be such a loving, generous, and useful wife to their son that they soon grow to love the girl as their own daughter.

Return of a Lying Brother

The greedy brother of One-Handed Girl soon hears word that the prince has taken a wife who has only one hand, and realizes this woman must be his sister. Since chopping off her hand, his life has been a terrible tale of ill luck, trouble, and difficulty. He had once again squandered his wife's dowry, along with the wealth he stole from his sister.

Hearing of his sister's good fortune, the brother's heart fills with envious rage, and he immediately presents himself to the king. He tells the king that the woman his son has married had her hand chopped off in another village because she was found to be a witch, and that his son has fallen under her deadly spell. The king has her exiled, along with her infant son, despite the brother's entreaties that she should be executed. The prince is away in a distant region of the kingdom, and so is not present to challenge his father's order. The girl's brother is given a place in the court by the king, as the bearer of his peacock-feathered fan.

The Snake's Gift

As she wanders in exile, the girl encounters a snake and helps it hide from a pursuer. In return, the snake shields her from the rain that night. When she awakens, she cannot find her baby. The snake tells her to search in the water among the reeds. She places her good hand into the water, finding nothing. The snake tells her to put both arms in the water. She does so and finds her baby and, when she pulls it from the reeds, she finds that her severed hand has come back.

The prince returns after a long delay, having fallen ill during his trip, and is lied to by his father. The prince is told that his wife and infant son are both dead.

Later, the girl returns, but isn't recognized because she now has her hand back. She begs entry into the king's palace; she is offered rest and is asked to tell them her story. Without telling anyone her identity, she begins to tell the true story of her life—her parent's deaths, her brother's treachery and thievery, and finally the loss of her hand and its miraculous return. As she speaks, her brother sits behind the king, sweating nervously, helpless to keep her from speaking. As she is about to end the story, the prince knows it is her and takes his wife and son into his arms.

She acknowledges her husband and weeps, but asks that she be allowed to complete the tale. She ends the story with how her brother has lied to the king and had her unjustly exiled. The king and prince leave judgment of the evil brother to the girl. His sentence? Lifelong exile from the entire kingdom … a fate worse than death in any tribal culture.

The Queen of Mycenae (Greek)

Queen Clytemnestra was the wife of King Agamemnon of Mycenae and the mother of Elektra (also spelled Electra). When Agamemnon goes off to fight in the Trojan War, Clytemnestra does not like having a cold bed, so she begins a love affair with a man named Aegisthus. When word reaches Mycenae that King Agamemnon is soon returning from the long war, Clytemnestra and her lover come up with a plan to get rid of the king. When Agamemnon returns, they murder him. In some versions, Aegisthus kills his lover's husband. In other versions, Clytemnestra herself takes the king's life.

Myth and Metaphor _____

Elektra was the inspiration for the naming of Sigmund Freud's "Electra Complex," a psychological condition in which a daughter desires to be rid of her mother to be alone with the father, or to murder her mother and have sex with her father. This is considered the female equivalent of Freud's "Oedipus Complex," named after the tragic hero who unknowingly killed his father and married his mother (see Chapter 8).

The young Orestes and Elektra, the son and daughter of Agamemnon and Clytemnestra, are rescued by an old nurse and escape the murderous hands of their mother and her regicidal lover. Eight years later, Orestes goes to the Delphi Oracle and is ordered by a prophetess to return home and avenge the murder of Agamemnon. When he arrives at his father's tomb, he finds Elektra, his sister, waiting for him there. With the help of a friend, Pylades, they kill Clytemnestra and Aegisthus.

Unfortunately, Orestes is cursed to suffer the wrath of the Furies (see Chapter 17), the terrible avengers that torment those who violate the bonds of family loyalty. His fate differs depending on which version of the myth you read. According to the writer Aeschylus, Orestes is put on trial by the gods and acquitted by the goddess Athena. In Euripides' version of the story, he is chased to the Black Sea by the Furies, but eventually escapes them by reuniting with his surviving family members.

A Hero's Ruin (Greek)

Medea is the daughter of King Aetes of Colchis and a priestess of Hecate. When the Greek hero Jason comes to Colchis in his search for the Golden Fleece, Medea falls in love with him. In fact, it is only because of her that Jason is able to obtain the Golden Fleece at all (see Chapter 10).

Jason flees Colchis aboard the Argo, with Medea in tow. They also take Medea's younger brother, Apsyrtus, as a hostage. King Aetes, outraged, boards his own ship with his warriors and pursues them. As he gains on the Argo, Medea takes up a knife and seizes her brother. She dices up her own brother and begins tossing his dismembered corpse into the ocean, piece by piece. King Aetes has no choice but to slow his vessel to retrieve his son's body parts so that he can be properly buried. Soon, Jason and Medea escape and the Argo is out of Aetes' vision.

Medea's Trickery

When Jason returns home with the Fleece, he finds that his Uncle Pelias had his father killed. Medea takes revenge on Pelias for her lover by convincing the man's daughters that she has the ability to rejuvenate the aging king with her magic. She brings forth an old ram, dismembers it, and places it into a boiling cauldron. A few moments later, she pulls a young lamb from the cauldron. After this display, she explains to the daughters of Pelias that if they do the same to their father, he, too, will be made young again.

Avoiding the Labyrinth

Medea's "witchcraft" was likely perceived as such because it is believed that she was probably of Persian ethnic origin. This might also explain why Jason never took her as a bride. Her murderous nature may have been based on the laws of revenge in the land from which she came, meaning that she was not so much insane or psychotic as acting in the manner of a woman from her native land.

Pelias' daughters, sadly, are a bit naïve. When they chop up their father and put him in the cauldron, obviously, nothing happens. Medea's trickery causes the girls to unknowingly kill their own father. As a result, she and Jason are forced out of Iolcos by Pelias' son.

Jason's Betrayal

Jason and Medea later settle in Corinth, under the welcome of King Creon. Though they never legally married, Medea and Jason live together for years and have two sons. However, when King Creon offers Jason his daughter Glauce's hand in marriage, Jason tosses Medea aside along with his children. He announces his marriage plans to Medea and explains to her that she and their sons will be exiled from Corinth.

As revenge against Jason, Medea sends a poisoned broach to Glauce as a gift. The poison is like fire, scorching Glauce from the inside out. When Creon tries to remove the fatal jewelry from his daughter, he, too, is consumed by the poison.

Avoiding the Labyrinth

In some versions of the Medea myth, it is not a poisoned broach that she sends, but a robe, dress, or other fine garment. Also, the nature of the poison varies from one version of the myth to another.

Medea's Revenge

While Jason is hearing the news of his murdered bride-to-be and future father-in-law, Medea is carrying out the second half of her plan of vengeance. After a short period of self-debate, she takes up a sword and traps her sons in their home. Sword in hand, she slays the sons she had with Jason.

Avoiding the Labyrinth

Medea's riding off in a chariot drawn by dragons is likely representative of the fact that her grandfather was said to be the sun god of her homeland. In the Greek myths, her grandfather is referred to as *Helios*, as this was the name of the Greek equivalent for the sun god. In some versions, her chariot is drawn by a pair of gryphons (for more on the gryphon, see Chapter 20) or she simply flies away.

When the hero Jason arrives at Medea's home, he sees her in the sky aboard a chariot drawn by dragons. In her arms are the small and limp frames of his murdered sons. Leaving him ruined and traumatized, Medea rides off into the sky on her dragon-drawn chariot, her shrill and mad laughter piercing the air.

Cursed Brides of Lemnos (Greek)

There is a Greek myth that says the women of Lemnos are some of the most beautiful in the entire world. However, they neglect to make sacrifices to the goddess Aphrodite and fail to offer her any worship. As punishment, Aphrodite curses the

Myth and Metaphor

In the Greek mythological tradition, goddesses were often prone to jealousy and had a vengeful nature. Many Greek myths tell of hardships, curses, and monsters that were set upon a region as a result of a goddess being spoken ill of, neglected, or replaced by another goddess as a matron deity.

women of Lemnos. Though they are allowed to remain beautiful to the eyes, they are made to have a scent so vile that no man will even come near them.

The men of Lemnos, repulsed by the terrible odor of their wives and brides, decide to leave Lemnos and seek new wives from Thrace. The women of Lemnos, however, refuse to be so easily cast aside. They arm themselves with spears and travel to Thrace, finding their husbands in their beds with their new Thracian wives. The murderous brides of Lemnos, with fire in their eyes and anger in their hearts, stab their husbands to death in their own beds. Even the new Thracian wives are not spared.

The Usurping Stepmother (Hindu)

During a battle, the wheel of the chariot of King Dasarath (Father of Rama) breaks and strands him dangerously on the field. Kaikeyi, the youngest of the king's three wives, comes bravely to his aid and repairs the broken wheel. In return for her service, Dasarath offers his young wife two *boons* that she can ask him to fulfill at any time.

Immortal Words

A **boon** is a favor, specific or nonspecific, that may be bestowed on a person as reward or compensation for service or help. However, a boon is an honor-bound obligation. In some cultures, denying a promised boon is equal to blasphemy, because one often swears to the deity/deities when a boon is made. The difference between a boon and a promised favor is that one has no choice but to fulfill a boon. Promises to humans may be broken, but promises to the gods cannot.

When Prince Rama is announced as heir to the throne of Ayodhya, Kaikeyi fears that it will diminish her importance to the king. Her handmaiden, Manthara, convinces Kaikeyi that Dasarath will now favor Rama's mother and forget all about her, perhaps even sending her into exile.

Boons Fulfilled

In a rage at the thought of this assumed future wrong, Kaikeyi decides it is time to call in her boons to Dasarath. For the first boon, she demands that Prince Rama, Dasarath's most beloved son, be exiled from Ayodhya for 14 years. For her second boon, she demands that her own son, Bharata, be crowned the King of Ayodhya. However, Rama is so beloved by even Bharata that her son later refuses to take the throne, placing Rama's sandals on it and acting as a regent for 14 years until his half-brother's return from exile.

Rama, in his wisdom and mercy, forgives his stepmother from the very start. When he learns of his exile, he approaches Kaikeyi and bows at her feet, telling her that he would have gone into exile if she had but asked, because his dharma as a son is to honor and obey his parents, even a stepmother. Kaikeyi, however, cares nothing for Rama. She is deaf to the pleas of her son, her husband, and all the people in the kingdom. No matter who appeals to her, she refuses to relieve Dasarath of these boons even though they break the poor king's heart.

All Her Sins Remembered

One must be careful and not be too quick to judge the young Kaikeyi. Not every version of Rama's tale portrays her as a vicious wife and malevolent woman. Some versions explain that Rama's exile was part of his dharma and that it was he who asked the greatest sacrifice of his stepmother, that she be the reason for his banishment.

In this version, he tells her that, if she accepts the task of having him exiled as he asks, she will be remembered for centuries on Earth as an evil woman and terrible wife. Realizing, however, that this is the Lord Vishnu himself in the form of an avatar asking this difficulty of her, she agrees to make the sacrifice of her reputation so that Rama can fulfill his destiny and bring peace and justice to the world. When the myth is considered in this light, Kaikeyi does not seem like such a wrathful character.

First Wife of Adam (Near and Middle Eastern)

In the Jewish mythological tradition, Lilith is the first wife of Adam in the Garden of Eden. In some myths, Lilith later becomes queen of demons or the wife of Satan. In the Genesis myth of the Jewish rabbinical texts, it is said that Lilith and Adam are created by YHVH, at the same time and in the same fashion, from the dust of the earth.

Adam, however, is not happy when he discovers that Lilith is not willing to be a servant to him, or to accept a role as secondary or inferior to him. She also refuses to allow Adam to be on top of her during sex. She leaves Adam and refuses to sleep with him. As a result, she is exiled from Eden. With Lilith gone, God then makes Eve from Adam's rib so that she will serve at his side. After leaving Eden, some myths say that Lilith becomes the mistress of the demon Sammael or, in other versions, Satan.

Lilith's Rebellion

In traditional Jewish myth, it says that YHVH, before creating Eve, sends out three angels—Semangelaf, Sanvi, and Sansanvi—in attempts to retrieve Lilith. If she will do as Adam told her, these angels explain to her, and "play nice," then she will be allowed to come back to Eden.

Lilith refuses and is punished by YHVH for her rebellious nature with a curse that causes her to lose 100 of her children every day. Myth also states, however, that she *does* have sex with Adam one more time before leaving Eden, and that her pregnancy results in the birth of a race of evil demons called the *Shedhim*.

Mother of All Monsters

In at least one version of the Lilith myth, the exiled first wife of Adam eventually returns to Eden in the form of a serpent. Her visit results in Adam's and Eve's expulsions from paradise. She also appears in one of the stories of the Babylonian goddess Inanna, making her home in Inanna's Huluppu tree until she is expelled by the goddess's warrior-brother Gilgamesh.

Lilith is also said to have given birth to other monsters, demons, and creatures of the deep. These monstrous children of Lilith are referred to as *lilim*, *lilum*, or *lilin*. They are sometimes described as winged creatures with the hindquarters of a jackass.

Lilith's War on Motherhood

In verbal transmissions of the Lilith myths, she eventually comes to be seen as a kind of female demon herself. As a result of the children YHVH took from her, it is said that Lilith is jealous of mothers and often hides in or near water, waiting to snatch up and devour children. She is also said to enter like a specter into the delivery rooms of birthing mothers and take the life of the baby as it is being born. Sometimes, she even does this after a baby is born.

According to old Judaic superstitions, the only way to keep Lilith's murderous powers at bay is to create and employ a special symbol or amulet upon which is inscribed the names of the three angels that YHVH sent to retrieve her, as well as the names of Adam and Eve, along with a Hebrew inscription that reads "Barring Lilith." This was sometimes carved into a special amulet that could be worn by the expecting mother or a child. At other times, it was drawn onto the floors of delivery rooms.

The Least You Need to Know

- The myth of the wrathful female sometimes serves as a reminder to men that betraying a woman can have fatal consequences.

- The wrath of the vengeful female in myth is often about more than just killing … it's about ruin and suffering.

- Sometimes, rebellious or independent females in mythology have been demonized or removed from their original myths during the passage of time.

- Never cross a woman in myth unless you are prepared to pay the price.

Chapter 13

Ladies of Tragedy

In This Chapter

- ◆ The tragic female: fatally flawed or an innocent victim?
- ◆ The fate of the tragic lover
- ◆ The ill-fated women of Irish tragedy
- ◆ The difference between females in tragedy and male tragic figures
- ◆ Why females in tragedy may in fact be more heroic than males

The women of tragedy are somewhat different when compared to men. Very rarely are their tragic fates the result of their own fatal flaws. In fact, more commonly their downfalls are caused by the fatal flaws and/or treacheries of men. Also more common among females in tragedy is the scenario of the ill-fated lover, where the woman's love of a certain man is forbidden but they engage in the affair regardless, which sparks a chain of events that leads to one or both of the lovers being killed or dying.

Sometimes, death is a voluntary choice made by ill-fated lovers. In some cases, the tragic female chooses to die when she is overcome by grief at the loss or death of her lover. In other cases, both lovers are faced with one of two choices—separation or death. Unable to endure a life apart, they choose to die together in what is often a romanticized situation, which serves as a metaphor of the male and female uniting as one.

Red Wolf's Daughter (Native American)

For quite some time, there is a bloody war fought between the Nez Perce and Black-foot tribes. The Blackfoot, seeing how plentiful the hunting and fishing grounds of the Nez Perce are, invade and seek to push out the native tribe. However, the Nez Perce chief, named Red Wolf, does not intend to give up the land without a fight. In the early battles of the war, the Nez Perce are victorious. Their victories, however, are primarily due to the Blackfoot warriors being somewhat unfamiliar with the land-scape and therefore easy to ambush.

As time passes, however, the warriors of the Blackfoot become more familiar with the land. Also, they have a new chief who is cunning and brilliant in the arts of strategy and waging war. He is called the Bloody Chief, and under his guidance the tables of the war soon turn in favor of the Blackfoot. The Nez Perce warriors begin falling in great numbers until eventually a small band is all that remains of this once great tribe of warriors.

In the Face of Oblivion

The Blackfoot are advancing, and total annihilation seems just around the corner. The daughter of Red Wolf is named Wahluna. As her father knows well, Wahluna is special, considered a shaman healer, a talented medicine woman who tends to the wounded after each battle. Wahluna, wishing to save her people from obliteration, prays to the spirits of Wallowa Lake. As she does this, a canoe suddenly appears at the water's edge. She climbs aboard and paddles across the lake, right into the ene-my's camp, and addresses the Bloody Chief.

At first, the Bloody Chief is indignant and cares nothing for her words of peace. His son Tlesca, however, is as impressed by the girl's bravery as he is enchanted by her beauty. The Blackfoot prince appeals to his father for mercy on the Nez Perce people by removing his cloak (a symbol of his authority in the tribe) and placing it across Wahluna's shoulders.

Peace at Last

As a result of Wahluna's act of bravery, a truce is made between the people of the Nez Perce and the Blackfoot. The war ends, and the land is shared for a time between the two peoples. Tlesca soon asks Wahluna for her hand in marriage. Unfortunately, there is a problem that makes a marriage between the two impossible. When Wahluna made her prayers to the spirit of Wallowa Lake, she promised her own life as a sacrifice in exchange for the peace and prosperity of their two tribes.

Tlesca is terribly grieved by this news, and believes that he cannot live without Wahluna. So the two make a pact and announce to their tribes the next day that they will be married. However, even now, just a short time since the truce was formed, old grudges are beginning to come to the surface and tensions start brewing between the tribes' people right up to the day of the wedding celebration that would unite them.

A Tragic Wedding

The ceremony is held next to Wallowa Lake. When completed, Tlesca and Wahluna board a canoe, presumably to paddle to their honeymoon spot. After they reach the center of the lake, however, a terrible wind strikes and a whirlpool swirls in the lake. From the whirlpool emerges an enormous creature, sent by the spirit of the lake to claim Wahluna.

The chiefs of both tribes, unaware of Wahluna's pact with the lake spirit, begin making their way to their children. The Blackfoot and Nez Perce warriors stand side-by-side, directly behind their unified chiefs, weapons drawn for combat against the monster before them. However, Wahluna screams to them over the howling wind and growling beast, telling them all to stop, that they must not interfere. She explains that this is what she and Tlesca had agreed to, and that to get involved will only cause the destruction of both tribes.

Two Die as One

Because Wahluna is obliged to give her life to the spirit of Wallowa Lake, and since Tlesca cannot live without her, the young lovers agree that they will die as one. Tlesca, brave prince of the Blackfoot, has volunteered to follow his beloved Wahluna into the jaws of death (literally). The great creature opens wide its jaws and descends upon the couple who, in their small canoe, hold one another tight in one final embrace before they are swallowed by the creature and taken to their deaths at the bottom of Wallowa Lake.

Never again will there be war between the people of the Nez Perce and the Blackfoot. Now joined together by their mutual loss, the chiefs of these two tribes remain forever a pair of sad friends. The Bloody Chief leads his people out of the lands of the Nez Perce … never to return.

Boann (Irish)

Boann is queen of a mythological race of people in Ireland called the *Tuatha de Danaan*, or "people of the hills." Her palace is in the legendary city of *Brug na Boinne*, which means "City of Boann." Unfortunately, her pride will one day lead her down the tragic path to self-destruction.

Immortal Words

Tuatal is a direction that means "counter-sunwise," or against the direction of the sun. Movement in this direction, by characters in Celtic or Irish myths, is often done as a way to counteract magic spells.

A beautiful, magical water well sits in a place called *Sid Nectan*, and belongs to Nectan, one of the *Side* people, another sect of the *Tuatha de Danaan*. Legend states that none but Nectan or one of his designated water carriers could look into the well without suffering a most horrible death. Boann, however, claims that the well cannot possibly have any power over one as strong as her. She travels to the well and walks around it three times in the direction of *tuatal*.

Just as Boann is about to look into the well of *Sid Nectan*, three waves rise up from its depths. The first wave snatches one of Boann's eyes out of her head. The second wave takes off one of her hands. The third and final wave tears loose one of Boann's thighs. Hideously maimed, the queen of the *Tuatha de Danaan* flees toward the sea. The waters of the well, however, pursue her and at last overcome her at the mouth of a river. There, Boann is drowned by the waters of the well. To this day, the river bears the queen's name. The river is now called Boyne.

The Ruin of Ireland

Deirdre is the name of one of the most tragic female figures in Irish mythology. Her name means "troubler," and upon her birth as daughter to Fedlimid of Ulster, at a feast for King Conchobar a soothsayer prophesies that she will cause the downfall of Ireland as well as the king's elite warriors, known as the Red Branch.

Upon hearing this prophecy, the warriors of the kingdom demand that she be killed immediately. King Conchobar, however, refuses to allow an infant to be put to death. Instead, Conchobar declares that the girl is to be sent away from men, raised in partial exile by his female confidante Levarcham, a male forester, and a royal nursemaid at one of his forest castles. Conchobar also makes one other declaration: when Deirdre comes of age, he will take her as his wife.

Calf's Blood and Raven's Feathers

When Deidre grows to a maiden, she witnesses the slaughter of a calf by the forester who cares for her. Soon, a raven flies down and begins to drink the spilt blood that stains the white snow. Having seen this, Deirdre returns home and tells Levarcham, the king's confidante, that she will only marry a man who has cheeks that are as red as blood, hair as black as a raven's feathers, and skin that is as white as the snow. Levarcham knows of only one such man—King Conchobar's nephew, Naoise, one of the three sons of Usnech.

Levarcham foolishly tells Deirdre of the young man named Naoise. The maiden asks Levarcham to invite the young man to the forest castle and, for some reason, Levarcham obliges her. Naoise is invited and soon arrives at the forest castle. When he arrives, Deirdre proclaims her love for him. After a little coaxing, Naoise agrees to elope with Deirdre to Scotland. Naoise's brothers, Ardan and Ainle, accompany them.

A Time of Happiness

Years pass as Deirdre and Naoise live happily and peacefully in exile in Scotland. However, Conchobar still desires to have Deirdre for his wife as he'd always planned. Eventually, the King of Ulster sends Fergus, one of the most legendary warriors of the Red Branch, to offer them a safe-conduct passage back to Ireland. Against Deirdre's pleadings, Naoise and his brother decide they will return to Ireland. Deirdre has no choice but to follow them.

Once they are all back on Irish soil, King Conchobar separates the three brothers from Deirdre by housing them in the barracks of the Red Branch, where she cannot enter. Levarcham, however, has learned of the king's desire to take Deirdre from them, and warns the sons of Usnech. However, her warning comes too late and the king's Red Branch warriors attack them. Only the sons of Fergus stand beside the sons of Usnech against the entire Red Branch. They fight valiantly and kill many adversaries before they are finally overtaken by a magic spell from Cathbad the Druid (the same soothsayer who prophesied that Deirdre would turn out to be Ireland's destruction).

Death of Deidre and Naoise

The sons of Usnech are taken away and executed, their heads removed. As they are being thrown into their large grave, Deirdre arrives. Horrified at seeing the beheaded corpses of Naoise and his two brothers, she breaks free and rushes to the corpse of her slain lover. She reaches into the grave and drinks his poisoned blood (presumably from the magic of Cathbad the Druid) before letting out a cry of lamentation for Naoise and his murdered kin.

She then jumps into the grave with Naoise's body, gives three kisses to the severed head of her one and only true love, and then dies at his side. Naoise and Deirdre are then together forever. In some accounts, King Conchobar has stakes driven through their intertwined corpses. These stakes, according to this version of the myth, grow into trees.

The Fall of Conchobar

The death of Deirdre, Naoise, and his brothers is not a victory for King Conchobar, however. In fact, this one moment eventually costs him his entire kingdom. Conchobar, it seems, pays a very heavy price for not heeding the warnings of Cathbad the Druid's prophecy, telling him that Deirdre would be the land's ruin. In the end, his words will ring true.

As a result of King Conchobar's treacherous ways, and the killing of Usnech's and Fergus' sons, many of his finest Red Branch warriors relieve themselves from the king's service and join the ranks of Queen Medb, enemy of Conchobar (see Setanta and Ferdiad in Chapter 8). In the terrible war that is soon to come, some of his greatest warriors will stand against him. As a result, King Conchobar's forces lose the epic struggle for supremacy in Ireland, the War for the Brown Bull.

Antigone (Greek)

Antigone is the ill-fated daughter of Oedipus and Jocasta, the infamous mother-son marriage of Greek tragedy (see Chapter 8). Her name comes from the Greek words *Anti* (against) and *Gon* (bend), so it could be translated to mean she who "bends against" or as "unbending." The most popular version of this tragedy, *Antigone*, written by Sophocles, is set in a time period that is after her father's death and her mother's suicide.

Thus orphaned Antigone and her siblings are taken under the care King Creon, their uncle. After Oedipus' self-exile, his two sons, Eteocles and Polynices, are told to rule Thebes in turns. However, Eteocles eventually refuses to give up the throne and has Polynices banished.

Seven Against Thebes

Antigone's brother Polynices joins with Thebes' rivals and stands against his former home in the war of Seven Against Thebes. Unfortunately for Polynices, he chose the wrong side. He faces his brother Eteocles in battle and the two kill each other. Creon, now the interim ruler of Thebes, is angered and insulted at this betrayal, so he has Polynices' body taken into the street and left there to rot. The King of Corinth decrees that anyone who attempts to give Polynices' body the proper funeral rites will be subject to execution.

Antigone's pleas to King Creon that she be allowed to bury her brother are scorned by the ruler of Thebes. Eventually, the daughter of Oedipus must make a choice to either obey Creon's order or bury her brother and face her own death. Antigone chooses the latter. She is caught and locked away in a cave until her execution.

Swaying a King's Heart

Two people come to King Creon in an attempt to sway his heart. Among these are Creon's son Haemon, Antigone's cousin as well as her fiancé (apparently, incest was a family tradition), and the blind prophet Tiresias. Creon refuses to be swayed by his son. However, Tiresias explains to him how his actions are not only immoral but against the will of the gods. Finally King Creon calms down and allows himself to be swayed by reason. He decides that he will not have Antigone executed and that he will allow Polynices' body to receive a proper burial. Unfortunately, his revelation has come too late. The king will not be able to hold back the flood of tragedy that is about to befall his life.

Tragically, Antigone does not realize any of what has transpired as she takes her own life by hanging herself in the cave, following her mother Jocasta's (who also committed suicide) tragic example. Had Antigone known that the king planned to allow a funeral for Polynices, perhaps she would not have been so willing to give up her life.

The Tragedies Continue

Sadly, the tragedy of Antigone does not end here. Haemon, who loves Antigone with all his heart, is rushing to the cave to release his beloved fiancé. As he pulls back the stone that seals the cave, Haemon sees the dangling body of Antigone. Upon seeing the hanging corpse of his suicidal lover, Haemon goes mad with grief. He draws his sword and plunges it into his side.

Upon hearing news of the death of her son, Queen Eurydice is overcome with grief and guilt. She runs to the top of the highest wall of the palace and jumps to her death. In a single day, and for nothing more than his own worthless pride, King Creon has lost a niece, a son, and his beloved wife and queen.

The Priestess and Her Lover (Greek)

The Greek myth of Hero and Leander is perhaps the oldest tragedy of ill-fated lovers. Hero was a priestess at a temple of Aphrodite at Sestos. Leander was a young man who lived at Abydos, a town that was located across the *Hellespont* from Sestos. Leander fell in love with Hero when he saw her at a festival in honor of the goddess Aphrodite. However, because of Hero's position as a priestess of Aphrodite, their love could not be and the two could not be married.

Immortal Words

Hellespont is also known as the Sea of Helle, which was the ancient name for the Strait of Dardanelles, which connects the Aegean Sea to the Sea of Marmora. The Hellespont was named after Helle, who is said to have fallen into its waters while escaping with the Golden Fleece on a flying ram.

Unable to endure being away from his beloved Hero, Leander swims across the Hellespont each night to meet with her at a secret rendezvous. To guide her swimming lover on his way, Hero holds up a lamp to serve as a beacon. One night, however, a terrible storm hits as Leander is swimming to her. The wind blows out Hero's lamp. Without a beacon, Leander becomes lost and disoriented in the raging waters and drowns. The next morning, his body washes ashore on the Sestos side of the Hellespont and is found by his lover Hero. Overcome with grief, Hero tosses herself into the sea and commits suicide by drowning, joining her lover in his fate.

Shakti's Tragic Fire (Hindu)

Daksha was a king and said to be one of the sons of Brahma. He prays to Shakti, the Mother Goddess, asking that she be born in avatar form as his infant daughter. He promises that if she grants him this request, he will never do anything to make her unhappy, so the goddess grants Daksha's wishes and allows herself to be born as daughter to the king, who names the child Sati.

Shiva, god of destruction, falls in love with Sati and she with him. Unfortunately, King Daksha despises Shiva (likely because his father Brahma is a creator god while Shiva is a destroyer god) and does not wish for his daughter to marry him. However, the king is completely powerless to stop Sati from marrying as she wishes (probably because he is bound by the promise he made to the goddess Shakti that he would never do anything to displease her as long as she came to Earth as his daughter).

Avoiding the Labyrinth

In some versions of this myth, Sati is said to have married the god Rudra, who is god of the storm and was a predecessor to Shiva in early Hindu mythology. Whether the myth states that Sati's husband is Shiva or Rudra, however, the basic chain of events in the myth remains the same for the most part.

The Wrathful Father-in-Law

Daksha, in his pride, tries to curse Shiva by demanding that the god pay an obeisance to him as his father-in-law. However, there is a law in the Hindu tradition stating that any revered being that pays obeisance to a less-revered being will be eternally cursed. Shiva, being a member of the *Trimurti* and therefore a part of the godhead, is one of the most revered beings in existence. Knowing the law, Shiva refuses to pay the demanded obeisance to his father-in-law and Daksha's hatred of him only grows. Soon, Daksha becomes obsessed with finding a way to hurt or insult the god of destruction.

Myth and Metaphor

Until abolished by British occupational law in 1829, there was a practice in India referred to as Sati (or suttee). Sati was the practice of burning Hindu widows upon the funeral pyres of their husbands. It is named for the myth of Sati, and is said to have allowed widows to continue to serve their dharma as wives into death. Begun sometime around 500 B.C.E., this practice was said to assure the widow a place in the heavenly realm of Svarga for 35 million years. Also, it was said that this act venerated the widow's soul of bad karma as well as pardoned her entire family of all sins, even those as serious as the murder of a Brahman.

To get back at his destroyer god son-in-law, Daksha arranges a sacrificial celebration and invites all of the gods except for Shiva. Daksha even invites his daughter Sati, though he rudely snubs her husband. A great sacrificial bonfire is constructed for this grand event.

Sati's Sacrifice

Sati arrives and immediately confronts her father, asking why he would refuse to invite her husband. Daksha says that someone such as Shiva, who dwells in graveyards and adorns himself with human skulls, does not belong at such a holy gathering.

Upon hearing her father's insults, and realizing that he will never accept Shiva as her husband, Sati declares that she will give up her life and return to the divine realm, as Daksha has obviously broken his vow to her (Shakti) by causing her unhappiness with his ill words about her husband. She tosses herself on the flames of the sacrificial fire and departs from her human body. Though Sati dies, she is still depicted as a wife of Shiva in her true form as the goddess Shakti in the pantheon of Hindu Dharma belief.

One Tragedy, Many Versions

The version previously offered differs somewhat from other versions. The version of the myth found in the epic *Mahabharata* states that the gods fail to apportion a part of the sacrificial offering (which Daksha arranged) to Shiva. Insulted by their neglect, Shiva dashes through the ceremony, knocks over the sacrificial altar, and maims several of those present. The gods and priests then decide to allow a share of the offering to be for Shiva, who restores those he maimed in his violent fit of indignant anger.

The *Puranas* offers another version of the myth which claims that the sacrifice at Daksha's palace is meant exclusively for Vishnu. However, the gods do not invite Shiva to the ceremony. In this version, Shiva's wife is called Uma, and she urges him to make a display of his power so that they will not dare fail to invite him again. Shiva attacks during the ceremony, striking down many of the gods with arrows and swords. The bloody mayhem is stopped only when Daksha takes a piece of the sacrifice and offers it as a devotion to Shiva. Shiva is satisfied, stops his attack, and departs peacefully. Daksha is portrayed in this version of the myth not as a spiteful father-in-law, but as a brave hero who restores peace to a holy ceremony that is being ruined by chaos.

The Least You Need to Know

- The tragic female is not always destroyed by her own fatal flaw.
- One common motif of the tragic female in mythology is that of the ill-fated lover.
- The tragic death of the female in myth is, more often than not, the result of a male character's fatal flaw.
- Often enough, the female of tragedy is in fact brave, strong-willed, and selfless … so perhaps she is not so tragic after all.

Woman Warriors

In This Chapter

- ◆ The woman as legendary warrior
- ◆ The pure maiden as blood-seeking warrior-hero
- ◆ The warrior woman as man-killer
- ◆ The untamable spirit of the woman warrior

Those who may only know of the male warrior-heroes might be surprised to learn that there are in fact a multitude of female warriors in mythology. Some of these woman warriors even defeated legendary male warrior-heroes in combat. Some are the product of a tyrannical world, leading them to rebel. Some are instruments of vengeance. Some are warrior-queens. All, however, have achieved victories in battle worthy of being immortalized in story.

The Kachina Warrior Maiden (Hopi)

Many years ago, Hopi legends tell of how there was once a family among them who lived outside the village, away from the tribe. The daughter of this family was named He'e'e. One day, as the mother of the family is putting up her daughter's hair, she spies enemy warriors coming toward the house. She has finished putting up only one side of her daughter's hair whirls, and one side is left hanging down.

Upon seeing the enemies of her people, the daughter He'e'e snatches up a bow and a quiver of arrows from the house wall. She speeds toward the main village, running as fast as her feet will carry her, hoping she will be able to warn the unsuspecting villagers in time. She gets to the village in the nick of time and raises the alarm. What few warriors are in the village assemble and begin preparing to defend their home territory. Their numbers, however, are far too few for them to last very long. He'e'e fearlessly steps forward among them and leads the defense herself. Under her leadership, the tribe is able to hold back the enemy long enough for the remaining men, who have been away working in the fields, to return and reinforce them. The tribesmen return and arm themselves immediately; thus they are able to defeat the enemy's surprise attack.

The myth states that, since her brave deeds that day, the girl He'e'e has been immortalized in the form of a *Kachina* doll. These He'e'e Kachina dolls are always portrayed with the hair up in whirls on one side and hanging down on the other. In her hands are a bow and quiver of arrows, the weapons she took from the wall of her home that day. Hopi legend says that He'e'e continues to guard her home village to this very day.

Immortal Words

Kachina, also spelled "Katsina," is a term used by the Hopi and other Pueblo Indian tribes. It refers to supernatural beings, the mythical predecessors of modern humans, who are said to return to our world for half the year during the winter months. They return to the underworld for the other half of the year. Their arrival and departure is acted out and celebrated through ceremonial dances. The term has also come to refer to small wooden dolls that are carved, painted, and given to children as gifts during the season when the Kachinas are in our world.

Battle of the Sexes (Czech)

The myth of what many refer to as the Maidens' War begins with the death of a woman named Libuse. Libuse had been a powerful matriarch of a tribe of warrior-women among the Czech tribes. During her reign, women had held most of the power. Now that she is dead, the Czech men throw insults at her mourning followers. Enraged, the women decide that they must wage war against all Czech males.

The powerful warrior woman Vlasta becomes the new leader. She has her fellow warrior women take up arms, organizes their ranks, trains them with harsh discipline, and has a mighty fortress constructed upon a high summit near the river Vltava. They name this fortress Devin Castle. Vlasta is made a queen of the women, and begins an aggressive recruiting campaign. Girls and women are recruited from all over, leaving everything they have behind so that they can come to Devin Castle.

Prince Premysl's Vision

As the newly recruited women begin to train for war at Devin Castle, the men who live in the region nearby watch with jovial disdain, throwing insults and laughing at them. After a time, the men become so arrogantly daring as to plan an attack that they believe will break the women's courage. They take this idea to the local prince, Premysl. As the men around him laugh and joke, Premysl remains serious because of a dream he recently had. In the dream, he had a vision of a terrifying warrior woman holding a sword in one hand and a goblet in the other. Her skin and armor were spattered with blood as she trampled over the butchered bodies of dead men. She then filled the goblet with the blood of the slain men and drank it voraciously.

While Premysl conveys his dream to the other men, the female army of Devin Castle are already arming themselves for battle. Each woman swears allegiance to Devin Castle, and to bring death to any man who stands against her on the field of battle, even if faced by a brother, father, or other kinsman. Vlasta appoints the most intelligent women as commanders. The strongest are made battle warriors, and the most beautiful are chosen to become spies and assassins.

The Battle Lines Are Drawn

The male warriors, however, pay no attention to Premysl's warnings, and they march to Devin Castle believing that these "fragile maidens" will lose heart and retreat at the mere sight of so many armed men. Unfortunately for the men, however, this does not happen. In fact, as the men begin making their battle formations, the women come out from the castle and begin to form up in front of them. The men then realize that these women truly intend to fight them in open combat!

Vlasta rallies the women into a rage before charging toward the enemy line. Close behind her, in full gallop, are the five mightiest among her warriors—Castava, Hodka, Mlada, Radka, and Svatava. As the men laugh at their charge, they fail to notice that the archers of Devin Castle have already released a wide and dense volley of arrows. Before they can recover from the rain of arrows, the female cavalry are already overtaking them, swords and spears at the ready. Soon an infantry division of battle maidens has closed in from behind the charging horsewomen, who are now turning to hit the male army from the rear in a strong pincer maneuver.

The battle is over quickly, and in mere moments every man on the battlefield is dead. Victorious, Vlasta soon orders all men to abandon the surrounding area of Devin immediately, under penalty of death. She declares that any man caught inside or near the walls of Devin Castle will be executed on sight. The local armies now decimated, the men of the region are left with no choice but to comply with Vlasta's order.

The War Rages On

The battle may have been short, but the war lasts for a very long time as army after army attempts to retake the areas surrounding Devin Castle. However, they are beaten back time and again, often because the male officers make the mistake of underestimating their female opponents.

Later, one of Vlasta's best assassins, a lovely girl named Sarka, devises a trap that leads to the murder of Ctirad, the Prince of Prague. The warrior queen then has the prince's body hung from the highest pole of the castle. When word of Ctirad's murder and how his body is being viciously displayed spreads among the land, all male warriors descend upon Devin Castle from every region inhabited by the Czech tribes, killing or enslaving any woman they meet along the way. Even Premysl, who had a dream of a woman warrior creating a path of destruction and even witnessed firsthand the terrible death dealt by Vlasta's army in the first battle, feels he has to rise to fight when he hears of what has been done to Ctirad.

So Falls the Queen of Devin

Vlasta has by now grown overconfident and she immediately leads a force toward Vysehrad, Prince Premysl's domain, intending to conquer the land and put an end to all male resistance. As usual, Vlasta rides out in front with her cavalry. However, she does not have her five best warriors with her at this time, and rides at a pace that is too fast for her normal cavalry riders to match.

Believing her cavalry women are riding right behind her, she rushes into the fray with the enemy. Too late she realizes that she is alone and surrounded by the male army. They come at her from all directions, drag her from her horse, and cut the Queen of Devin Castle to pieces. With Vlasta dead, her followers soon fall apart and are defeated shortly thereafter. Any woman found to be a compatriot of Vlasta is hunted down and brutally murdered. Eventually, Prince Premysl becomes the undisputed ruler of the Czech tribes.

Hervor the Shield Maiden (Scandinavian)

Hervor is perhaps the most famous female warrior among the Norse sword maidens, and her deeds are told of in the epic *Northvegr.* Treachery and the flaws of men lead to the tragic death of King Heidrick the Wise, King of Gothland. A conflict soon arises between his sons, Hlod and Angantyr. Angantyr is crowned the new king of the Gothland throne. Hlod, half-Hun in blood, has been brought up in Hunland under the tutelage and mentoring of King Humli, his grandfather (mother's side).

Hlod learns of his father's death and returns home, and with his brother drinks to the honor and name of their late father. However, his birthright of half the kingdom is not given to him. Hlod, now angry, gathers an army and marches upon his brother. This time, he demands that he be given the half of the kingdom that is rightfully his. Angantyr, however, refuses to give up any of his power. Instead, he offers weapons, warriors, gold, and women to Hlod as compensation. Despite being offered such a vast fortune, Hlod wants only what he believes is his by rights.

Avoiding the Labyrinth

Hlod's refusal of Angantyr's bribes has nothing to do with any heroic virtues. Angantyr voices that his reason for denying Hlod is because he is a "bastard son of a thrall," primarily because his mother is a Hun. The fortune being offered is overly generous compensation for such a lowly son, he tells Hlod. This reasoning puts Hlod in a tough spot. Accepting the offer means that Hlod acknowledges he is in fact an illegitimate thrall's son and of lowly birth. Unwilling to accept the shame of this, he refuses Angantyr's offer.

Hlod's Return

Denied his demands, and not having enough men to lay a proper siege to his brother's castle, Hlod returns to Hunland and explains to his grandfather King Humli that Angantyr has refused to surrender to him his birthright. The Hun king is extremely displeased with this, and devotes a large portion of his army to his grandson's cause.

Humli and Hlod assemble hordes of warriors and wait out the harsh winter, taking their time to plan a large-scale invasion. Spring comes soon enough, and with it the vast Hun army begins its march, planning to take Gothland by violent force. The story tells that the Hun army is numbered at nearly 350,000 men. At this time in Gothland history, an army of such incredible size would have been almost unheard of.

Hervor Rides to Mirkwood

Hervor is the greatest shield maiden in Gothland, a daughter of the late King Heidrick the Wise, and sister to the current King Angantyr. When she receives word that the Huns are on the warpath, she knows there is no time to lose. She assembles as much of the army as she can and quickly marches them to a Goth battle fortification near Mirkwood Forest, which runs along the border separating Hunland and Gothland. She reaches the battle fortress only a day ahead of Hlod's and Humli's forces. By sunrise the next morning, the Hun army begins to emerge from the treeline of Mirkwood Forest. As they take up battle formations on the open plains in front of the Goth fortress, Hervor calls for the trumpeter to sound the alarm that the enemy has arrived, sending every man to his battle station.

Hervor knows that her forces do not have the necessary provisions or equipment to withstand a siege. She sees only two options … victory or death. As her men prepare for battle, she sends out her best rider, Orman, to challenge the enemy to open combat in a field outside the South Gate of the battle fortress. The Huns, knowing that they have the enemy woefully outnumbered, agree to the challenge.

Last Stand of the Shield Maiden

In a brave last stand rivaling that of the Alamo, Hervor rides out to meet the Hun army. She gallops at the front of her army, clad in full battle gear. Outnumbered beyond belief, the Goth forces of Hervor are soon outflanked and surrounded. Before long, only Hervor and a handful of Goth warriors remain standing. They are surrounded. They are exhausted. And all hope of victory has been extinguished.

However, they do not surrender. These few brave souls, with Hervor out front, ride into the face of an enormous enemy and meet their deaths with courage. Hervor dies a true warrior's death, and her sacrifice becomes a rallying battle cry to the rest of Gothland's warriors. The tale of her sacrifice gives strength and bravery to her countrymen.

In the *Northvegr*, when Angantyr hears of his brave sister Hervor's death, he says, "Unbrotherly is the bloody game they played with you, excellent sister … I see no man in my army (even though I offer rings and riches) who would ride boldly and bear a shield, or hasten the Hunnish hosts to find."

Scathach and Aoife, Warrior Sisters (Scottish)

Scathach is a strong and highly skilled warrior woman of Scottish mythology. She is head of Dun Scaith, a school of warrior arts and a mighty fortress that is located on an island. Normal people cannot reach the island, as to do so requires one to pass through treacherous lands and across the Plain of Ill-Luck and the Glen of Peril. If one is "lucky" enough to reach the magical bridge that crosses over to Dun Scaith, one must then pass the test of crossing it. The "Bridge of Leaping," as it is called, is enchanted, said to be created by one of the ancient gods. When a person steps onto one end of the bridge, the center whips up, throwing the person back in the direction from which they came. One story tells of how the famed warrior, Setanta (also called *Cu Chullain*), jumps completely over the bridge to reach the other side so that he might be schooled by the legendary warrior woman Scathach.

Immortal Words

Cu Chullain was a name given to Setanta when he was a youth. The name means "Hound of Cullan." When Setanta once arrived late to a celebration at Cullan's castle, he found that Cullan's ferocious guard hound had already been loosed (Cullan believed that all the guests had already arrived). Attacked, Setanta killed the hound. As compensation to Cullan, who was terribly sorrowful at the loss of his great hound, Setanta served as guardian of Cullan's castle until a new guard hound could be raised and properly trained. Hence his nickname, "Hound of Cullan."

At the end of Setanta's training, Scathach receives a challenge to combat from her wild warrior twin sister, Aoife (which means "incredible beauty"). The challenge sent by Aoife declares that the champions of both schools should meet in combat. Knowing that her sister is strong and treacherous, and that she will try to kill

Setanta, Scathach drugs her warrior student with a sleeping potion. As Setanta slumbers, Scathach leads the other champions of Dun Scaith to the place of the battle. Although the potion makes any normal man sleep for four hours, it only affects Setanta for about one. He soon wakes and realizes what has happened. He mounts his war chariot and takes off in pursuit of his teacher and fellow students, following the tracks left behind by the wheels of their chariots.

As both sides prepare at opposite ends of the battlefield, Setanta comes riding over the horizon in his chariot. Needless to say, Scathach is quite shocked at how quickly he has recovered from the sleeping potion. The champions soon clash in a bloody battle of shields, spears, and swords. Setanta, alongside all of Scathach's warrior sons, slays the strongest six of Aoife's warriors. Seeing that the warriors of Dun Scaith are gaining the upper hand, Aoife challenges her sister to single combat, knowing that she is stronger than Scathach. Setanta, however, steps forward and claims the "champion's right," meaning that he may fight in Scathach's stead.

Sword and Man

Single combat between the leaders of opposing armies, in Scottish warfare, was sometimes used to end a battle that had drawn out too long. Other times, it was a trump card that could be used when one faced a superior army led by an inferior combatant.

Before closing with Aoife in combat, Setanta inquires of Scathach as to what her sister cherishes most. Scathach tells him that Aoife cherishes her two chariot horses above all other things. The single combat challenge, however, will be fought on foot, so she does not understand how this information could be of use to Setanta.

Setanta and Aoife clash with one another. Aoife's sword strike is strong enough to shatter Setanta's buckler (a small shield). Setanta is pushed to his back by the blow. However, as Aoife closes in for the killing blow, Setanta points at a spot behind her and cries out, "Your chariot and horses are going over the cliff!" Distracted, Aoife snaps her eyes in the direction Setanta has pointed. The boy warrior jumps up and throws Aoife to the ground. He draws his knife and presses it to her throat. Aoife has no choice … she must yield. In return for sparing her life, Aoife must agree to make a binding and permanent peace treaty with her sister and with the warrior school of Dun Scaith. Setanta will later marry Aoife and they will have a son. However, the boy warrior Setanta's heroic life will one day turn tragic (see Chapter 8).

Fa Mu Lan/Hua Mulan (Chinese)

The Chinese tale of the warrior girl, Fa Mu Lan (also known to be spelled Hua Mulan) is perhaps one of the most extraordinary among such myths of the female warrior-hero. The peculiar nature of the myth is because it originates from a culture that was dominated by males during the period in which she is said to have lived. In recent years, a series of animated films have been made regarding Fa Mu Lan, none of which remain true to the power of the actual myths.

As a little girl (some stories say she was seven years old), Mu Lan wanders away from home one day and becomes lost on a mountainside. As the sky grows dark and the hour late, she meets an old sage who takes her to his home, which is cut directly into the rock of the mountain face. Hungry and exhausted, she stays the night in the sage's cave home. The next morning, the sage tells her that she will stay with him to train in the martial arts for the next seven years! Mu Lan wishes to see her parents, and the sage offers her a magic gourd of water that shows them in its reflection. This gourd continues to allow Mu Lan to see her family on occasion.

Training of a Woman Warrior

For the first five years, Fa Mu Lan studies the animals, learning their ways and abilities. At the end of five years, when she begins her menstrual cycle, the sage takes her to the bottom of the mountain and tells her that she must journey back up alone this time. He leaves her alone to meet the test before her. As she travels, Fa Mu Lan is able to survive with the lessons she learned from the animals. She knows the plants from which she may gather berries, nuts, and fruits. She knows how to create fire and has great speed. She eats what she needs and gathers fuel from nearby when she needs a fire, but she does not take any extra with her.

After three days, she reaches a long section of the mountain in which there is no food to be gathered. Because she has brought no food or wood with her, she goes without food for many days. She eventually finds wood for a fire, but no food. She drinks melted snow for water. Eventually, she completes her journey up the mountain.

Mu Lan's Return

When her seven years of training are complete, Fa Mu Lan prepares to return home to her family. Not until now, gazing in her magic gourd at her family one last time before going to meet them, has she understood the reason for her odd tutelage. Her father has no son, and there is too much evil in the world. Being too old to fight the evil himself, Mu Lan realizes that she will have to fight in his stead.

The sage and his wife give Fa Mu Lan a number of supplies that she is going to need as a warrior—a horse, men's clothes, a sword, and armor. Her hair is cut short and tied back in the style of men. Dressed in this manner, she returns home to meet her destiny. When she arrives home, she is treated to a great feast.

The Rise of Fa Mu Lan

When Mu Lan arrives at her first military unit, she sees that the men despise and alienate their commanding officer. Wanting to know the truth in this, she sneaks into the commanding officer's tent that night to find him counting out portions of the men's pay … to himself! He is corrupt! Having been raised as an avenger for justice, Fa Mu Lan draws her sword and takes off the officer's head.

When morning comes, the other men in the unit find Mu Lan holding the corrupt officer's severed head in her hands. Most of these men had been forced to fight, taken from local villages as the army marched. Having freed them from the commander's tyranny, they now become her loyal army.

The Road to Justice

Fa Mu Lan, with her army now behind her, begins a long march for the capital city. On the throne sits a corrupt man who is ruining the country. Her destiny, she realizes, is to end his reign of despotism. As Fa Mu Lan travels with her army, they kill corrupt officials, military officers, and criminals. Soon, word of her and the army she leads becomes the stuff of legend, all the while no one knowing that she is a woman.

Avoiding the Labyrinth

Much of ancient Chinese history is intermingled with mythological tales. As a result, it is unclear as to whether or not Fa Mu Lan was ever an actual woman. Although it is entirely possible that she could have been, there is no solid evidence aside from her myth to support or refute Fa Mu Lan's existence.

Eventually, Fa Mu Lan reaches the capital city. She fights her final battle even though, the legend states, she is pregnant at the time. Because her armor is too big anyway, it does a good job of hiding her swollen belly. In some versions of the myth, it is said that she actually gives birth to the child on the battlefield. After being victorious, and having dethroned the corrupt emperor, Mu Lan returns home with the father of her child and lives out her days in peace.

Tsunade and the Gallant Jiraiya (Japanese)

Tsunade is the wife of a warrior-turned-bandit-chief-turned-ninja named Jiraiya and is perhaps the most powerful *kunoichi* (female ninja, see Chapter 16) warrior in Japanese Shinto mythology. Her abilities in fighting are said to be greater than those

of most of her male colleagues. Some claim she is even stronger then her legendary husband, Jiraiya "The Gallant." Tsunade is said to have superhuman strength. She is also a talented sorceress, having mastered the arts of snail magic. Her husband, Jiraiya, is a master of frog magic, which was taught to him by the immortal Echigo Fuji of Myoko-yama. The immortal promised to teach Jiraiya so that he might avenge the destruction of his family by a man named Sarashina, but only if he gave up the life of a bandit chief. Jiraiya agreed to the arrangement and reformed his ways.

 Myth and Metaphor

In Shinto mythology, there are five primary types of animal magic: Snail, Frog, Snake, Bird, and Spider. In myth, it is stated that users of Snail and Frog magic are incompatible and often at odds with one another. The fact that Tsunade and Jiraiya are of opposing magic types is a testament to love's power to overcome any obstacle.

Jiraiya, whose name means "Young Thunder," falls in love with and marries Tsunade after failing to defeat Sarashina in combat. As time passes, a number of students seek out Jiraiya and Tsunade, hoping to receive instruction in the magical arts. One stu-

dent in particular will become troublesome for the couple. His name is Yashagoro, an ambitious young man with a lust for power. One day, Yashagoro finds himself in a confrontation with a master of snake magic. He fails, and the venom of the snake magic spells turn his blood black and his heart evil. He leaves Jiraiya and Tsunade behind and takes the name of Orochimaru, meaning "Son of the Giant Eight-Headed Snake." When Orochimaru returns, he challenges Jiraiya and Tsunade to combat.

Myth and Metaphor

In the anime series *Naruto*, the character of Tsunade is based on the Shinto myth. The Tsunade of *Naruto* has superhuman strength, can summon a giant snail/slug, and is a very talented healer. All these traits can be attributed to the Tsunade of mythology.

In what is said to be the greatest showdown in the history of animal magic, the couple fight Orochimaru with all they have. Jiraiya's frog magic overpowers the snake magic. Tsunade's snail magic counters most of the poisonous venom attacks.

In the end, it is uncertain whether Orochimaru is defeated. Some myths say yes. Other myths say he survives. The only written record claims that, eventually, Jiraiya and Tsunade become exhausted and are overcome by the poison of Orochimaru's snake magic. Fortunately, however, a loyal student who studied under the arts of both Jiraiya and Tsunade finds them and nurses them back to health with the healing arts they taught him. At this point, the only written record suddenly comes to an end, leaving a number of things unanswered.

The Rider in the Roman Helmet (Persian)

Gordafarid is the famous Persian woman warrior in the epic poem, *Shahnamah*. When the Turanian prince, Sohrab of the Samengen, invades the domain of King Kavus, his army comes upon a great battlement, called the "White Fortress." This great fortification is located on the Persian side of the Oxus River, which acts as the border between Persia and their enemies.

Hojir, one of the best of Persia's male warriors, challenges Sohrab to single combat. The two clash, with Sohrab overpowering Hojir and sending him to serve as a slave to one of the Turanian commanders. Seeing this, the Persian warriors become demoralized. Not a single Persian man dares to step forward to challenge Sohrab.

Gordafarid Rides Out

Witnessing the defeat of Hojir and the fear rising in the eyes of the Persian warriors, the brave girl Gordafarid tucks her long hair into a Roman helmet, takes up her weapons, and mounts a warhorse. With a cry that is said to shatter the sky like a thunder clap, Gordafarid gallops up to the enemy line.

She defiantly challenges any man among the Turanians to step forward and face her in single combat. None dare accept, seeing how strong and confident she appears. The Turanians are scared to death of her after seeing how fearlessly she approached their ranks. In fact, her true identity concealed by her helmet and armor, the Turanians believe that Gordafarid is a *man*, especially after witnessing the strength and power with which she holds herself.

The Battle of Gordafarid and Sohrab

Sohrab, seeing how his men now falter in the face of this mysterious warrior, rides out to meet the challenge. Gordafarid draws her bow and sends a hail of arrows into the air, which come raining down at Sohrab. Overcome with dodging these lethal arrows, Sohrab has no way to defend himself as Gordafarid advances on him with her sword. Sohrab barely has time to get his spear up, only to have it cut in half by Gordafarid's swift blade. Disarmed and held at the tip of Gordafarid's sword, Sohrab is defeated.

As Gordafarid begins riding back to the White Fortress, however, Sohrab chases her down and knocks off her helmet with the remaining shaft of his spear. He is shocked beyond belief to realize that he has just been handed his first defeat in battle by a *maiden!* Enraged with embarrassment, he captures her with a lariat.

Fearing what terrible things will be done to her if Sohrab drags her back to the Turanian battle line, she decides to try reasoning her way out of the situation. She convinces Sohrab that his shame will be far greater when his men discover her true identity and learn that he has been bested by a woman. Lovestruck and/or realizing the truth in her words (that his shame will be less if the truth remains a secret), he releases her. Gordafarid wastes no time in riding like the wind back to the White Fortress and into the immortal pages of warrior legends.

Avoiding the Labyrinth

There are various opinions as to why the warrior prince Sohrab sets Gordafarid free. Some say it is because he is entranced, lovestruck by her unexpected beauty. Others are of the opinion that when Sohrab sees that he's just been beaten by a woman, he does not drag her back to the Turanians for punishment because he fears that his men will be demoralized and his reputation damaged if the truth becomes known. Both are valid possibilities.

The Least You Need to Know

◆ Female warriors are not as uncommon to mythology as many would believe.

◆ The woman warrior may become so as a result of exceptional circumstances that force her to assume a combative role not commonly held by women.

◆ There is a strict balance kept by female warriors of legend: they are warriors, but rarely do they cease acting as women.

◆ Woman warriors are rarely portrayed as inferior to males. In fact, the opposite is true in that they are often portrayed as superior to male opponents.

Seductresses and Enchantresses

In This Chapter

- ◆ The enchantress in mythology as savior and destroyer
- ◆ The terrible fate of those who fall prey to the mythical seductress
- ◆ The mythological enchantress/seductress as guide to the underworld
- ◆ The archetypal symbolism of the mythological enchantress/seductress
- ◆ The fall of the hero as a result of the seductress or enchantress

Seductresses and enchantresses can be the saviors and the ruin of heroes in mythology. Their ways are mysterious, sometimes deceitful, and, if rubbed the wrong way, they are often fatal. These women of mythology represent Man's fear of falling victim to his own lust for power and knowledge, and/or becoming the victim of his own weakness for the opposite sex.

Men Are Pigs ... Literally! (Greek)

When the Greek hero Odysseus lands on the island of Circe, he sends out a scouting party to explore the interior. The scouts find a powerful sorceress named Circe, singing and weaving as she sits in a stone cottage in the middle of the islands. Mountain lions and wolves stand all around her. She gives the men some wine to drink. Unfortunately for them, it has a magical potion in it. Once they have consumed the wine, Circe waves her wand and transforms them all into pigs. One of the men manages to escape, and reports back to Odysseus on the fates of the other crew members.

Intrigued by the account of Circe's allure, Odysseus succumbs to temptation and sets off to meet the sorceress. As he journeys out to her stone cottage, the messenger god Hermes appears and gives Odysseus some crucial advice. If he wishes for Circe to return his men to their natural forms, then he must accept and go to bed with Circe when she offers. However, before he does this, he must place an antidote into his wine (a plant called Moly), to avoid being transformed himself. After this, he must make Circe swear an oath that she will release him from her island when he desires to leave. The hero does as Hermes has instructed, allowing him to avoid peril and rescue his transformed men.

Odysseus enjoys the fruits of Circe's flawless bed of love for an entire year. Eventually, however, his crew members get irritated and restless, as they are anxious to return home. They beg him to make plans for their departure. Understanding the desires of his men, Odysseus concedes and tells Circe that he will soon leave her.

Before he leaves the island, however, Circe tells Odysseus that he must journey into the domain of Hades before he will be able to return home. She gives him directions to Hades. In addition, Circe provides Odysseus with specific instructions on what he must do to summon the shades of the dead and avoid becoming trapped in the underworld forever. Without her instructions, Odysseus never could have made it out of the underworld alive, let alone succeeded in finding the knowledge he needed to make it back home. Also, she warns him of the danger of the Sirens.

Song of the Sirens (Greek)

After Odysseus departs from the island of Circe, he sails beneath the perilous cliff where the Sirens dwell. These fatal seductresses sing an alluring song that drives men mad with desire. Rolling in the waves of the surf below and littered among the base of the cliffs are the bones of shipwrecked sailors who have succumbed to the temptation of the Sirens' songs. The song of the Sirens causes men who hear it to lose all sense of self-preservation, and they are killed when their vessels smash upon the rock sides of the cliff.

Avoiding the Labyrinth _____

The Sirens' song has nothing to do with sex, as many have wrongly assumed: the temptation of the Sirens is one of knowledge, for the Sirens sing of all that is past, present, and to come. While listening to the song, overcome by its allure, even the hero Odysseus cannot resist. He begs his men to untie him from the mast. However, they refuse to release him, as he has ordered, and by doing so are able to pass the Sirens in safety.

The Sirens are wasplike creatures, with female breasts and beautiful heads. Some myths claim that the Sirens are servants of Persephone, wife of Hades and Queen of the Dead. To safeguard them against the maddening affects of their song, Odysseus plugs his crew members' ears with beeswax. However, Odysseus wishes to hear the song with his own ears. Knowing well the fatal affects of this, he instructs his men to tie him securely to the ship's mast. He also tells them not to release him until they are safely past the Sirens, no matter how much he begs, pleads, or threatens them. As he predicted, when the sound of the Sirens' song reaches his ears, Odysseus begins screaming at his men to release him. However, they remain loyal to his orders and keep him bound until they are safely past the seductive Sirens.

The Maiden of the Rhine (German)

There is a famous German folk ballad that all Germans sing as they pass beneath a spectacular cliffside that is located along the River Rhine. This ballad tells the story of Die Lorelei, a beautiful maiden who sits combing her golden hair and singing.

At twilight, the light of the sun falls on her shining hair and the jewels that drape her beautiful breasts. Sailors who pass by this cliff at the time of twilight are so mesmerized by her song that they neglect to notice the swirling rapids beneath the cliffs. Trapped in such a trance state, these poor men drown as they are sucked below by the powerful whirlpool that has torn their boats to splinters.

Myth and Metaphor _____

There are a number of parallels that can be drawn between the myth of the Sirens and that of Die Lorelei. Both are female entities that seduce men with their songs, leading them to their deaths by causing the men to crash their vessels into the rocks.

A Wife Not Seen on Saturdays (French)

While out hunting one day, Prince Raymondin becomes separated from his men and wanders into the forest alone. Deep within the woods, he comes upon a beautiful spring with a mysterious woman sitting beside it. Immediately smitten by her beauty, Raymondin proposes marriage to the maiden, asking her to return to his castle as his wife. The girl agrees to marry him, with one very specific condition—he must never see her on Saturdays. Love-drunk, the prince agrees to her condition without hesitation. After all, not being able to see his bride only one day a week would not be so difficult a thing to endure. Her name, he learns, is Mélusine.

The new lovers return to Raymondin's castle and spend several happy, carefree years together. When their children are born, however, they have a number of curious deformities. The first son is born a three-eyed ogre, and is appropriately given the name Horrible. Another son, named Antoine, is born with a lion's foot growing out of his cheek. Despite these oddities, the couple remains deeply in love.

One Saturday afternoon, however, Raymondin's jealous brother convinces him to spy on his wife while she is taking her bath. He peeps in on her, and sees her immersed in the water. However, as he continues to watch he realizes that she has a long, twisting, serpentine tail from the waist down. Even this, however, is not enough to sway Raymondin's love for his wife. He does not publicly denounce Mélusine, in fact, until one of their strange sons accidentally (or perhaps not so accidentally) sets fire to an abbey, burning alive all the monks inside.

Raymondin's loyalty to Mélusine finally falters, and he denounces his wife publicly, calling her a "Vile Serpent." Upon hearing these words from Raymondin, Mélusine leaps out the window. As she falls, her body suddenly transforms into that of an enormous winged dragon. She then disappears into the sky, returning only on an occasional night to nurse the two youngest of her sons.

The Song of Wandering Aengus (Irish)

One evening at twilight, a lonely hermit named Aengus leaves his cottage to go fishing. He fashions a rod out of a hazelwood wand and uses a berry hooked to a thread as bait. Soon, his rod shakes from the pull of a catch. He pulls up, dragging a little silver trout from the water. He takes the quivering fish back to his cottage as the first stars are flickering in the night sky. When he lays the silver fish on the dirt floor and kneels down to blow upon the kindling of his fire, however, the fish suddenly transforms into a stunningly beautiful girl with apple blossoms in her hair.

Without a word, the young maiden runs off into the night. Lovestruck, Aengus pursues her. However, he is never able to catch up to the elusive girl. For the rest of his life, the hermit Aengus wanders in pursuit of the silver trout girl/apple blossom maiden, lost in the hollow hills of the Irish countryside and dreaming of the day when he will find her at last. They will finally kiss only when the silver apples of the moon and golden apples of the sun glimmer in the sacred orchard of their love.

 Myth and Metaphor

One interpretation of the myth of Aengus is that the apple blossom maiden represents virginity and chastity. When lost, virginity cannot be regained. This is why after the maiden runs away and is lost to Aengus, he is never able to recapture her.

The Green Knight's Lady (English/Arthurian)

During one extraordinary Christmas dinner in the court of King Arthur, a mysterious Green Knight appears and challenges the knights to play a Christmas game: "You cut off my head within three strokes of the axe," he says, "and I will return the favor next year." Only Gawain takes up the challenge, swiping the Green Knight's head off with a single blow of a huge Danish axe. Then the Green Knight picks up his own severed head, climbs onto his horse, and rides out of the court. As he departs, the Green Knight repeats his challenge for Gawain to appear at his Green Chapel within a year's time.

On Halloween, Gawain sets off on the journey to keep his promise. On Christmas Eve, the knight arrives at a mysterious castle that sits amidst a grove of towering oak trees. He is welcomed rather hospitably by The Lord of the Castle.

A Game of Gifts

Upon Gawain's entry into the castle, his host proposes that they play a game. The Lord of the Castle knows well where the Green Chapel is located. Therefore, Gawain can stay with him until New Year's Day, when the knight is honor-bound to fulfill his promise by meeting the Green Knight. Every day between Christmas and New Year's Day, the Lord of the Castle goes hunting. Upon his return, he gives anything he kills to Gawain. Meanwhile, Gawain is invited to sleep in every morning, but must exchange the winnings by giving the Lord anything he might have obtained during the day. In truth, this turns out to be a test of Sir Gawain's knightly integrity.

Gawain's Test

Each day while the Lord of the Castle goes hunting, the beautiful young Princess of the Castle, wife of the generous Lord of the Estate, comes tip-toeing into Gawain's bedroom for a little love play. Taunting and teasing in an effort to seduce him, she gives him a kiss on each day, which Gawain dutifully returns by giving the Lord of the Castle a kiss when he comes back in the evening from the hunt. In turn, the lord gives Gawain a deer, a boar, and a fox killed on each day.

On the third morning, however, the Lady of the Castle comes into Gawain's bedroom dressed in a transparent nightgown, and offers him all her body. When he refuses, she offers him a ring, which he in turn refuses. However, when she then offers him a green girdle to strap around his thigh, Gawain accepts, because she tells him that whoever wears the girdle cannot be harmed. Knowing he will meet the Green Knight the next day, and that he will most likely be decapitated, Gawain keeps the girdle and does not give it to the Lord of the Castle when he returns that evening.

Facing the Axe

On New Year's Day, Gawain awakens early and rides to the Green Chapel, where the mysterious knight appears. As before, he is all garbed in green. As the young knight draws closer, he can hear the sound of the axe being grinded on a stone wheel. The Green Knight tells Gawain to kneel down and stretch out his neck. Gawain does as honor demands, and takes a knee before the Green Knight so that he might receive the blow of the axe.

 Myth and Metaphor

The symbolism of blood on snow is a commonly employed device in mythology, literature, and even cinema. The symbol of blood on snow can be interpreted in two possible ways, the first being as a symbol of lost virginity. Secondly, however, and more universally, the symbol of blood on snow represents the death of innocence or the staining of purity. Blood being shed symbolizes violence and/or death while white snow symbolizes innocence and purity.

The Green Knight swings his huge axe once, and misses. He swings a second time, and again the sharp head of the axe falls harmlessly to the ground. On the third swipe, however, the Green Knight connects, putting a nonlethal gash in Gawain's neck that will leave a scar to forever remind him of the moment. A spurt of blood spills onto the white snow. Gawain leaps to his feet, exclaiming that the Green Knight has taken his three strokes as the contract of honor required.

A Scar of Shame

The Green Knight laughingly explains that the knick he gave to Gawain's neck is punishment for not giving him the Green Girdle that his wife had tempted him with in the castle. We now learn that the Green Knight and the Lord of the Castle are one and the same, and that the magical events of this situation have been presided over by Morgan the goddess/enchantress.

Gawain is humiliated by his failure of bravery and honor. He is terribly self-critical and accuses himself of cowardice and covetousness. Infuriated, he verbally blames all women for Man's downfall, saying that men are but victims of the seductive allure and wicked manipulations of treacherous temptresses. However, in the end, the blame and shame are only Gawain's to bear ... and he will carry that scar for the rest of his days.

Morrigan and Morgan Le Fay (European/Arthurian)

You may remember Morrigan the Celtic war goddess from Chapter 5. Over time, Morrigan as well as a number of other European goddesses were absorbed into Arthurian legends under the name of the enchantress Morgan (or Morgan Le Fay). Aside from the Celtic war goddess Morrigan, Morgan Le Fay also displays attributes of the widely worshipped Celtic Matrona, a goddess who was venerated from the Rhine River of Germany to the lands of northern Italy. From the other geographical direction, Morgan shares traits of Modron, the wife of Urien and mother of Owein from the popular tales of Welsh mythology.

In Arthurian legend, Morgan Le Fay is the half-sister of King Arthur. One night, during Arthur's younger years, she enters Arthur's bedchamber and enchants him (in other versions she changes her form to a disguise or to that of Guinevere). As a result of her incestuous seduction, Morgan becomes pregnant and gives birth to the illegitimate son of Arthur, Mordred (sometimes spelled Modred). From the early years of Camelot, Arthur had already unknowingly sealed his own fate by succumbing to the seductive enchantments of Morgan Le Fay.

The Seductive Stepmother (Greek)

Phaedra is the sister of Ariadne, who helped Theseus kill the Minotaur on the island of Crete, and then escape the labyrinth where the Minotaur was imprisoned. Theseus takes Ariadne with him on his voyage back to Athens, but abandons Ariadne on the island of Naxos. After returning to Athens, and several years and exploits later, Theseus marries Ariadne's sister Phaedra.

He brings to the marriage a child born to his previous wife, an Amazonian queen. His name is Hippolytus, and he grows up to be a magnificent young man who seems completely uninterested in love. That is until one day, during one of his father's long absences, he falls in love with Aricia, the princess of a rival family, and therefore a forbidden spouse. The situation is further complicated when Phaedra notices the beauty of her stepson and becomes completely smitten with him. She falls passionately in love with Hippolytus; at first, she struggles to restrain and repress her desire.

Phaedra's semi-heroic self-denial eventually crumbles, and one day, thinking her husband Theseus will never come home—because rumors of his death begin to circulate—she confronts her stepson and indirectly confesses her love for him. She does so by retelling the story of the slaying of the Minotaur, making critical changes in the tale: she, not Ariadne, would be the one to help Hippolytus, not his father Theseus, in killing the Minotaur and escaping the labyrinth. In fact, she would lead Hippolytus into the labyrinth herself, dispensing with Ariadne's trick of the red thread. By the time she has finished her speech, which is an elaborate attempt to seduce her stepson, Hippolytus is forced to recognize the horror of his stepmother's passionate desire.

Myth and Metaphor

A comparison may be made of this myth to that of King Pelops, the ancestor of Oedipus told of in Chapter 8. In that myth, Pelops' wife is named Hippodameia. The phonetic similarity between the names Hippodameia and Hippolytus might explain how they became intermixed. Considering both myths are of Greek origin, it is of no surprise that the details of the older myth of Pelops became integrated with that of the newer myth of Hippolytus and Phaedra. Also, Hippolytus is thrown from his chariot and into the sea by the curse of his father, just as Myrtilus was thrown from the chariot of Pelops.

Hippolytus then escapes the palace, riding on his chariot by the sea. When his father suddenly appears, Phaedra accuses his son Hippolytus of attempting to seduce and rape her. Enraged, Theseus calls down the wrath of the sea god Poseidon upon his son. Poseidon concedes to Theseus' request and sends a huge monster into the surf along the shore where Hippolytus is riding in his chariot. The horses are terrified by the presence of the creature and overturn the prince's chariot, dragging unfortunate Hippolytus to his death.

The Least You Need to Know

- The enchantress can be either Man's savior or his ruin.

- Seductresses often lead men to their deaths by tempting them with not only sex, but also knowledge and power.

- The enchantress represents Man's fear of his own lust for pleasure, knowledge, and power.

- The seductress represents Man's fear of his own weakness for the opposite sex.

Part 4

Monsters, Creatures, Demons, and Dangers

In the darkest recesses of the human psyche lurk the greatest fears of the human imagination. These creatures are angels and aids, beasts and abominations, which can serve as humanity's greatest hope or bring about its most certain doom. Some can be helpful yet mischievous, such as the Tengu, winged demons who are said to have conveyed the secret arts of death to the legendary Ninja warriors of Japan. Others are harbingers of mankind's ultimate destruction, such as the seven-headed dragon of the Judeo-Christian Apocalypse. Still others represent our own fears about our most hidden desires, such as the blood-consuming vampires or mind-shattering banshees of the Western mythological traditions. Whether angel, demon, imp, or monster … you don't want to get on their bad side.

Chapter  16

Angels and Demons

In This Chapter

- ◆ The angels and demons of Jewish, Christian, and Muslim mythology
- ◆ The orders of angels and the role of the archangels
- ◆ The Japanese Tengu demon's relationship to martial arts
- ◆ The myth of the Japanese Kitsune fox demons, plus their relationships with gods, humans, and Tengu

There are some who believe that our physical world is but an imperfect reflection of a perfect spiritual world. The struggles that are fought by the forces of good and evil, between we humans and within our own selves, are represented in religion and mythology by the conflicts of angels and demons. These mysterious and elusive beings maintain the balance of physical existence by playing it out in the spiritual realm, hidden from human sight. Angels and demons represent the spiritual forces that protect and guide us, tempt and corrupt us. They are unseen actors on the stage of war that is the battle between the creative powers of light and the destructive harbingers of darkness.

The Order of Angels

Angels, as with most human organizations, have their own hierarchy that is broken up into a number of angelic orders. Depending on what religion, denomination, or text one goes by, the entirety of the angelic hierarchy may differ. As far as biblical/Judeo-Christian mythologies are concerned, there are three angelic types that are the most active: the Metatron, the Grigori "Watchers," and Archangels (which will be covered in another section of this chapter). There is a general consensus that biblical angels are androgynous, neither male nor female, so please understand that the use of the gendered term "he" and "him" in reference to an angel is done only for linguistic convenience and nothing more.

The Metatron

The Metatron (also known to be spelled in some texts as Mittron, Metaraon, and Metratton) has a multitude of names and titles. This angel has been referred to as the King of Angels, Chancellor of Heaven, Prince of the Divine Face, the Voice of YHVH, and the *Tetragrammaton* ("lesser" YHVH). The easiest explanation for the Metatron is that he is an angel that acts as the voice of YHVH. According to the Jewish *Talmud*, the angel Metatron acts as a link between the physical world in which we live and the spiritual realm/Heaven of YHVH.

The Judaic lore of the *Enoch* explains that Metatron is the tallest and greatest of the angels. However, it is also said that he was once mortal. The Jewish legend states that when Metatron's spirit was received into Heaven, he was given new form as a being of light and fire. From his back spread 36 pairs of enormous wings and more eyes than could be counted. When not relaying YHVH's will and wishes to humanity, Metatron resides in the seventh level of Heaven (where the throne of YHVH is located).

As a result of the Metatron's multifaceted nature, a definitive mythological explanation of the angel is hard to pin down. He has been credited as an angel of such contradictory tasks and roles as wisdom, wrath, light, dark, and even death. In addition, the origins and exact meaning of the name Metatron is uncertain. Many theories exist, most of which are speculative at best and none of which are absolute or completely verifiable.

The Angelic Watchers

Those appointed to the Grigori Angelic Order (also spelled *egregori* or *egoroi*) are called Watchers for a good reason, as it is their task to watch over the entirety of humankind. In Judaic myth, the Grigori are able to carry out their task because they have been given the appearance of men. However, though they appear of normal size to human eyes—unless they choose to reveal themselves (which they almost never do)—in truth they are the size of giants. The Grigori dwell in both the second and fifth levels of Heaven.

Because these watcher angels are meant to observe but not interfere (except on *very* rare occasions) with human affairs, the Grigori do not speak … ever. It is not certain, though, whether the eternal silence of the Grigori is due to their choice, some unknown necessity of their position in the Angelic Order, or if YHVH simply chose not to grant them the ability of speech. The highest-ranking angel in the Angelic Order of Grigori is named Salamiel, which means (oddly enough) "the one who rejected YHVH."

You see, apparently Salamiel is no longer a Watcher, though he seems to have somehow retained his title as their prince. One myth explains that Salamiel, though he does not seem to be one of the original fallen angels that sided with Lucifer, rejected his creator YHVH. However, the exact nature of his rejection is unclear. This could simply mean he refused to obey an order from YHVH or that he rejected his creator entirely.

Archangels: The Order of High Angels

The Order of Archangels is often misrepresented as one of warrior angels. However, archangel is actually a title for very high-ranking angels. An archangel is any angel above the generic angelic rank. Of this order, there are seven angels who are considered the highest among them all—Michael, Uriel, Gabriel, Raphael, Simiel, Orifiel, and Zachariel. Of course, the names and ranks of angels differ depending on what religion, denomination, or text you are going by. This list is the most common. The next few sections will look at the three most active of the seven head archangels.

The Angelic Prince of Israel

Michael's name means "The one who is as YHVH." In biblical mythology, no matter which text or denomination one subscribes to, Michael is undisputedly the greatest of all the angels. One might look at Michael as being kind of like the "general of angels." When Lucifer made his play against Heaven, it was Michael who led the angelic hordes against the usurping angels.

Avoiding the Labyrinth

According to the Muslim tradition, the Archangel Michael resides in the seventh level of Heaven (instead of the fourth), where the Heavenly throne of YHVH is located. In Muslim lore, Michael's wings are said to be emerald green and his body is covered with hairs of saffron. On these hairs are millions of mouths that speak in all the different languages in existence, all of them crying out praise for Allah and begging for the pardon of Man for his sins.

The Archangel Michael serves as a leader in many levels of existence, not only in the angelic hierarchy but in the realms of both Heaven and Earth. He is chief of the Order of Virtues, the Prince of the "Presence," as well as the patron angel of righteousness, justice, mercy, repentance, and sanctification. For his loyalty to his creator and devoted service to the battle against evil, YHVH appointed Michael ruler over the fourth level of Heaven and made him the Angelic Prince of Israel. Lastly, Michael serves as one of the Ten Angels of the Holy *Sefiroth*.

Immortal Words

Sefiroth (also spelled Sephiroth; though sefira/sephira is the singular form) is a pairing of polar opposite Angelic Orders that consist of the Ten Holy Sefiroth, the most powerful archangels in Heaven, as well as the Ten Unholy Sefiroth, a group of evil counter-entities. Although the Angels of the Holy Sefiroth come from the right hand of YHVH, the Ten Unholy Sephiroth come from the left hand of YHVH. The Ten Angels of the Holy Sefiroth represent the elements of Jewish *Kabbalah* mysticism, and they are Metatron (crown), Raziel (wisdom), Tzaphqiel (understanding), Tzadqiel (mercy), Michael (beauty), Raphael (splendor), Gabriel (foundation), Camael (strength), Haniel (victory), and Shekinah (kingdom). In some texts, Metatron assumes a second form in place of Shekinah, as these two angels are sometimes said to be one and the same.

Despite his many titles, Michael's primary title is "Conqueror of Satan," called so because he is credited with defeating the adversary of YHVH. Adversary is the English translation of Satan, the name given to Lucifer after his fall from Heaven. This role of Conqueror of Satan is the one in which the Archangel Michael is most frequently portrayed. For a number of centuries, multitudes of artists have created works that depict the scene of Michael's victory over Lucifer in battle. The common theme is that Lucifer is often on his back while the Archangel Michael stands over him, sometimes pinning the usurping angel down with his foot. In such artworks, Michael is often shown wearing shining armor (which is often close to the style from the period during which the painting was created), pointing the tip of either a sword or lance at the defeated Lucifer's chest or throat.

Michael is very much a warrior in his role as archangel, and is almost always shown with a drawn sword or spear in his hand. He can also be wrathful, and in Judaic lore is credited (acting under an order from YHVH) with the destruction of the ancient city of Babylon. He is also spoken of in a part of the somewhat recently discovered *Dead Sea Scrolls*, which tells of a war between the Sons of Light and Sons of Darkness. In this tale, Michael is referred to as the Prince of Light who led the angels of Heaven against the Angels of Darkness (who followed a demon commander by the name of Belial).

Gabriel

Gabriel's name means "My Strength is From God." In both the Muslim and Judeo-Christian angelic mythologies, the Archangel Gabriel is second in rank only to Michael. He is one of only two angels that are specifically mentioned by name in the biblical Old Testament (the other being Michael).

Avoiding the Labyrinth

Some might say that there are three angels mentioned by name in the Old Testament. This is based on a text called the *Book of Tobit,* in which the Archangel Raphael is mentioned. However, this book's authenticity is disputed among Catholics, Protestants, and Jews. Therefore, Raphael's place as the third angel named in the Old Testament by the *Book of Tobit* was not included in this section (see the next section, "Raphael").

Most people think of Archangel Gabriel as being something similar to YHVH's announcer, or they perceive him solely as Heaven's messenger, bugler, or trumpeter, causing him to be seen as a Christian form of the Greco-Roman god Hermes/Mercury. Although these are among Gabriel's responsibilities, the angel's duties are far more complicated than simply making announcements and blowing a horn. What makes Archangel Gabriel so interesting when you compare him to his fellow angels is that he displays a balanced (some might say paradoxical) and somewhat binary nature.

You see, Gabriel occupies a number of roles that many would perceive as contradictory (or, at the least, certainly not complementary) to one another. For example, Gabriel is the patron angel of both mercy and vengeance, of annunciation and revelation, and of death and resurrection. In all three cases, it would seem that he is performing tasks that are counter to the other. However, one would do better to view this as a symbol of balance, of conflicting forces in harmony. Through this perception, Gabriel's binary nature becomes easier to understand.

In Islamic mythology, Gabriel is the Angel of Truth, and the *Qur'an* tells that, when the dust thrown up by the hooves of Gabriel's divine steed entered the mouth of the Golden Calf that Moses' people had erected, the statue began to move and came to life. According to Jewish lore, it was the Archangel Gabriel who rained down a fiery death upon the cities of Sodom and Gomorrah.

Raphael

Raphael means "God Has Healed," and he is the third highest angel in rank (next to Gabriel and Michael). The oldest text he is known to be named in is called the *Book of Tobit*, which is a text that is a cause of debate among Jews, Protestants, and Catholics (see the previous section's sidebar). However, according to this text, Raphael acts as a guide and protector for Tobias, son of Tobit, as he journeys to the city of Nineveh. However, the archangel disguises himself as a mortal and does not reveal his true form until they have reached their destination. When in Nineveh, Raphael "uncases his wings," so to speak, and tells Tobias that he is one of the Seven Holy Angels that stand before the throne of YHVH.

Immortal Words

The **Cherubim** (Cherub is the singular form) are now seen as a lower order of angels. However, they were not always seen in such a positive way. Cherubim are Assyrian in origin, and Cherub is believed to have meant "one who intercedes" or possibly "one who knows." To the ancient Assyrians, Cherubim were enormous winged beings with the heads of lions (sometimes of men) and the bodies of bulls or eagles. In the *Talmud*, Cherubim were seen as an order of "Holy Beasts" that occupied the sixth level of Heaven. In modern depictions, Cherubim are childlike angels, often shown singing or playing musical instruments.

Raphael, similar to Gabriel and Michael, has a multitude of names, titles, and posts. He is said to be the Guardian of the Western Horizon, Prince of the Second Level of Heaven, and Protector of the Eden Tree. The Archangel Raphael is the patron angel of light, love, prayers, and happiness. Raphael seems to be popular with other angels, and is a member of many angelic orders. He is a member of both the *Cherubim* and *Seraphim*, and is counted among the Ten Holy Angels of the Sefiroth.

As suggested by his name, Raphael is also the angel of healing, medicine, science, and knowledge. One day, however, it is said that the time for healing will come to an end, and when that time comes, Raphael will be among the Seven Angels of the Apocalypse.

> **Immortal Words**
>
> Seraphim (singular form is Seraph) is the higher order of angels above the Cherubim. These are the angels that surround the throne of YHVH and constantly call out "Holy! Holy! Holy!" In general, the Seraphim are an order reserved for angels of light, fire, and love. Seraphim are said to have four faces and six wings (though, oddly, they are rarely depicted this way in art).

Angels of the Fall

When Lucifer led a third of the angels in a rebellion against YHVH, a war broke out in the realm of Heaven. When it was over, Lucifer was cast from above. He was stripped of his title as Lucifer ("Light Bringer") and given the shameful name of Satan, meaning "adversary," before being exiled to the physical realm for the rest of existence. Misery, however, loves company, and the cast-down Lucifer would have plenty of fallen angels to join him.

According to the Judaic text *Enoch I*, 200 angels were cast from Heaven for their roles in Lucifer's rebellion. Also, excluding some beliefs from certain sects of Christianity, those who sided with Lucifer are not the only angels to be cast out of Heaven. Take Salamiel, for example, the former Angel Prince of the Grigori who was cast out for refusing YHVH (see the earlier section "The Angelic Watchers" about Grigori). They are only the most well known. In the following sections, however, you will find descriptions of just a few of the worst offenders to ever be cast down from Heaven.

Demon of the Flies

Beelzebub (also spelled Belzaboul and Belzebud), whose name means "God of the Flies," was originally a god of the Syrians that was integrated into Jewish mythology and transformed into a demon. In Kaballah, this terrible demon is lord over hell's Nine Hierarchies of Evil.

Beelzebub is the chief of demons and a prince of hell, but should not be mistaken for Lucifer/Satan. This is a common mistake due to past misinterpretations of Judaic lore that were the result of mistranslations of the word "Satan." In such cases, the word was taken to mean the fallen angel Lucifer instead of its intended use as adversary. However, they have since been clearly established as being two separate entities.

The Poison Angel

Sammael's name translates as "Poison Angel." He was the Angel of Death and may still be, as it is unclear whether he retained his role after the fall. He is called Chief of the Adversaries (Satans) and is said to be one of the most cruel and horrible creatures in all existence—Heaven, hell, Earth, and beyond. There exists at least one reference to Sammael that claims he had his way with both Lilith and Eve (the first two women of creation in Judaic mythology). As with Beelzebub, Sammael has frequently been confused with Lucifer due to misunderstandings/mistranslations of the word "Satan" as adversary.

However, continued research into the figure of Sammael becomes confusing, because he is often referred to as still being an angel. In fact, some texts claim that he resides in the seventh level of Heaven alongside the greatest of the archangels. However, he is not one of the Seven Holy Angels that stand before the throne of YHVH.

Leviathan

Leviathan is often thought to be the name of an enormous whale that swallowed Jonah in the Christian Bible. Although Leviathan was, in fact, the creature who swallowed Jonah, she is certainly *not* a whale. Leviathan, actually, may not even be a demon (at least, not in the way we commonly think of demons) and she is definitely not a fallen angel. Leviathan was a large female sea monster that terrorized the seas of the ancient world. Some myths claim that she was spewed forth from the mouth of Lilith after she was demonized by Jewish mythology (for more information on Lilith, see Chapter 12).

Some believe that Leviathan may have been the Jewish transformation of the Babylonian goddess Tiamat, who mothered a brood of monsters to avenge her husband's murder by her divine children (see Chapter 2). In the Rabbinical tradition, Leviathan is said to be the consort of Behemoth, another large monster/demon. She and Behemoth are said to have been created during the fifth day of the Genesis creation (though the texts that provide direct references to this claim are noncanonical and rare).

Lords of the Ninja: Tengu (Japanese)

Tengu are perhaps one of the most powerful supernatural entities in Japanese mythology, or at least among the most troublesome. These beings exist in Japanese myths from both Shinto and Buddhism. The Tengu myth was probably introduced to Japan sometime between the sixth and seventh centuries B.C.E.

The name Tengu means "Heavenly Dog" (which is weird, because they look *nothing* like dogs). This name could have two possible origins. It could have been derived from the name of the Chinese mountain god, Tiangou. However, there is also a similar creature in Chinese mythology called a Tien Kou, which means "Hound of the Celestial Realm," a name with obvious similarities to Tengu, both in meaning and phonetics. In Shinto myths, the Tengu are said to have been created by the god of destruction, Susanowo. The Tengu king goes by the name of Sojobo.

What *Can't* a Tengu Do?

The Tengu seem to feel most comfortable when they are among nature, and therefore reside in the mountainous forest regions of Japan, such as Koga and Iga. The appearance of a Tengu depends on what type it is. There are three main types of Tengu demons: Yamabushi (Monk), Konoha (Leaf), and Karasu (Crow/Bird). Though all three are considered Tengu, and have similar abilities and traits, their appearances are very different. No matter what type, all Tengu are said to be hatched from eggs.

A Yamabushi Tengu lives in the regular guise of a Mountain Monk (Yamabushi = Mountain Monk), and that's exactly what your eyes will see until it chooses for things to be otherwise. A Konoha Tengu (or Leaf Tengu) looks somewhat like a man. However, the Konoha Tengu have red faces, long beaklike noses, and are often said to have wings (but they may be able to conceal them with their powers). Karasu Tengu (Crow Tengu) are perhaps the most common and popular depiction of a Tengu demon. They are extremely birdlike in appearance, with a pair of wings and beaks instead of mouths.

No matter what appearance or type they assume, Tengu have a number of powers that are as useful as they are beyond belief. Just for starters, Tengu have the ability to assume nearly any shape—animal, human, even plant. They are also able to communicate with humans (and each other) without speaking (as though using a form of telepathy).

Though Tengu have wings, they don't appear to need them because they have the ability to instantly move from one place to another (an ability that is akin to teleportation). The powers and movements of these mischievous goblinlike creatures are not restricted to the waking realm, either. Tengu are said to have the magical ability to enter into and manipulate one's dreams (whether or not one wants them to).

The Warrior Tengu

Of the three Tengu demon types, the one most commonly told about in Japanese mythology is the Karasu Tengu. This is likely due to the fact that, of the three, the Karasu-type Tengu are the most skilled warriors. As a matter of fact, Karasu Tengu are considered the patron spirits of the Japanese martial arts and are said to enjoy practicing *Bushido*.

As a warrior spirit of sorts, the role of the Karasu Tengu is somewhat similar to that of the Furies of Greek mythology in that they carry out violent justice upon the wicked, especially those who misuse or abuse power and/or knowledge. Their rebellious natures make them especially good at their job, and class is no protection from the wrath of a Karasu Tengu. Whether a peasant, priest, monk, or even samurai, the Karasu Tengu will punish those wicked, vain, and arrogant souls unlucky enough to cross their paths.

Also, the Karasu Tengu are said to have an especially harsh dislike for vain people and drunken braggarts (however, they are also said to enjoy drinking *sake* and are often rather egotistical) and often play rather cruel pranks on these kinds of people. Though the Karasu Tengu can certainly be mischievous, tricky, and even wrathful (at least against the wicked), they are not usually portrayed as evil, unnecessarily (or, at least, unjustifiably) violent, or malevolent beings.

Immortal Words _____

Bushido literally means "The Way of the Warrior." It comes from a combination of the words *bushi* (warrior) and *do* (way or path). This term refers not only to the disciplined practice of the martial arts, but also to the application of a warrior mindset and lifestyle.

Immortal Words _____

Sake, pronounced *sah*-kay, is Japanese rice wine, often served warm. For hundreds of years, sake has been the alcoholic beverage of choice among the Japanese. Sake should not be confused with *soju*, which is a far more bitter Korean rice wine that is made by a different process.

Tengu and Bushido

A number of myths surround the interaction and relationships between Karasu Tengu and the legendary warriors of Japan. Stories tell of Tengu appearing to ninja, samurai, and *ronin*. Because they are said to be rather fond of fighting, this is not surprising.

Immortal Words _____

A **ronin** is a samurai who is without a daimyo (feudal lord) to serve. Often, ronin are viewed negatively, because samurai who did not have a daimyo were likely either banished or had failed to commit *seppeku* when ordered, appropriate, or called for. *Seppeku* was a form of ritual suicide by way of performing self-disembowelment until one was aided by a skilled swordsman (called a *kaishaku*) who cuts off one's head, also called *tsuifuku* and *hara kiri* ("stomach cutting," often mispronounced by Westerners as "hairy carry").

There are a number of stories about Karasu Tengu and their encounters with warriors. One such story tells of a confrontation between a Karasu Tengu and famed Japanese swordsman Miyamoto Musashi (for more information on Musashi, see Chapter 11), who defeats the demon and therefore receives instruction in secret fighting arts. This is a common element in such myths, that of warriors being taught secret fighting techniques or magical arts after defeating a Karasu Tengu in a fight. However, they are sometimes willing to do this for no other reason than to punish powerful men who have become arrogant in their stations.

Immortal Words _____

Shinobi literally means "to hide" or "to steal away." This word is often used in reference to male ninja warriors, and comes from their legendary abilities of stealth and infiltration. The term for female ninja is *kunoichi*.

One rather obscure myth suggests that the legendary *shinobi* ninja warriors were taught secret killing arts and the ways of dark magic by a Karasu Tengu. However, considering the fact that ninja were well known for being masters of psychological warfare, these myths were likely created and encouraged to spawn fear and paranoia in the hearts and minds of their enemies. Ninjas are even known to have worn frightening masks that resembled the face of a Karasu Tengu or other demon.

Avoiding the Labyrinth

Westerners often misperceive the relationship between ninja and samurai, seeing them as enemies. However, this wasn't the case. Ninja were often employed by samurai. In fact, some samurai and daimyo are believed to have been ninja. In contrast to portrayals of ninja as silent assassins, it's more accurate to see them as rebels who wished to undermine the oppression of the Japanese feudal system. Ninja could be male or female, and came from all walks of life—peasants, ronin, samurai, daimyo, and (in some cases) Buddhist monks and Shinto priests. One common thread was their resistance to authority, loyalty to the group/clan, and use of any technique that worked (even if it violated traditional *Bushido* codes of samurai conduct).

In truth, it is now believed by many Ninpo ("ninja way") or Ninjutsu ("skills of ninja") practitioners that the arts have a more historically realistic origin. Grandmaster Stephen K. Hayes is credited with bringing knowledge of Ninjutsu to the West, and as a result of his research claims that the origins of the art likely came from China. This does not mean that the ninja came from China, however. He claims that Chinese refugees who fled to Japan, escaping the wrath of the violent T'ang Dynasty, likely bestowed arts of fighting (Kung Fu/Wushu) and illusion (using gunpowder for smoke devices, for example) to the political insurgents of medieval Japan.

Two main ninja groups are known to have originated from the mountainous Japanese regions of Iga and Koga. Because Tengu were a familiar creature of the local mythology, the ninja of these regions learned to take advantage of the superstition. The Tengu myth may have originally been used by Chinese refugees and/or Japanese rebels, hiding in the mountains, to discourage accidental encounters with innocent civilians as well as to frighten away spies and intruders. Apparently they did one heck of a job. At one point in Japanese history, belief in the Tengu became so strong that, in 1860 B.C.E., the government officials of the Edo region posted notices all over the city that directly addressed all local Tengu demons. The notice was posted due to an upcoming visit from the Shogun to Edo. It requested that all local Tengu demons vacate a nearby mountain until the Shogun's visit had ended.

Ninja: Demon, Refugee, or Rebel?

The ninja's ability to hide had less to do with donning black outfits or magic arts of invisibility, and more to do with their amazing skills at blending in. They were hard to find because they looked just like everyone else (often, because they were someone familiar). The ninja, truthfully, only *seemed* able to appear and disappear at will (a belief that was likely inflamed by spread of the Karasu-Tengu-Ninja myth).

In truth, the reason ninja were never seen was simple. They were often already actively involved in familiar roles within their victims' lives, and often had been doing so long before they struck. Such infiltrations took an unknown length of time, even to the ninja involved, which required amazing discipline and devotion. An infiltration mission could require days, months, years, or (amazingly) an entire lifetime.

Avoiding the Labyrinth

Although ninja are known to have worn black for nocturnal operations, this was not their normal dress. The popular image of the black-suited ninja is actually a carryover from their portrayals in Japanese *Kabuki* (theatre). These black suits were worn by performers who were playing ninja parts (as well as stagehands, puppeteers, and prop masters) to symbolize to the audience that they were invisible to the other actors onstage.

Imagine, for example, a female *kunoichi* who received an assignment to spy on a daimyo would likely have first sought employment within the lord's home as, perhaps, a nanny, maid, or other kind of servant. This would have allowed the *kunoichi* to remain close to her target while gathering information without attracting any unwanted attention.

Eventually, it was entirely possible that the *kunoichi* would finally receive a kill order from her group/clan (often hand-delivered by another ninja and written in some form of code or secret scripts). Because she had already made herself a fixture in the home of her target, it was easy enough for her to walk freely on the premises and kill him. If captured or placed in a situation where she was unable to readily escape, the *kunoichi* would likely take her own life by either swallowing poison or plunging a *tanto* (Japanese word for a roughly 12- to 24-inch-long knife that was carried as a weapon) into her heart or abdomen. One might see the ninja as precursors to the modern-day "sleeper cells," employed by special military units, intelligence operatives, and global terrorist organizations.

The Fox Messengers (Japanese)

In the Japanese language, *Kitsune* is a word used to refer to your average, everyday, run-of-the-mill fox. However, in Shinto mythology, Kitsune also refers to the race of fox spirits/demons who act as messengers for Inari, the Rice *Kami* god. Kitsune have a close relationship with Tengu and they share a number of attributes, such as the ability to assume human form.

Avoiding the Labyrinth

Tengu and Kitsune, though they are certainly not human, should not to be thought of as monsters. In fact, they are more like demon-angel hybrids, in that they have capacities for good and evil that are similar to those of humans. In Japanese mythology, *bakemono* is the word used for beings (usually evil and/or destructive) that are considered *monsters* (see Chapter 21). Tengu and Kitsune fall into the category of *yokai*, which are a type of nature spirit or demon.

Kitsune spirits enjoy playing tricks on people nearly as much as the Tengu (though they are not quite as cruel in their pranks as the Tengu). Whereas Tengu are trickster demons of a somewhat wrathful nature, Kitsune are more playful in nature and are almost always portrayed as helpful allies to humans (as long as they are treated with respect). Because normal foxes often reside near humans (attracted by domesticated pheasants and discarded food), they were a common sight to those living in ancient Japan. So perhaps it should not be surprising that the myths of the Kitsune arose.

The Kitsune are strong, stubborn, wise, and clever beings. The level of a Kitsune's power can be measured by counting the number of tails it has. Kitsune can have between one and nine tails. The more tails it has, the wiser, older, and more powerful a Kitsune is. Therefore, one should be careful around a Kitsune that is a *Kyuubi*, which means "nine tails." In fact, myths warn that you should be kind to foxes if they are not doing any harm, because you might accidentally end up offending a Kitsune, and that is something you *really* don't want to do. An offended or provoked Kitsune (especially a "nine-tail") can do *a lot* of damage.

Myth and Metaphor

In the popular anime series *Naruto,* the main character (Naruto) has the spirit of an angered Kyuubi (a nine-tailed Kitsune) sealed with him when he is an infant. The Kitsune within him makes the boy's fellow villagers wary of him. However, he proves himself a powerful warrior and eventually learns how to utilize the powers of the Kyuubi Kitsune. He and the Kitsune develop an uneasy symbiotic relationship, in which the nine-tail loans his *chakra* (energy) to the boy in the hopes of tempting Naruto into eventually releasing him from his seal. However, Kitsune are not forgiving beings and for Naruto to release the angered nine-tail fox demon would be disastrous.

One Kitsune myth tells of a samurai who encounters a fox one evening while returning home from the residence of his daimyo. Though he is still some distance from his residence, the samurai draws his bow and nocks a special flash-bang arrow that is normally used to scare away wild dogs. He fires the arrow at the fox, hitting it in the back of the leg. As the samurai draws a second arrow, the animal darts into a nearby bush. The warrior comes up to the bush, bow drawn, planning to finish off the fox with a second shot. However, when he aims at the fox, it suddenly disappears. As he goes to retrieve his first arrow, the fox suddenly reappears in front of him! He quickly draws his bow to shoot, only to have the fox disappear before his eyes once again.

A bit unnerved, the samurai decides to get back on his horse and continue on. Less than a mile from the warrior's home, the same fox emerges from the forest onto the road ahead of him. In the animal's mouth is a burning torch, which puzzles the samurai. Then, the fox darts off in the direction of the samurai's home. Overcome by a strange panic, he spurs his horse into a full gallop.

When the samurai's home is within his sight, he spies the fox sitting next to the door with the flaming torch still in its mouth. Before the samurai can reach it, the fox transforms into the shape of a human. This "fox," the samurai now realizes, is a *Kitsune!* This thought bellows within the warrior's mind as the Kitsune lights the house on fire. As the flames rise, the samurai draws his bow once more, seeing that the Kitsune is now within range. Before he can fire, however, the fox spirit returns to its original form and disappears into the nearby woods. The samurai's home, and everything within it, is reduced to ashes.

The Least You Need to Know

◆ The three highest-ranking angels in canonical Judeo-Christian and Muslim myths are the Archangels Michael, Gabriel, and Raphael.

◆ Satan means "adversary" and the context in which it's used should be carefully noted to avoid confusing references to other demons with those to Lucifer.

◆ Tengu and Kitsune are both talented pranksters, though the Tengu are far more cruel.

◆ A Kitsune's power is measured by the number of tails it possesses, between one (Ichibi) and nine (Kyuubi).

◆ A provoked Shinto nature spirit, whether Tengu or Kitsune, can do a serious amount of damage.

Chapter 17

Dragons and Fairies

In This Chapter

◆ The difference between dragons of the East and dragons of the West

◆ The multi-headed female dragons of the Greeks

◆ The classifications and purposes of fairies, brownies, gnomes, and pixies

◆ The war between the fairies and the pixies

Dragons and fairies are perhaps two of the most commonly seen nonhuman entities in Western mythology. Fairies, and similar nature spirits and sprites, are more commonly seen in the mythologies of Western cultures and play only a small role (if any) in the myths of the East. In similar fashion, dragons maintain a much stronger presence in the mythologies of Eastern cultures than they do in the West, where they are often employed as little more than lethal representations of evil and greed that must be slain to save a maiden or seize a treasure.

Western Dragons vs. Eastern Dragons

Dragons are perhaps one of the best mythological examples of how the perceptions of Easterners and Westerners differ. There is a distinct difference between the portrayals of dragons in Eastern and Western cultures.

In the East, dragons are seen as wise creatures that often aid the human race. Eastern dragons are teachers of supernatural wisdom and can be powerful allies to humanity.

In the mythologies of Western cultures, however, dragons are portrayed in a polar opposite way. Western dragons are usually portrayed as evil creatures that burn villages, kidnap helpless maidens, and horde vast treasures in their dark abodes. In the Western view, dragons are harbingers of destruction. The Western dragon is humankind's enemy, not its ally.

Scylla (Greek)

Before Odysseus leaves the island of Circe (see Chapter 15), she gives him instructions regarding his voyage. The only path he can take is not a pleasant one, and will send him between two terrible female monsters named Scylla and Charybdis. Charybdis, according to some myths, is a woman whom Zeus casts into the sea as punishment for stealing from his half-god son Herakles. Forever after, the myth says Charybdis is cursed to suck down seawater and spew it forth three times each day. The result of this curse is a deadly whirlpool near which no ship can pass without being capsized. As a result, Circe tells Odysseus that he must sail closer to Scylla to avoid Charybdis. However, the option of Scylla isn't a whole lot more appealing than that of Charybdis.

Scylla is a female dragon with six heads, each of which has three rows of razor-sharp teeth. The most popular myth surrounding the origins of Scylla says that she was once human. However, Scylla was transformed into a multi-headed sea monster when she somehow incurred the wrath of a goddess or nymph (some say it was the witch/nymph Circe that cursed her; others credit her curse as the work of Amphitrite, wife of Poseidon). Nonetheless, there is not one definitive myth that tells the exact origins of Scylla.

> **Myth and Metaphor**
>
> Odysseus' difficult, no-win choice between Scylla and Charybdis has long been viewed as a metaphor for a choice between two bad alternatives. A choice between a rock and a hard place (or, in this case, between a whirlpool and a man-eating dragon) is one no one wishes to make. Unfortunately, one alternative must be chosen, often the "lesser of the two evils," one might say.

Scylla's domain is a rock along what some think might have been the Straights of Messina (though there is some debate about this), directly opposite the whirlpool Charybdis. Circe tells Odysseus that he will have no choice but to lose six of his men while passing by Scylla, as each of her six heads will snatch a man up and devour him. If he passes near Charybdis, however, his ship will be sucked to the seafloor and everyone aboard (including Odysseus) will die. She tells him that he *must* sail near Scylla and that he *must not* try to make it by Charybdis (no one would ever succeed in, or even survive, doing so).

Odysseus, needless to say, is terribly distressed by the choice put before him. The knowledge that six of his men are going to die so that he can save his ship and remaining crew members weighs heavily on the hero's conscience. However, Odysseus does as he has to and, when he and his men sail speedily past the terrible jaws of Scylla, six of them are devoured, lost to the sea monster's horrible appetite.

The Hydra (Greek)

The ancient Greeks seem to have had a thing for multi-headed monsters, especially when it came to their dragons. The Hydra is no exception, sporting nine grotesque heads. During Herakles' Twelve Labors, he slew the Hydra with the help of a friend. You see, the Hydra was hard to kill because every time one head was severed, two more would sprout up in its place. Herakles was able to defeat the monster by having his companion sear the wounds shut with a hot iron, thereby preventing the new heads from sprouting.

The part of the myth that states that the Hydra would grow two heads for every one that was severed creates an interesting problem when you look at it mathematically. How, exactly, did the Hydra maintain nine heads if two would replace one when severed? By that rationale, when the first head was severed, the Hydra would have a total of 10 heads. When the second was severed, it would have a total of 11 heads. This would continue until, theoretically, the Hydra had a plethora of new heads. However, in no myth does it ever state that this creature ever experienced any change in its number of heads.

The Slaying of Fafnir (Teutonic)

The dragon Fafnir, as with many dragons of European myth, was the guardian of a vast horde of wealth that was beyond imagining. Guided by an ill-fated man (some say a dwarf) known as Regin the Bard (called so for his skill at playing the harp), the Scandinavian hero Siegfried (also associated with the hero Sigurd; see Chapter 11) went to slay the terrible creature.

Fafnir was once human it is said, but became a dragon as a result of his own brooding and bitter heart (this turns out to be only partially true later on in the myth).

What made Fafnir so powerful was the fact that he possessed two very dangerous items—the Helmet of Terror and Ring of Power. Unbeknownst to Siegfried, Fafnir was actually Regin's brother. To gain a power that was not rightfully his, Fafnir killed their father and used the power of the ring to transform himself into a dragon. Regin, however, also lusted after the power of the ring and hoped to take it from Siegfried after the dragon was defeated. Basically, Regin planned to kill the exhausted hero Siegfried when his battle with the dragon was over.

Knowing that a stand-up fight is a bad idea, due to the fact the dragon scales were nearly impossible to penetrate, Siegfried digs a hole along the path that Fafnir frequents. He then hides there and waits for the dragon to pass over him. When Fafnir goes by, Siegfried thrusts his mighty sword Balmung into the monster's soft underbelly. Drenched with Fafnir's blood, Siegfried emerges from the hole and sees that he has succeeded. Fafnir is dead.

Myth and Metaphor _____

The mythological theme of a ring of power that drives the wearer mad with greed and lust for strength, as that seen in this tale of Regin and Siegfried, is one that greatly influenced the writings of J. R. R. Tolkien, author of *The Hobbit* and *The Lord of the Rings* trilogy. In recent years, the latter has been made into a successful series of live-action films by director Peter Jackson. A movie of *The Hobbit* is said to be in the works.

Luckily, Odin's crows arrive just in time to warn Siegfried of Regin's lust for the Ring of Power and his murderous intentions. At this point, Regin turns on Siegfried and becomes angry, accusing the warrior of having slain his brother. Siegfried tells him to keep the treasure as a blood ransom, but Regin has become mad with his lust for the ring and attacks. As Regin charges at Siegfried, he loses his footing and falls forward onto the sharp tip of the sword Balmung.

The Four Dragon Kings (Chinese)

In Chinese Taoist mythology, there are four primary Dragon Kings who have domain in the Four Oceans, and live in crystal palaces on the ocean floor. These Dragon Kings are called Long Wang, and serve the greatest deity of Taoism, Yuan-shi Tian-zong, from whom all things came into being. Annually, these dragons must deliver reports to Yuan-shi Tian-zong, who will then use them to deliver orders to the other deities of Taoism.

The Long Wang Dragon Kings are organized directionally, and are as follows: Ao Ming (also called Ao Shun), Dragon King of the North Sea; Ao K'in (or Ao Qin), Dragon King of the South Sea; Ao Guang, Dragon King of the East Sea; and Ao Ji, Dragon King of the West Sea. The Long Wang Dragon Kings are most well known for their connection to the myth of the Monkey King, Sun Wu Kong, who bullied all four of them into giving him precious magical gifts (see Chapter 2).

Dragon King of the Sea (Japanese)

Ryujin is somewhat considered a Shinto God of the Sea, but he is always shown in the form of a dragon. However, it is said that he also has the ability to transform into a human. Ryujin's palace exists at the bottom of the Sea of Japan, a beautiful castle carved from red and white coral.

Myth and Metaphor

Ryujin shares a trait with Poseidon, the Greek God of the Sea—a nasty temper. Sea gods, commonly, are depicted in myth as being temperamental and moody deities. This personality trait is believed to be a metaphor for the unpredictable and violent nature of the oceans/seas. A calm sea can turn into a raging tempest in the blink of an eye, so it is no surprise that sea gods are often easily provoked to anger.

Once, long ago, Ryujin's skin was stricken with a painful rash that could only be cured by eating monkey liver. So he called on the jellyfish to go get him a monkey (at this time, the jellyfish still had bones). They soon captured one but, as they began bringing the monkey back to the sea, the clever animal thought of a way to trick them into letting him go.

If it was his liver they wanted, the tricky monkey explained, then he would have to go back and get it because he'd put his liver in a jar years ago. He told the jellyfish to return to the sea and to tell Ryujin that he would bring the liver right away (which, of course, was a lie). The naïve (and fairly stupid) jellyfish released the monkey and returned to Ryujin to report this. The Sea God Dragon became so enraged at the stupidity of the jellyfish that he beat them senseless, crushing every bone in their bodies into powder. Since that time, jellyfish have not had skeletal structures.

Yamata-no-Orochi (Japanese)

Orochi (full name Yamata-no-Orochi) is the eight-headed dragon of Japanese Shinto mythology. Orochi was very serpentine, looking a lot like a mix between a gigantic snake and a traditional dragon. This mythical creature is troublesome indeed, even giving the *kami* gods a difficult time.

Immortal Words

In the Japanese language, the word *no* denotes attachment and/or ownership. The first item/person is owner of/related to the second item/person, which follows the word *no*. For example, Yamata-no-Orochi translates to mean Orochi of Yamata.

Avoiding the Labyrinth

In the well-known Japanese manga/anime *Naruto*, one of the most evil villains is named *Orochi*maru (meaning "Born of/ Son of the Orochi") and has the ability to summon a giant snake that he rides up. From his mouth, he spits forth a sword, perhaps symbolic of the Kusanagi katana blade that was in the body of Yamata-no-Orochi.

Unlike most dragons in Asian mythology, Yamata-no-Orochi is purely evil in nature and there is not a single tale of the creature choosing to act for the benefit of humankind. For example, Orochi attacked and threatened the Kusanagi clan until they gave him the special katana they possessed, which he then swallowed so that it might never be used against him. Also, Orochi is known to enjoy eating people and has a preference for devouring virgins.

After Orochi took over the region of Izumo, he began terrorizing the people. The dreadful eight-headed serpent demanded that they sacrifice virgins to him regularly. The people had to comply to stave off Orochi's destructive nature. Sadly, the myth says that the virgins were taken from the ruling clan, who had only eight daughters.

When the daughters of the sorrowful couple were taken from them, the trickster god Susanowo appeared. Actually, he'd just been banished from Takamagahara for causing trouble there and was looking for a new place. Even the heart of a god as troublesome as Susanowo was enraged at what Orochi was doing.

Myth and Metaphor

Many of the characters from the *Naruto* story are taken from Japanese Shinto mythology. In *Naruto*, the character Orochimaru's rival is a ninja named Jiraiya. There is a character named Orochimaru in Shinto myth who murdered his teacher, Jiraiya, with snake magic. The mythological Orochimaru is said to have learned his magic from the evil Yamata-no-Orochi.

Susanowo prepared eight giant jugs of *sake* and disguised them to look like women. When Orochi arrived, in his arrogant haste he gobbled up the eight jugs of sake without question (thinking he was devouring the virgin sacrifices he'd demanded). Soon enough, the giant snake-dragon's eight heads were all extremely drunk and Susanowo sprang into action. With his mighty katana, he severed all eight of Orochi's heads, saving the daughters of Izumo, including the beautiful Kushiinada-*Hime*. Susanowo and Kushiinada are said to have married.

Immortal Words

Hime is the Japanese word/title for princess, and is often followed by the honorific title of -Sama when one is addressing said princess. In Japanese, there are three primary titles by which people are addressed: -Kun/-Chan, used to address a boy/girl; -San, used to address most people, and means something similar to Mister/Miss in English; and -Sama, which is used to address a person of honor, superior rank, higher status, or greater age.

Fairies

The word *fairy* comes from an older word, *fays*, that is no longer in use. Some think that the word may have been an anglicized form for the Three Fates of Greek and Roman myths, and eventually came to mean female spirits that guided the destinies of men (however, this has never been 100 percent confirmed). Eventually, the concept of fairies found its way into the myths of the Celts, Anglos, Saxons, and Scandinavians.

Fairies are often portrayed as winged beings. Depending on the culture, they vary in size from as large as a human to a few feet high to as small as an insect. The appearance is also dependent on what type of fairy it is. There are two main types of fairies—domestic and wild. Domestic fairies are often kinder and involve themselves in the affairs of humans. Wild fairies, however, are far more dangerous and will harm or kill any human who tries to interfere with them.

Fairies from these two main types are further divided into elemental subtypes—air, subterranean, and water. Air fairies are sprites that live in the mist, clouds, and air. They are often invisible to human eyes. Subterranean fairies are sprites of the earth and stone. When swamp or bog gas would ignite upon reaching the surface, this was often called a *fairy fire*, and was attributed to subterranean fairies. Water fairies have their domain in lakes, rivers, streams, the sea, and just about any other body of water. They are often portrayed as very beautiful. These fairies are often the saviors of sailors and fisherman who are lost or in peril on the water.

Gnomes (European)

Gnomes are often misclassified. Understand, however, that gnomes are *not* fairies. Gnomes actually have more in common with the concept of the *homunculus* (see Chapter 18) than with fairies. They were a large part of the elemental sciences that later gave rise to the practice of alchemy. Gnomes, basically, are Earth elementals and are therefore often portrayed as dwarves that live underground. However, the truth is that gnomes are able to move through Earth as easily as humans move through air. Also, unlike fairies, gnomes are often portrayed as male.

> **Myth and Metaphor**
>
> To this day, it is common to see garden gnomes in people's yards. These pointy-hat-wearing statues were originally meant to attract real gnomes, who were thought to protect one's garden and nourish the surrounding soil with minerals. Today, however, a gnome statue is not viewed as anything more mythically motivated than is a plastic pink flamingo.

A second association can be made to alchemy regarding gnomes, because one of the earliest written records telling of them comes from the legendary alchemist Paracelsus (see Chapter 18) who also wrote of the *homunculus*. The function of gnomes, according to Paracelsus, is to protect the subterranean elements and other treasures that are kept within the earth.

The Bane of Travelers (Welsh)

Fairies, especially wild ones, are not always good to have around. The Gwyllion are a perfect example of this. In Wales, it is said that the Gwyllion are an evil race of fairies that have haunted the mountain regions of the country for thousands of years. The faces of these female fairies are gruesome and deformed. They are the enemies of travelers, and often create illusions and other such tricks to confuse, mislead, or harm them.

Because the Gwyllion have an aversion to the element of iron, it was said that they can be frightened away by drawing an iron knife in front of them. Perhaps in a reference to pagan or malevolent figures (the mammal most commonly associated with evil is the goat), the Gwyllion are the friends of the goats. As a result, whenever they choose to shape-shift it is often into the form of a goat. If a Gwyllion visits one's house (which they will normally only do during violent storms), it is suggested that they be greeted with the utmost hospitality and generosity. Otherwise, one might incur the visiting Gwyllion's anger and wrath. This is a problem that, trust me, you *really* do *not* want.

Little Brown Men (Celtic)

Although brownies are one of the most widely used beings in all of Celtic myth, they are more commonly seen in the tales of Scotland. As with gnomes, brownies are often portrayed as male in gender. Unlike gnomes, however, brownies are thought of as a race of earth-elemental fairies. Also, of all fairy types, the way brownies look is very well established and fairly consistent from one myth to the next. Brownies look like *very* small men, between one and three feet in height. Their clothing is usually rather tattered and brown in color, sometimes made from the skins of mice or rats. Their faces are also brown and almost completely covered with bushy hair.

Avoiding the Labyrinth

Brownies were brought to the attention of mainstream pop culture by director Ron Howard's 1988 fantasy adventure film *Willow*. The portrayal of brownies in this film is impressively accurate. However, the size of the brownies was reduced to serve the movement of and provide comic relief for the story.

Brownies are nocturnal fairies, doing almost all their work under the cover of night. The main purpose of brownies, you see, is to complete work that was left unfinished by peasants and/or servants at the end of the day. This is considered a kind of symbiotic arrangement. Brownies often take charge of helping out in whatever farm or home they choose to reside in. A brownie's choice of home often has to do with the residents. For some reason, brownies will usually be attracted to one particular member of a household. As a result of this, on top of helping to finish work, brownies will often also see to the protection of this family member.

War of the Fairies and Pixies (English)

Pixies (also called piskies or pigsies) are winged fairylike creatures that always dress in green. They always have red hair and pointed ears. Also, they are said not to be quite as beautiful as fairies. This is not to say that they are ugly, however. Compared to humans, they are quite fair-faced. Pixies also have total control over their size. They have been known to change their sizes from human-size down to too small for human eyes to see.

Pixies are good friends with the brownies and sometimes help them in their tasks. As with the Gwyllion, however, pixies enjoy misleading travelers. However, they are more mischievous than malevolent (as are the Gwyllion) in this activity. In fact, pixies are very good pranksters who enjoy having a laugh at human expense every now and then.

Avoiding the Labyrinth

In J. M. Barrie's work *Peter Pan*, the character Tinkerbell is a pixie. Often, she is misidentified as a fairy. However, if this was the case, then Tink would have used fairydust to allow the children to fly, instead of pixiedust.

Pixies also have a sense of moral justice. Although they might play a trick or two on a human who accidentally passes into their territory, they rarely cause them harm. However, a person of evil intentions or dark heart who treads past the borders of Pixyland should pray for mercy and deliverance from whatever god will listen, for the pixies are wrathful against men of evil. Few men of dark heart escape the realm of the pixies unharmed (or, sometimes, alive).

At some point, according to fairy lore, a war broke out between the pixies and the fairies. This war appears to have been fought over domain or territory. The pixies are said to have been the victors, pushing back the fairies as far east as the Parrett River. When the war ended, this river became the border between the two fairy races. Everything west of the Parrett River is now called Pixyland, while everything east of the river is the last domain of fairies, a place now called Fairyland.

The Least You Need to Know

◆ Western dragons are destructive, while Eastern dragons are commonly creative.

◆ Yamata-no-Orochi, the eight-headed snake-dragon of Japan, is one of very few evil dragons in Asian mythology.

◆ Gnomes are elementals, and have nothing to do with Fairies.

◆ The Brownies and the Pixies are friends, but the Pixies and the Fairies are mortal enemies.

Chapter 18

Cursed Humans and Man-Made Abominations

In This Chapter

- ◆ The transformation of humans into monsters by the curses of the gods
- ◆ The creatures and abominations created by the intellectual follies of Man
- ◆ The infamous cursed anti-heroes of mythology
- ◆ The fate of the damned in mythology

Human beings are often the creators of their own monsters. Whether by actions that cause them to be cursed or by misguided intellectual ambition, humans sometimes cross the boundaries of safety. This trespass into the territories of the gods can lead to the creation of frightening abominations. These characters of mythology stand as tragic examples of what can happen when human beings commit transgressions and/or trespass against the gods.

The Gorgon (Greek)

The gorgon was originally portrayed as a single monstrous creature in Attic mythology of the Greeks. Usually, it is serpentlike in appearance. According to the Attic version, the gorgon is a gigantic and terrible being created by Gaea as an aid to the *gigantes* during the war between them and the gods. However, during the battle, Athena comes forth and slays the gorgon. The goddess of wisdom takes the head of the gorgon and places it on her own shield.

Immortal Words

Gigantes are a race of giants in Greek mythology that sprung up from the earth (Gaea) when the blood of Uranus fell upon her. The gigantes are said to have been enormous beings with serpents for feet. In an act of revenge for the death of Uranus, Gaea had the gigantes attack the Olympian gods. She made the giants invincible with a special herb that protected them from the gods. The only way for them to be destroyed was with the help of a mortal. In most myths, the last of the gigantes were defeated when the Olympians were aided by Herakles.

Immortal Words

In Greek myth, an **aegis** is a part of clothing from Zeus and/or Athena. This item symbolizes magical power. The aegis is meant to provide protection to the wearer and, when shaken, it is said that an aegis has the power to send one's enemies running away in fear.

As a result of the alterations from the transition of the Attic version to the Greek, the myths surrounding the gorgon are often confusing, as they frequently use contradicting details from both. Homer also claims that the gorgon was a single creature of Hades. However, Zeus (or, in some versions, it is still slain by Athena) killed it and wore the monster's carcass (or head and skin, in some versions) over his left shoulder as an *aegis* or as a part of it. In early depictions of Zeus, the snake-riddled head of the gorgon is often seen dangling from his aegis.

Three Terrible Sisters

As time passed, and the gorgon myth became adopted by the whole of Greece, the nature of the creature was subsequently altered. The gorgon came to be portrayed as three gruesomely hideous sisters, known as Euryale (Wide-Springer), Medusa (the Queen), and Stheno (Mighty). Among the three sisters, Medusa alone is said to be mortal. Commonly, the gorgon sisters continued to be portrayed as serpentine in appearance. The hair of a gorgon is often depicted as a mess of writhing snakes. Such depictions are common elements of *Gorgoneion* art.

> ### Immortal Words
>
> A **Gorgoneion** is a portrayal of the head of a gorgon that often adorned city walls, the shields or breastplates of warriors, and/or special amulets/necklaces. These were often used for protection against harm or evil. When worn in amulet form, a Gorgoneion is believed to have been used as a talisman against the "evil eye." This makes sense, considering the paralyzing power attributed to the eyes of the gorgon.

These three gorgons are said to be the daughters of Phorcys and Ceto. They have wings of gold, claws of bronze, and piercing eyes that have the power to paralyze anyone who dares look into them. In later versions, the eyes of the gorgon are said to actually turn the bodies of men into stone.

As the Greek version of this myth progressed, the hideousness of the gorgon sisters was diminished. In later myths, they are portrayed as beautiful but fatal seductresses like the Sirens.

The Fate of Medusa

The most well-known gorgon sister is Medusa, who is slain by the hero Perseus. As a matter of fact, when later myths tell of "the gorgon," they are referring specifically to Medusa. As a result of this, it is a common misconception that Medusa is the only gorgon.

On a quest assigned to him by the wicked Polydectes, Perseus uses the head of the gorgon to rescue the beautiful princess Andromeda from her fate as a sacrifice to sea monster Titan (in some versions, the Titan is named specifically as the "Kraken"). Before obtaining the head of one of the gorgons, however, Perseus had to find them.

Under the advisement of Athena and Hermes, Perseus first goes to the three wicked sisters known as the *Graeae*. These three witches share a single eye and tooth between them. To locate the nymphs, Perseus steals their eye and tooth and then uses these to extort the Graeae for information on where to find certain nymphs who know the whereabouts of the gorgon sisters. Unable to see or eat without their precious tooth and eye, the Graeae divulge the whereabouts of the nymphs to Perseus. The hero then travels to see the nymphs, who tell him of the gorgon Medusa's mortality and where the gorgon may be found.

> **Myth and Metaphor**
>
> Metaphorically, the gorgon(s) is thought to be a personification of and metaphor for the human nightmare. This theory is based on the idea that the fear one feels in a dream can have a paralytic effect that is very similar to the paralyzing power of the face, head, and/or eyes of a gorgon.

Because Perseus is a son of Zeus, he receives quite a bit of help from both the nymphs and the gods. Before Perseus sets out to kill Medusa, the nymphs bestow upon him Hades' cap of darkness, which renders the wearer invisible; a pair of winged shoes, which give him inhuman speed; and a special wallet/pouchlike item in which to store Medusa's severed head, which is referred to as the *kibisis*. From Hermes, Perseus receives a sickle forged out of a mythic and unbreakable metal called adamantine. The goddess Athena gives the hero a special mirror (or, in some versions, she loans him her shield).

The Face That Felled a Titan

Armed with the special items bestowed upon him, Perseus sneaks up on the gorgon sisters. He avoids their paralyzing gazes and/or being turned to stone by walking backward and looking at the gorgon through the reflection in the mirror (or Athena's shield). He then locates Medusa, the only mortal gorgon, and cuts off her head with the adamantine sickle. As soon as he has accomplished this task, Perseus places Medusa's head in the kibisis and dons the cap of darkness before darting off with his winged shoes of swiftness. Talk about a dramatic getaway plan!

> **Avoiding the Labyrinth**
>
> In the early 1980s, a film was made that portrayed the myth of Perseus called *The Clash of the Titans*. Although it was, perhaps, entertaining, this film is an extremely inaccurate interpretation of the actual myth of Perseus and Andromeda, and should in no way be used as a resource for mythological analysis.

On his way home, Perseus passes through the land of Ethiopia and sees the beautiful princess Andromeda chained to a rock. The Kraken arises from the ocean depths and advances toward the sacrificial girl. Before he reaches her, however, Perseus draws the head of Medusa from the kibisis and holds it before the Kraken, turning the Titan to stone. Later, he returns the special items given to him by the Hermes, Athena, and the nymphs. Perseus also presents the head of Medusa to Athena as a gift for her to use as an aegis for her shield.

Talos the Colossus (Greek)

Hephaestus, the Greek god of the forge and blacksmith of the Olympians, created the bronze giant called Talos (sometimes spelled Talus). Zeus commissioned this creation from Hephaestus as a gift for his lover Europa. The giant automaton was to serve as her personal bodyguard, and was brought to her home island of Crete.

Talos diligently patrolled the island of Crete, circling the whole of its shores three times a day. Any unauthorized vessels or invading forces that came close to the shores of Crete are driven back by this colossal guardian, who throws enormous boulders at them.

The destruction of Talos came when he tried to prevent Jason and the Argonauts from leaving the island of Crete (in some versions, Talos prevents the Argonauts from landing on Crete). Aided by the magic of Medea, they are able to defeat him. You see, Hephaestus had created Talos with only one weakness. All the blood in the creature was held in by a nail-like plug in his ankle.

Avoiding the Labyrinth

Though commonly Talos is said to have been a creation of Hephaestus, there are other versions of the myth. In some versions, Talos is said to be a giant bronze bull. In other versions, he isn't a creation of Hephaestus but the last member of a race of bronze giants. Also, in some versions of the myth, Talos is not created as the bodyguard to Europa, but is a gift to King Minos of Crete meant to act as a protector to the island.

In some myths, Medea tells Jason of this flaw in Talos' design and he pulls the nail out with the assistance of the other Argonauts. In other versions, Medea uses her magic to drive the giant mad, giving the Argonauts an opportunity to remove the nail. In still other versions, the ankle nail is dislodged by an arrow from the bow of Herakles.

Crossing Into God's Territory (European)

Homunculus is a Latin term meaning "little human." Although there are a number of accepted definitions of this word, here it is used to refer to one of the most bold and frightening pursuits of medieval alchemists. One of the earliest, if not the first, mentions of a homunculus in *alchemy* is found in the writings of Paracelsus. In his writings, he claimed to have successfully created a miniature human being that stood about a foot tall. In his writings, the brilliant (or mad?) alchemist called this creature a homunculus.

Immortal Words

Alchemy is a primitive school of chemistry that was the predecessor of modern science. Unlike its modern counterpart, however, alchemy was far more speculative in nature. Alchemy often mixed religious or supernatural beliefs with science. The most common pursuit of medieval alchemists was turning lead or other common metals into gold. Failure to accomplish this feat likely led to the alchemy-specific myth of an item called the "Philosopher's Stone." According to legend, this stone would allow the possessor to transfigure any metal into gold, among other things.

Also, Paracelsus wrote down a detailed explanation of the process he used to create his own homunculus. However, he appears to have left out the specific details of key steps in the instructions, supposedly to prevent others from attempting the endeavor. The ingredients for Paracelsus' process included wheat, wine, blood, human bones, hair, and pieces of flesh. Also, if one wished the homunculus to have the traits of a certain animal, then the hair of that animal would be used in place of human hair. This alternative process created a type of hybrid homunculus.

Myth and Metaphor

It is possible that the writings of Paracelsus influenced Mary Shelley in her creation of the literary work *Frankenstein*. Seeing as how there is strong evidence to support that both her father and husband were quite familiar with Paracelsus' alchemical writings, it is not unlikely that she would have been aware of them as well.

Paracelsus' explanation is not the only known recorded process for creating a homunculus. Another method involves the use of a mandrake root. This method likely originated from the misguided belief that the mandrake root only grew in places where the semen of dying or hanged men had dropped to the soil. This homunculus process is also far more supernatural than scientific. For example, this version for creating a homunculus requires that the mandrake root be picked on a Friday morning. Also, the picking of the root must be done by a black dog. After this, the root must be washed and then fed with milk and/or honey. Sometimes, the mandrake homunculus process calls for human blood in place of or in addition to the use of milk and honey.

Although the creation of the homunculus may have been seen as a great accomplishment by alchemists, it was seen as an abominable act by the church and others. To create a life without a union between Man and Woman, it was reasoned, was an attempt to do that which was reserved solely for God. Such a thing was blasphemous and could only result in monstrosity, they believed. As a result, in the late seventeenth century, Thomas Browne denounced the claims of Paracelsus in his work *Religio Medici*.

Myth and Metaphor

In recent years, the myth of the mandrake root homunculus has been portrayed in cinema via the miracle of modern CGI. For example, in director Guillermo del Toro's film *Pan's Labyrinth*, his young heroine uses the mixture of milk, blood, and a mandrake root to create a homunculus that heals her ailing pregnant mother.

From Men to Monsters (Japanese)

The Oni are large, cannibalistic demons from the mythology of Japan. Although some Oni are born as such, humans could also be transformed into these monstrous creatures. For example, you may remember the tale of the Oni named Shuten Doji from Chapter 11. Originally, he was a human. Considering accounts such as this, it would seem that any human who becomes consumed by bloodlust has the potential to become an Oni.

Myth and Metaphor

The Oni demons are, metaphorically and literally speaking, debauchery incarnate, the personification of the most savage parts of human nature. Oni eat people by the dozens, and their appetites are voracious. They rape women and prefer to defile the most chaste of virgins. They have even been known to deflower nuns on rare occasions. These demons have murderous natures, killing women and even children without hesitation. Also, their vaults swell with spoils taken from robbing and raiding villages.

In Japanese mythology, there is a multitude of stories with accounts of the Oni in them. Depictions of these demonic creatures vary from one tale to the next. One absolute about the Oni is that they have fangs, though these are sometimes feline and other times wider and more tusklike. They almost always have horns protruding from the foreheads above their hideous faces, which are often shown to have noses that resemble a pig's. Commonly, Oni are said to have either red or blue skin. More often than not, they are rather hairy and animal-like in appearance. Sometimes they have hoofed and somewhat piglike feet and/or hands. The clothing of an Oni is usually made up of animal skins (sometimes their clothing is even made of human skin).

Though sometimes an Oni may wield a sword, they are more popularly depicted with rather barbaric instruments of death, such as large clubs or a spiked, macelike weapon known as the kanobo.

The Exile of Cain (Judeo-Christian/Muslim)

Cain is the firstborn son of Adam and Eve, as well as the older brother of Abel. In Judaic myth, Cain is the first person to take a human life. When Abel's offerings are favored by YHVH over Cain's, the older sibling goes into a rage. He attacks his younger brother Abel and kills him. As a result of his *fratricidal* act, Cain is cast into exile and forced to wander the wasteland known as Nod.

> **Immortal Words**
>
> Fratricide is the murder of one's brother or sibling.

In the Muslim version of the myth, both Cain and Abel were born with twin sisters. When they come of age, Adam decides to marry each brother to the other's twin sister. However, Cain's sister is far more attractive than Abel's. Angered that he would be forced to marry the less attractive of the two sisters, Cain begins throwing stones at Abel. Eventually, he hits his younger brother in a spot that causes fatal injury.

Murder or Tragic Accident?

Cain is unsure what to do with Abel's body, until he sees two ravens quarrelling. Afterward, the victor raven scrapes a trench in the earth to bury his defeated opponent. This inspires Cain to do the same, and he buries Abel's body in the earth. YHVH is said to have put a curse on the earth for allowing Abel's body to be buried within it. YHVH then exiles Cain along with his twin sister to the Land of Nod.

> **Myth and Metaphor**
>
> There is some uncertainty as to why YHVH favored Abel's offerings while rejecting Cain's. One of the most commonly accepted theories is that Abel's sacrifice is an animal and therefore a blood sacrifice, making it more appropriately sacrificial. Cain's sacrifice, on the other hand, is one of grain. However, there is one fact that is extremely contradictory to this theory. If the blood of Abel's sacrifices makes the earth fertile, then why is it said that the land becomes infertile to the hands of Cain when he spills Abel's blood on it?

Although at first glance one might view Cain as evil, there are those who do not see him in this way. Some reason that, because no human being had yet to kill or be killed, there was no way Cain could have known that murder was possible. Therefore, there are some who view Cain's killing of Abel as a tragic accident and not as an act of intentional fratricide. In fact, Cain verbally expresses his guilt and remorse for what he has done. As a result, some versions say that YHVH marks Cain to protect him from those who might do him harm because of his curse and exile.

The Mark of Cain

The nature of Cain's mark is a matter of some debate, as there are a number of different schools of thought and the myth does not offer any specifics regarding its function or appearance. Also, it is unclear if the mark of Cain is meant to serve as a warning to those who might harm him or if it actively protects him from harm. Since Cain came to be associated with a tribe known as the Kenites, who are believed to have worn some unique mark on their bodies, this may be the origin of this part of the myth. Some believe that the story of Cain is an *allegory* for the fall of a somewhat primitive Hebrew tribe referred to as the Kenites.

Immortal Words _____

An **allegory** is a story, legend, or myth that is a symbolical representation of a concept, situation, archetype, or idea.

After his exile, Cain is said to have created the first city of humankind and birthed a tribe of his own (Kenites) with his twin sister. Yet again, this detail contradicts the earlier half of the myth, which states that Cain's curse for killing Abel is to wander the earth for the rest of his days. His children/subjects were said to be an evil people who created a number of inventions and concepts that further served to destroy the already dwindling freedom of humankind—walls, boundaries, property/land ownership, measurements, and laws. Such evil inventions, it is said, brought about the destruction of human freedom which to this day has not been restored.

Myth and Metaphor _____

A mythological comparison can be made of the myth of Cain and Abel to that of Romulus and Remus, the founders of the city of Rome (see Chapter 10). In both stories, the tale consists of the building of the first city, with one brother murdering the other before its completion.

The Vampire Misconception of the Cain Myth

As a result of the blood aspects of the myth, Cain has come to be regarded in pop culture and by vampire enthusiasts as a kind of vampire patriarch. However, there is no substantial or factual evidence to support this theory. The main reason for this misconception comes from the mistaken assumption that the mark of Cain (meant to protect him from retribution) was in fact a curse of immortality.

 Avoiding the Labyrinth

In some obscure Judaic versions of the myth, Cain is not the son of Adam and Eve, but of Lilith (see Chapter 12) and Adam. In some versions, the father of Cain is said to have been the angelic Lucifer (before his fall from grace after the war in Heaven) or the demon Sammael.

Cain eventually meets his end at the hands of his descendent Lamech, the son of Methushael. Methushael is Cain's great-great grandson, suggesting that the son of Adam lived for as long as 300 years. Some see this as further support for the vampire aspects of the tale. However, many other characters of Old Testament myths lived for hundreds of years. As a result, one cannot associate Cain with vampires without doing so with every other character of the Old Testament who had an unusually long lifespan.

The Least You Need to Know

- The gorgon evolved from a single creature into three sisters, who were then changed from hideous murderesses to beautiful seductresses over time.

- A homunculus can refer to many things, but in mythology it refers to a small living creature created through the use of alchemy.

- Oni are often human at first, but are transformed into demonic creatures as punishment for their murderous natures.

- Cain is often misperceived as a murderous brother, when in fact he may have been the victim of a tragic accident of ignorance.

- Cain is not and was not a vampire patriarch, and such perceptions are based on extreme assumptions. There is no evidence to support this belief.

Chapter 19

Shape-Shifters

In This Chapter

- The difference between therianthropy and lycanthropy
- The myth of Lycoan and its connection to the werewolf myth
- The evolution of the perception of the werewolf myth in modern society
- The shape-shifters of Japan
- The serpent/snake shape-shifters of ancient and modern mythologies from across the globe

Sometimes, shape-shifters in myth serve as a personification of the human fear that people may not be who or what they appear to be. This fear further stems from the possibility that what lies beneath the illusion, when revealed, will turn out to be dark, gruesome, and/or deadly. Sometimes, such as in the case of the werewolf, a shape-shifter represents the human fear of our more beastly and savage origins. The werewolf is a regression toward an animal state, somewhat representative of a human de-evolution into unchecked animal savagery. What's worse, a werewolf attacks his own kind (humans), further revealing another human fear of a reversion to cannibalism. In any case, humans who have acquired the traits, appearances, and/or abilities of animals are not only considered powerful … they are often portrayed as a danger to the rest of the human race.

Therianthropy vs. Lycanthropy

The term therianthropy comes from the Greek words *therion* (wild animal) and *anthropos* (man), and refers to the state where a human has the ability to transform into the shape of an animal ... *any* animal. As a result, all animal shape-shifters (including werewolves) fall into this category. Although lycanthropy is a type of therianthropy, therianthropy is not restricted solely to lycanthropes.

The term lycanthropy comes from the Greek words *lykoi* (wolf) and *anthropos* (man), and refers to the state where a human has the ability to transform into a wolf. However, this change can be whole or partial. This means that a lycanthrope may either change into a wolf, or assume a shape in between. The hybrid state of a half-man, half-wolf has become the most commonly accepted depiction of a lycanthrope, or werewolf.

Aside from the myths discussed in the following section on werewolves, all animal shape-shifters discussed in this chapter fall under the label of therianthropes.

The Curse of Lycoan

In this myth, Lycoan is a king over the early race of men (in some versions, he is said to be a king of ancient Arcadia). Arrogant and drunk with power, however, Lycoan began to refuse the gods of the respect due to them. Eventually the blasphemy of this king of early humans exceeds the tolerance level of the Olympians. When he finally commits an act of inhuman savagery toward Zeus, the God of Thunder punishes Lycoan by transforming him into a wolf.

Avoiding the Labyrinth _____

The name Lycoan (also spelled Lykoan, Laocan, or Lycan) is often mistakenly thought to be the origin of the term lycanthropy, which refers to the state of a human who transforms into a wolf (commonly called a werewolf). Although the Lycoan myth does relate to werewolves, the term lycanthropy comes from the Greek words *lykoi* (wolf) and *anthropos* (man). His name does, however, survive in the classification of the grey eastern timberwolf species, called *canis lupius lycoan*.

In the version provided by Ovid, when word reaches Zeus' ears of the wicked atrocities being committed on Earth, he comes down from Olympus and assumes the form of a man. Zeus' tour of creation eventually leads him to the land of Arcadia, ruled by the savage King Lycoan. When there, the thunder god reveals his true form to the Arcadians. All begin to worship and pay homage to Zeus. Lycoan, however, doubts Zeus' power and schemes against the god. Feigning hospitality, King Lycoan invites Zeus to a feast (with the intentions of slitting the god's throat that night as he sleeps).

Avoiding the Labyrinth

Most versions of the Lycoan myth state that Zeus transformed the cruel king of men into a large wolf. However, many images depict the myth during the middle of Lycoan's transformation. As a result, such depictions show Lycoan as a man with a wolf's head or in some other half-man, half-wolf state. It is not impossible that such depictions have influenced the now common portrayal of the man-wolf hybrid we call a werewolf.

Recently, Lycoan had taken a hostage from the Molossians. He slits the captive man's throat and cooks his flesh. When Zeus sits down at the banquet table, Lycoan presents him with a plate of cooked human flesh. Zeus, in his divine insight, knows the truth of what is before him and is disgusted by what Lycoan has done. In his anger, Zeus brings the entire house of Lycoan crashing down. All inside perish. Lycoan escapes the falling rubble, but not Zeus' wrath. As he runs, grey hair sprouts up all over his skin and he transforms into a large wolf (in some versions, he becomes half-man, half-wolf).

The Modern Werewolf

Similar to perception of the myths of vampires and zombies (see Chapter 20), the perception of werewolves has evolved from one of superstition to one of science. The werewolf was originally portrayed as a supernatural creature, often said to be cursed with an affliction that caused him to involuntarily transform into a beast on the night of a full moon. Because silver was thought to have magical powers and/or purifying qualities, a lycanthrope was believed vulnerable to weapons made from this rare metal. Later, after the widespread introduction of firearms in the West, the previous belief in the weaponization of silver gave rise to the legend that a silver bullet was the only way to kill a werewolf.

Modern depictions of werewolves by movies and fiction have evolved to offer scientific explanations for the condition of lycanthropy. As the shadow of the supernatural world is increasingly brought into the light of reality, the myth had to be changed to retain some sense of believability. The "boogie man" of the common era is not the result of a curse … but of a virus. As with vampirism, the lycanthropy condition is said to be passed through blood or by a bite. This means that lycanthropy mimics the behavior of viral microorganisms. Therefore, to the modern mind, it makes more sense to think of lycanthropy as the cause of a viral infection than as some kind of mystical curse.

The Monster Kitty

Bakeneko begins as a cat, not as a human as do werewolves. However, when fed too much or for a certain amount of time, a Bakeneko will first become unusually large. Soon after, the animal will display abilities of magic or shape-shifting. In Japanese culture, cats were closely associated with the concept of death. Therefore, perhaps it should be of no surprise that many of the myths surrounding the "monster cat" Bakeneko, one of the *bakemono,* do not end well.

Immortal Words

Bakemono is a Japanese term that refers to spirits or monsters with supernatural powers. Bakemono can be a blessing or a curse, depending on their dispositions and moods when encountered. They are often skilled deceivers, and many of them are known to eat humans.

One of the most famous stories of an evil Bakeneko tells of a poor gentleman by the name of Takasu Genbei. Takasu kept a cat in his home, as many did, to keep rodents out. One day, however, his cat goes missing. Shortly after this, Takasu begins to notice that the behavior of his mother has become rather odd. She rarely speaks, refuses to have company, and always takes her meals in private, eating only in her room.

Suspicious of this sudden change in his mother, Takasu decides to spy on her during one of her evening meals. As he peeps in on her, what he sees gives him a terrible shock. Sitting there gnawing on the carcasses of dead rats is a giant cat wearing his mother's kimono! Now certain that he has a Bakeneko in his home, Takasu takes up his sword. Sadly, he has no choice but to slay the creature as it attempts to fool him by transforming back into his mother. A day after the monster is killed, it returns to its original form as a normal housecat.

Takasu now wishes to know what has become of his mother, who he now realizes has been missing for as long as the cat has been thought gone. With trembling hands, he tears up the *tatami* mats of his mother's room. His heart breaks when he discovers her skeletal remains beneath them. The Bakeneko had eaten every bit of her flesh, leaving nothing behind but bones.

The Raccoon Dog

The Tanuki was a "raccoon dog" spirit in Japanese mythology, often related to the Kitsune (see Chapter 16). Often, the Tanuki is depicted as standing upright. He is potbellied, with masklike markings on his face similar to those of raccoons (hence the name). As with many of the bakemono in Japanese mythology, Tanuki are born tricksters and love to stir up a little harmless mischief. However, unlike the Bakeneko, they are usually kind and bring good fortune to those they come across (as long as you do not try to bring them harm).

One myth about the Tanuki begins at the temple of a Shinto priest on a mountain in Japan. This priest loves the *chanoyu* and his favorite pastime is to repair and restore old tea kettles. One day, while at a nearby town, the priest buys an old rusty tea kettle from an alleyway kettle shop. He brings the kettle back to the temple, scrubs away the rust, and gives it a shining polish.

Immortal Words

Literally translated, **chanoyu** means "hot water for tea." However, the term has evolved to refer to the very ritualistic practice of the Japanese tea ceremony. The tea ceremony is perhaps one of the most venerated traditions in Japanese culture, and the ability to perform the ritual is viewed as a pursuit of perfection. The chanoyu, when performed for someone else, is considered the highest form of honor and etiquette in Japanese culture.

The Tanuki and the Tile-Maker

The next day, the priest brings the kettle before his pupils and sets it upon a nearby stove for the midday tea. Soon, the kettle begins to shake and spin, shouting out as if in pain *"Ittai,"* which is Japanese for "Ouch!" Suddenly the kettle sprouts arms and legs, and a raccoonlike face appears from it. Everyone in the room recognizes it as a Tanuki.

The priest, believing the tea kettle must be cursed, decides it should be taken out of the temple. He walks the kettle away from the temple. When he reaches the road, he comes across a tile-maker. He offers the kettle to the tile-maker as a gift, making no mention of the strange things that happened with the kettle before. The tile-maker graciously accepts the kettle and takes it home.

When his day is over, the tile-maker places the kettle on his stove. As before, the kettle jumps and shouts. The man begins to cry out in fear when the Tanuki speaks to him, saying, "Take me off this fire and I'll make a deal with you!" The man obliges and Tanuki tells him that he will make him rich as long as he is kind to the creature, cares for him well, and never again puts him on a fire. The man agrees.

The Dancing Tea Kettle

The next day, the tile-maker takes the Tanuki into town. The creature reveals his true form and begins to sing, dance, and perform acrobatics. People crowd around and give money. Day after day, for quite some time, the two go to town and return home with bundles of money. It isn't long before the tile-maker is quite rich, and he uses some of his wealth to buy the Tanuki his favorite rice cakes and to ensure that the creature is well cared for. However, not wishing to be greedy, he offers to return the Tanuki to the temple. The Tanuki says that he would like to go back there, but that there needs to be some conditions.

Avoiding the Labyrinth

In Japan, from the 1600s to early 1900s, a tile-maker's job had nothing to do with floors (which were covered with tatami mats). These tiles, made from clay, were used as covers for roofing homes and other structures. As cities in Japan began to expand in size, a number of devastating fires led to the use of tiles for roofing. Before tiles were used, many homes and structures in Japan used straw or other such flammable materials, which cause a one-house fire to spread from roof to roof extremely quickly. In their search for the right kind of clay, tile-makers often had to travel out from cities.

The tile-maker brings the Tanuki back to the temple and presents it to the monk, explaining that it is an enchanted creature and laying out the details of the conditions he'd been given. The first condition is that the priest is never to put him on the stove again. Second, the Tanuki is to be fed his favorite rice cakes. Third, he is always to be treated kindly and to be well cared for. The priest, realizing his mistake, welcomes the Tanuki into the temple. The creature, returning to tea kettle form, is placed on a table next to a stack of his favorite rice cakes, where he remains to this very day.

People of the Serpent

Perhaps one of the most frightening forms of therianthropy is that of humans who take the shapes and/or traits of serpents. Almost always, snakelike creatures and/or serpent therianthropes are portrayed in mythology as superhumanly powerful (and, more often than not, evil). This depiction could be attributed to the venomous traits and predatory natures of many snakes. Certain snake species are cold-blooded carnivores that feed almost entirely on warm-blooded mammals, so it only makes sense that normal humans would be the prey for these serpentine therianthropes. However, in the East, there are myths of a special race of ancient serpentine beings who lived alongside humans during the long-forgotten centuries of the past.

The Hooded People of the Cobra (Asian)

The Naga exist in a large number of Indian and Asian myths, from India to China to Laos and beyond. These serpentine beings are a common thread among the mythologies of the East. Although some myths state that the Naga could assume an entirely human shape, their ability to shape-shift is more easily attributed to their alleged connections to the divine and the powers that come from this than to the phenomenon of therianthropy.

According to the myth, the Naga are semi-divine beings with the heads (and sometimes torsos) of humans and the bodies of snakes. However, Naga are not necessarily evil but instead have the potential to be of help. If insulted or mistreated by a human, however, they are quick to lash out with lethal power. This dual nature is further confirmed by the fact that the Naga possess both deadly venom as well as an elixir that can heal and/or grant immortality.

When one considers the popular worship of serpents, seen as a symbol of the life force in India, it is of no surprise that they are the most prolific culture when it comes to myths of the Naga. However, these myths are not restricted to Hindu Dharma beliefs. In shrines of both Hinduism and Buddhism, stone images of Naga are placed at the entrances as protective guardians. In Punjab, a northern region of the Indian continent, many of the Gaddi people continue to give interesting offerings to the Naga—bee stingers, male lambs, firstborn male goats, and first-picked fruits.

The Naga live in the bejeweled palaces of their underwater city, called Bhagavati. This city is so enchanted that it is said even the plants that grow there have the power to dance and sing. Naga females, called *Nagini*, are said to be unbelievably beautiful, clever, charming, and finely dressed. In some myths, Nagini have been known to wed mortal males. In fact, a number of noble bloodlines in India claim lineage from the Naga, and the existence of a Nagini within a family tree is considered by them to be of the utmost importance.

Due to the very ancient and widespread existence of the Naga myth, it is extremely difficult to make any definite statements regarding its origins. However, these beings are mentioned in the Hindu Dharma *Vedas* and play an increasingly large role in later Hindu epics such as the *Mahabharata*, in which the serpentine race is destroyed as a result of Janamejaya's sacrifice.

The Reptoids (Modern)

The common occurrence of the half-human, half-serpent figure in mythology has recently given rise to an unusual sub-culture of people who believe in a species of reptilian humanoids, or "reptoids." Very similar to the claims made by alleged victims of UFO abduction, those who believe in reptoids believe that the creatures are among us. Often enough, accounts of reptoid encounters involve the victim being taken away to a ship (UFO). Reptoids are commonly described as having skin or scales that are grey/silver, blue, or green in color. They are bipedal and stand upright, usually described at a height of between 4 feet and 7 feet tall.

As the reptoid hysteria moved into the realm of conspiracy theory, people began to claim that these beings were an extraterrestrial race with the ability to shape-shift. Although some scientists are legitimately researching the possibility that a species of beings such as this could exist, there are those who are more alarmist in their pursuit. The conspiracy theorists of the reptoids are led by a man named David Icke. Icke claims that our world and our species have been under the control of reptilian humanoids for centuries. In fact, he has stated that most figures of political power are reptoids (including George W. Bush and the entire British Royal Family). He's also been known to refer to these beings as Draconians, because he claims that they travelled to our solar system from a faraway star system he calls *Alpha Draconis*.

The motivation behind the alleged Draconian occupation and domination of our planet is simple, claims Icke: we are their food. The reptoids/Draconians feed on fresh human blood. Because, of course, they are large, cold-blooded, carnivorous reptiles, they need mammals of appropriate size on which to feed. We are, according to Icke, the intergalactic equivalent of cattle to the Draconians. This is perhaps one of the most interesting and elaborate myths created in recent years and stems from ancient myths involving serpent/snake archetypes.

A Rooster Worth a Soul (Lithuanian)

Aitvaras are spirits of the household in Lithuanian mythology, and can be a blessing or a curse. An Aitvaras can be hatched from the egg of a seven-year-old rooster (yes, that's right, the male equivalent of a chicken, which does not lay eggs). Another way to acquire an Aitvaras is to buy one. Unfortunately, the only person who sells them is the devil, and the price of an Aitvaras is your immortal soul.

An Aitvaras does not really fall into the category of therianthropy, primarily because it never assumes a human shape. Instead, it begins as a white- or black-feathered rooster with a tail the color of fire (or, according to some, a tail *of* fire). When hatched, an Aitvaras will immediately take up residence in the nearest home. To make matters worse, it will then refuse to leave. However, this may be a blessing in disguise, because after an Aitvaras steps outside the house, it turns into a dragon.

Immortal Words

The origin of the word **Aitvaras** is, strangely enough, completely unknown. No record can be found to explain the roots of this word. In addition, even the meaning of the word is unknown, other than as a title for the creature explained in this section.

Aitvaras should be well cared for, because they have the potential to bring good or bad luck to a household. A mistreated Aitvaras could do quite a bit of damage. However, even an Aitvaras with good intentions can bring troubles to the household. For example, these creatures are skilled thieves who often venture out at night to take things from surrounding homes, and quite often they will bring stolen goods (such as grain, corn, milk, and even gold or coins) to the houses of their owners. This often causes their poor owners to be mistakenly charged with stealing.

If a person is having problems because of an Aitvaras, he or she will find it extremely difficult to get the creature to leave. In fact, one of the only known ways to rid oneself of an Aitvaras is to kill it. Apparently, when in rooster form, an Aitvaras is just as vulnerable as your everyday, run-of-the-mill pheasant.

There is one Lithuanian myth that tells of a young bride who goes to the barn of her mistress every morning to hand-grind grain. Mysteriously, the grain bucket is full every morning, even though no one ever went into the barn. Finally, one night the young bride creeps into the barn and finds a black rooster with a fiery tail, coughing up (or, in some versions, vomiting) grains into the grain bucket by the light of a candle. Thinking that such a thing must be evil, she picks up a large knife and kills the creature.

When the young bride returns to her mistress to tell of what she'd seen and done, the old woman flies into a fit of tears. Apparently, the black rooster was an Aitvaras, and was the source of the woman's entire wealth. Without it, she is left with no means to support herself. The tale ends there, so it is unclear what became of the woman or the young bride.

The Least You Need to Know

- ◆ Lycanthropy is the state of changing from human to wolf or a wolflike shape.

- ◆ Therianthropy is the state of changing from human to any animal or a human-animal hybrid shape.

- ◆ Although the Naga have roots in Asian mythology, they've been loosely used by conspiracy theorists as evidence of the existence of aliens called reptoids or Draconians.

- ◆ An Aitvaras is usually more trouble than it is worth and is probably not worth the price of a soul.

Chapter 20

Vampires, Zombies, and the Undead

In This Chapter

◆ The vampire as metaphor of destructive desires and/or depravity of human beings

◆ The roots and history of the vampire myth

◆ The reason human perceptions of the mythological undead have shifted away from the supernatural

◆ The zombie: voodoo magic or a doomsday "super-virus"?

◆ The viral zombie as a metaphor for the most commonly shared fears of the human race

◆ The undead of world mythology

The undead are a myth that represents all that is worst in human nature and all that we most fear. Vampires, violent and nocturnal, represent the human struggle against succumbing to depravity. They offer immortality and superhuman abilities, but the price for these gifts is damnation to a life of darkness and murder. Zombies are all that is worst in humans, a representation of the savagery from which we evolved. They are driven by the unchecked primary urge of human existence to feed.

Viral zombies (see "The Viral Zombie" section later in this chapter) are also a metaphor for extreme conformity, transforming all they infect into mindless machines that have the same needs, behaviors, and drives. At its foundation, the zombie myth represents a fear of physical decay as well. Not allowing the body to be laid to rest, zombie infection offers a fate that seems, to most humans, worse than death. Vampires and zombies, as well as all undead creatures of myth, represent the instinctive human fear of death and the intellectual fear of being stripped of one's self.

Vampires of the Past

The origins of the vampire myth were supernatural and superstitious in nature. They were demonic beings, capable of changing shape into a wolf or bat, or even turning into mist. They were unholy, damned creatures. Basically, vampires were treated as unclean abominations of the devil that were therefore vulnerable to the holy power of Christianity.

The weapons against a vampire were, in the past, primarily supernatural or religious in nature. For example, the vampires of old could be warded off by strings of garlic (said to have magical properties) or held at bay with a simple cross. Holy water would burn or even kill a vampire, an effect often portrayed as similar to that of hydrochloric acid on human skin. A wooden stake could do the trick, often followed by beheading and/or cremation.

Secondary actions such as burning the body or cutting off its head were performed to prevent resurrection, which some myths claimed was possible. For example, certain older vampire myths claimed that if a vampire's impaled corpse was exposed to the light of the full moon, it would somehow allow the stake to be removed and the body to regenerate. Also, there were even pitfalls in the use of the wooden stake, the "old faithful" of vampire slaying. For example, stakes that were cut from evergreen woods such as pine were said by some myths to have no effect. Such woods, in European superstition, were associated with immortality. Therefore, it only stood to reason that a stake cut from an evergreen wood would not work on a being that was all but immortal itself. Also, a weapon made from silver was effective when used to pierce the heart of a vampire. In some myths, silver would not only kill a vampire but cause it to disintegrate or burst into flames.

In the early days of the vampire myth, especially in Europe, there were also a number of odd rules surrounding how one could detect, and avoid falling victim to, a vampire. For example, it was said that vampires could not enter a residence unless they were invited. They also could not tread on holy ground or enter a church. When a mirror was held before a vampire, no reflection would be cast. Often enough, however, vampires were credited with the actions of mortal men, or as scapegoats to explain away what early science and medicine could not.

Vlad Dracula

Vlad III, also known as Vlad Tepes, Vlad *Dracula*, or Vlad "The Impaler," has been the target of much sensationalism in the evolution of vampire lore. Most believe that this cruel warlord was Bram Stoker's inspiration for his well-known vampire, Count Dracula. However, the real Vlad Tepes was in many ways far more frightening than Stoker's fanged menace.

Immortal Words _____

Dracul/Dracula was a name given to Vlad Tepes III, which can be translated a number of ways. Dracul, the name of Vlad II, means "dragon," when taken with the root word *Drako* of the same meaning. However, in the Romanian language, this name can also be read as "devil" or "demon." Therefore, Vlad III's given name of Dracula has multiple possible readings as well. This name means "Little Dragon" or "Son of the Dragon," but can also be read as "Son of the Devil/Demon." Needless to say, the name was a powerful psychological weapon in the deterrence of possible rivals against the Tepes clan.

Vlad III's father, Vlad II (or Vlad Dracul), lived in forced exile in the region of Wallachia. Vlad III was born sometime during the last two months of the year 1431, the middle sibling of three boys. His older brother was named Mircea. His younger brother, an exceptionally fair-faced young man, was called Radu "The Handsome."

By the time Vlad III was five years old, his father had eliminated all rivals (namely, a group known as the Danesti) and taken the throne of Wallachia, making his sons princes. As a result, the boys were now to be educated accordingly. Vlad began his education in the ways of warfare and administration, and the usual common instruction given to Christian knights of the period.

The Hostage Princes

Unfortunately, Vlad II had few allies on the Christian side of the conflict between Western Christianity and Eastern Islam. As a result, he had to make a number of pacts with the Muslim Sultan. When Vlad III was 13 years old, his father was ordered to send him along with his younger brother Radu to live at the home of the Sultan in Adrianople, Turkey. For all purposes, Vlad and Radu were hostages. This was done to ensure that their father remained loyal to agreements he'd made with the Sultan, as any betrayal by Vlad II would result in his two youngest sons being immediately executed. However, it appears that the boys were treated quite well while living in Turkey.

Avoiding the Labyrinth _____

Though it cannot be concretely confirmed, it is believed that Vlad Tepes was first exposed to the practice of impalement during his time in Turkey. As a boy, Vlad seemed to display an early interest in the ways of warfare, both physical and psychological. Seeing as how impalement was effective for both, it is no surprise that he brought the practice back with him upon his violent and vengeful return to Wallachia.

In 1448, when Vlad III was 17, he was finally released and returned home. Because he had been partially educated in Turkey, Vlad received the Sultan's endorsement as the successor for the throne of Wallachia. Radu chose to remain in Turkey. Radu "The Handsome" was so young when he arrived in Adrianople that he had spent more time there than in Wallachia, and viewed Turkey as his homeland.

A Short Reign

Only two months after Vlad Tepes had returned home to assume the throne of Wallachia, he was the victim of usurpation. Attacked by his fellow Wallachian nobles, called *boyars*, Vlad was quickly dethroned. To make matters worse, he soon caught word that during his absence these same boyars had murdered his father. In a horrible act of cruelty, they also seized his older brother, Mircea, and buried the poor young man alive. Vlad turned to Hungary for help.

In 1456, with the powers of both the Sultan and the Kingdom of Hungary supporting him, Vlad returned to Wallachia with death on his mind, fire in his eyes, and vengeance in his heart. By this time, it appears that Vlad's heart had fallen into darkness, transforming the warrior prince into a cruel warlord who was only happy when his hands were covered in blood.

Vlad's Revenge and Castle Dracula

After he had secured his place on the throne, Vlad Tepes arranged one of the most cunning setups in human history. He sent out notices of amnesty to all the noble families of Wallachia. In addition, these notices informed the families that, to celebrate a newfound period of peace and prosperity, all were invited to a lavish feast and celebration at a small castle near Tirgoviste, Wallachia. Everyone who was anyone was in attendance—and every single one of them would regret it. Vlad Tepes, it would seem, had an excellent memory, and he was not of a forgiving nature.

All who entered the celebration were asked to disarm at the door. This was not an unusual request, of course, especially when one was in the polite company of fellow nobles. Outside, Vlad had a large contingent of his men waiting. Inside, however, were only a few formal guards. As soon as all the noble families had been assembled in the banquet hall, those responsible for the murder of Vlad's father and brother among them, the Lord of Wallachia gave a subtle predetermined signal to his guards. They shut and barred all but one door to the hall. Through the only open door came Vlad's contingent of warriors. Before the surprised boyars knew what hit them, every nobleperson in the banquet hall (men, women, and children) was either Vlad's prisoner or dead.

Now that Vlad had all the boyar nobles at his mercy, he stripped them of all property and forced them to march to the peak of a mountain near the Arges River. Those who were too old, weak, sick, or feeble to make the trip were either executed (most by way of impalement) before their departure or died in transit. Those who actually managed to survive the march may have later wished they had not.

Some of the first and most terrible atrocities for which Vlad Tepes is credited took place during the construction of Castle Dracula. He oversaw the work of his imprisoned former-nobles with torturous vigilance, literally making their lives a living hell. Any who dared oppose him were publicly tortured, impaled, and/or executed in some other gruesome manner. In the end, however, Vlad built his Castle Dracula through the toil, blood, and suffering of his enemies.

He's Called "The Impaler" for a Reason

Vlad Tepes' preferred form of torturous execution was a cruel and gruesome procedure known as impalement. This was a horribly painful way to die that involved impaling a victim's body on a long, sharp wooden pole. Vlad Tapes seemed fond of carrying out this form of execution by having a horse tied to each of the victim's legs, with the business end of an impaling stake pointed in between them. The horses would then pull the poor person into the direction of the sharpened tip. This was not a fast or easy way to die. Death by impalement was slow and excruciatingly painful.

Other, less-elaborate methods of impalement also existed, such as simply stabbing the person in the abdomen or back, then lifting them up until they were suspended by the stake. The blunt opposite end of an impalement stake, after the sharp end had been plunged into the victim's body, would be placed in the earth, allowing gravity to drag the person down the shaft. For those unfortunate enough to still be alive during this part—well, one can only imagine.

Though gruesome, impalement was also a very effective psychological weapon. One could see how a road lined with impaled bodies could be a morale crusher. It is said that an invading Turkish army turned around and went home, abandoning the campaign into Wallachia, where they witnessed thousands of impaled corpses along the banks of the Danube River. Another such incident in which Vlad Tepes used impalement as a psychological deterrent occurred in 1461 when Mohammed II, the famed conqueror of Constantinople, was so sickened by the sight of 20,000 impaled corpses that he marched his army straight back to Constantinople and never again ventured into Wallachia. This incident came to be referred to as the "Forest of the Impaled."

How Vlad Became a Vampire

There could be a number of explanations for why Vlad Tepes became a prominent figure in vampire mythology, all of which are primarily speculative. The most obvious explanation would be to attribute this to Bram Stoker's novel. There is not, however, any evidence to support the idea that Stoker used much historical fact in his work. If anything, Vlad Tepes was little more than a template for the character of Count Dracula.

However, many argue that there are references to Vlad Tepes in correspondence of the period that refer to him as a vampire or at least suggest it, predating Stoker's work. However, this could also have been caused by an error of linguistics. The name Dracula, as you saw earlier, has a number of different meanings. A hastily transcribed letter could have referred to Vlad Dracula as "Vlad the Son of the Devil." Linking a man who is called the "Son of the Devil" to a vampire is not much of a stretch.

Another explanation as to why Vlad Tepes has been connected to the vampire myth has to do with dated correspondence. Letters that were allegedly written by or to Vlad Tepes have some unusual dates, suggesting that the man lived for an unusually long time—such as a couple of centuries. However, this could be written off as an error in dating. Also, names were often passed from noble to heir, as the name Vlad Dracul was passed to Vlad "Dracula" Tepes. It is not impossible that Vlad Tepes had an heir or son who assumed a name similar to his father's, which later led to this misunderstanding.

One explanation for the belief in Vlad's vampirism, perhaps the easiest to swallow, is that Vlad Dracula was known to collect the blood of a recently impaled victim into a chalice and drink it. It is also suspected that Vlad may have been prone to cannibalism, eating the roasted flesh of the recently executed. Anyone who witnessed such practices, considering the superstitions of Romania, would have immediately associated Vlad Dracula with the vampire belief.

Lastly, perhaps Vlad Tepes was transformed into a monster in the minds of the people. After all, how could any human be so cruel, merciless, violent, and bloodthirsty? Perhaps the only way people could wrap their heads around the idea that a man could do something as terrible as impaling 20,000 people and arranging them into a forest of death was to think of him as some kind of inhuman creature. How many people does a man kill before he becomes a monster or devil? Perhaps Vlad Tepes found out.

Peter Plogojowitz: History or Hysteria?

The incredible (and, in a fashion, *true*) tale of Peter Plogojowitz can be seen as one of two things. Either the tale is the first recorded case of vampirism, or it is a record of the most extreme case of mass hysteria in human history. Throughout Europe (and especially in England) in the early 1700s, there was a surge of interest in the subject of vampires. So perhaps it is no surprise that these alleged events, dubbed by some vampire enthusiasts as the "Plogojowitz Incident," took place in 1725.

Avoiding the Labyrinth

The Plogojowitz Incident took place in a village called Kisilova, which is geographically located in Serbia. You may find other translations or accounts that place it elsewhere. A number of past summarizations and translations of the account mistakenly claim that Kisilova is located in Hungary. Most of the time, this mistake is made due to an error of geography or from a general lack of familiarity with the political history of the region. In 1725, this area was in political chaos, with several countries (one being Hungary) claiming it as their own. Such political confusion could also have caused this error.

According to the actual record of what transpired, which was written down and logged by a German official sent to investigate, a villager from Kisilova by the name of Peter Plogojowitz had recently died. However, 10 weeks after his burial, Peter began appearing to people in the night—a total of 10 people, the first of which had been Peter's recently widowed wife. Making things even more suspicious was the fact that 9 of the 10 people who reported seeing Peter died within roughly 24 hours from an unspecified and mysterious illness.

The Vampire Who Wanted His Shoes

The only person said to have received one of Peter's nocturnal visits and *not* died was his wife. She claimed that he had come to their home in the middle of the night and demanded his *opanki* (shoes), which she gave to him. After giving her apparently undead hubby his shoes, and conveying this story to at least some of the other villagers, Mrs. Plogojowitz hastily packed up her things and got the heck out of Dodge. Of course, having the reanimated corpse of one's late spouse show up at your door in the middle of the night asking for his shoes would probably be enough to motivate anyone to move to another village.

Sword and Man _____

Belief in vampires and/or the undead phenomenon became so strong in Northern and Eastern Europe at one point that caskets were constructed by a special design meant to prevent the dead from ever having a chance to rise. The lid was fitted with a sharp stake that, when closed, would impale the heart of the deceased. Some were also equipped with the secondary measure of a sharpened metal blade that fitted to the lid at neck level so that, when closed, the corpse would also be decapitated.

Considering that there was (and, in some of the most rural regions, still *is*) a strong belief in the undead phenomenon in this part of the world, it is no surprise that the villagers were soon convinced they had a vampire in their midst. Peter Plogojowitz, they were certain, was now one of the undead, coming back to those of his home village and preying on them to satiate his unholy appetite. Because the only way to be sure was to check the body for the tell-tale signs of vampirism—the body not having decomposed and showing new growth of the hair, nails, and beard—they decided to dig old Peter up. They then informed the Imperial Official of the neighboring district of Gradisk.

Enter the Bureaucrat

The German Imperial Official pleaded for the villagers to wait until he could get the proper authorization for an exhumation of Peter's corpse from his superiors in Belgrade. The villagers, in what was certainly the most polite way possible, told him to take his authorization and shove it! As far as they were concerned, everyone would likely be *dead* by the time word came back from Belgrade! So he had no choice but to travel to Kisilova to witness the body himself. Just to be safe, the official took the Pope of Gradisk along with him. After all, if this fellow was a vampire, it couldn't hurt to have a holy man on standby.

By the time the Imperial Official arrived in Kisilova, the villagers had just finished digging up Peter Plogojowitz's body. They then began inspecting the corpse for the signs of vampirism previously mentioned.

Peter Gets Staked

According to the official's own record of what he witnessed, the body of Plogojowitz did not have any odor of decomposition. However, the man's nose is said to have collapsed somewhat. His hair and beard showed signs of recent growth. His nails had fallen away, and new ones had grown in their place. His pale-white skin seemed to have peeled away to reveal a new, flush skin underneath.

Observing that Plogojowitz's body was in such a state, the villagers were confirmed in their suspicion that he had become a vampire. So they did what any reasonable person would do—they ran a wooden stake through the guy's heart. According to record, upon being impaled, Plogojowitz let out a horrible shriek. Just to make sure the job was done, the villagers then burned the corpse.

Avoiding the Labyrinth _____

Although this story seems rather incredible, modern science can now rationally explain all the signs Plogojowitz displayed. But what about the shriek Plogojowitz gave out? That, too, can be explained. A dead body accumulates gases in the chest cavity. When suddenly compressed by the entry of the stake, these gases were likely shoved into Plogojowitz's throat, producing a sound similar to a shriek.

Chiang-Shih

The Chiang-Shih means "Hopping Corpse," and is often called the "Chinese vampire." However, this creature has more in common with a zombie than with the traditional Western vampire. Unlike the vampires of Western lore, the Chiang-Shih does not possess any significantly amazing supernatural powers. Also, it does not seem to retain any kind of human intelligence after reanimation. These vampires are said to be the reanimated bodies of people whose souls were unable to ascend after death, often due to the manners of their deaths. Those who committed suicide, for example, were said to be at high risk of becoming a Chiang-Shih.

The reason the Chiang-Shih is called the "Hopping Corpse" is due to the fact that it cannot walk or move very well. As *rigor mortis* sets in, the undead person's limbs become painful and stiff. As a result, they can only hop to reach their victims (however, they are said to be *very* good at doing so). Despite the difficulties caused by rigor mortis, the Chiang-Shih still have a savage sexual appetite and will sexually assault any young woman who happens across their path.

How to Spot a Chiang-Shih

A Chiang-Shih is often depicted with long, sharp, and/or serrated teeth. It has a long, pointed tongue and clawlike fingernails. Sometimes, Chiang-Shih are depicted as having greenish skin (which, in some cases, is said to give off an eerie glow).

These "Hopping Corpse" vampires are somewhat weak and awkward when first resurrected, but the Chiang-Shih grows stronger over time. This increased strength can be measured by looking at how much of the hair has turned white. If all of a Chiang-Shih's hair has turned white, this means it has become quite powerful, and likely now has superhuman strength, the ability to fly, and can shape-shift into a wolf.

The Chiang-Shih vs. Western Vampires

In addition to the ability to change into a wolf, there are some interesting similarities between the Chiang-Shih vampire and the traditional Western vampire. For example, these undead bloodsuckers are also bound by a set of terribly odd rules which can be taken advantage of by an escaping mortal. One such rule states that a Chiang-Shih either cannot or simply will not cross a body of running water. Because the breathing of the living is how Chiang-Shih track their prey, one can become invisible to the monster by simply holding one's breath. Chiang-Shih can also be warded off with garlic, just as with the Western vampire.

Any extremely loud noise can be enough to frighten off a Chiang-Shih, especially if that noise resembles thunder. This works because a few known ways to kill any Chiang-Shih are a direct hit from lightning, a loud clap of thunder, or shooting one with a bullet. A young Chiang-Shih, with little or no white hair, can be held back with a broom and is unable to cross a border made out of iron filings, red peas, and grains of rice. After being killed, however, the body of a Chiang-Shih must be immediately cremated (perhaps to prevent resurrection similar to that of Western vampires).

The Slayer Priests of Taoism

After a Chiang-Shih has been undead long enough to reach the Long White Hair stage, they are very difficult to kill. A village that believed it was being victimized by a powerful Chiang-Shih would often employ the services of a *Taoist* priest, some of whom appear to have been specially trained in the arts of slaying the undead. These priests would first subdue the vampire with small slips of paper which had to be tacked to its forehead, upon which were written magical inscriptions (often written in blood or, more likely, red ink). This paralyzed the Chiang-Shih and rendered all its powers impotent. When subdued, the priest would then use a special bell that forced the vampire to hop his way back to his grave. However, stories don't really specify what the priest did after that to prevent the Chang-Shih from simply coming out once again the following evening.

Immortal Words _____

Tao, pronounced "dow," literally means "the path." This is the Chinese root for the Japanese term *Do*, which also means "path or way." The religion of Taoism is founded in the search for hidden truth and walking a righteous life path. Taoist priests dedicate their lives to the service of good and the combat of evil. As a result, it is not a surprise that they would also seek to combat Chiang-Shih vampires (no matter how crazy it sounds).

Sometimes, however, a Chiang-Shih became too powerful to be subdued by the paper inscriptions. In such a case, the slayer priest would employ the use of a special type of sword. The most interesting type of sword was made from copper coins bound strongly together by red string. The less impressive type was a simple wooden sword. Needless to say, these Taoist priests had an interesting job.

The Modern Vampire Myth

Modern myths have evolved along with common perceptions of the vampire. As superstition fell to the advancements of science and medical technology revealed the mysteries of illness, the vampire myth changed. Most modern stories portray vampirism as a virus, not a kind of demonic possession. Because vampirism passes through a bite or through contact with infected blood, it mimics the behavior of modern viruses of which humans have learned to be terribly fearful—AIDS, for example.

 Avoiding the Labyrinth

One part of the vampire myth that is still a matter of debate is the question of whether vampires can procreate. When they were supernatural, it was believed that they had a sexual appetite but were all but sterile when it came to producing off-spring. However, one interesting and fairly recent addition to the vampire myth is the *Damphir*. A Damphir is the offspring of a vampire and a human, perhaps suggesting that vampires are only unable to procreate with other vampires. Because they are no longer believed to be truly dead, but just an infected person who has mutated into a new form with unusual attributes due to a virus, this idea makes sense (although in a really whacked-out sort of way).

The strengths, abilities, and weaknesses of vampires have been altered. For example, vampires rarely shape-shift in modern depictions. Crosses and holy water are rarely shown to work against vampires anymore. Today's vampire myths commonly retain the belief that vampires cannot bear sunlight, and that it is either harmful or fatal if they are exposed to UV rays. Stakes still work, as does garlic most of the time. The shift of the vampire from demon to virus is an amazing example of how a mythology can (and perhaps *should*) be changed to fit into the scope of common knowledge. Otherwise, the myths can take on a feeling of being somewhat ludicrous and cease to be interesting.

Zombies

Quite commonly, there are two primary zombie types in mythology—voodoo zombies and viral zombies. Voodoo zombies are supernatural, believed to be the resurrected and enslaved corpses of the deceased. They are said to serve the whims of whichever priest raised them from the grave. Viral zombies, however, which are often portrayed in films and pop culture, are the cause of some strange virus. The so-called

Z-virus or *Solanum* virus is often said either to be a man-made experiment gone wrong or to have reached our planet by riding on the back of a meteor (in recent years, the "man-made virus" explanation seems to have become more popular).

The Voodoo Zombie

The concept of the so-called voodoo *zombie* comes from a practice of the *vodun* cult priests of Haiti. Recently, however, this myth has been debunked due to the persistent efforts of some rather brave scientists. Because voodoo is dependent on the beliefs and superstitions of others, they tend to react rather violently when someone seeks to reveal their powers as little more than elaborate illusions.

At great risk, a number of samples of a vodun priest's so-called "zombie powder" was obtained and tested. Research revealed that the one common element, which existed in nearly all the samples, was puffer fish poison. Puffer fish poison is extremely toxic and usually fatal. In just the right dose, however, it can also cause a person to enter a state close to that of suspended animation and resembles hibernation. To an unobservant doctor or medic, the person would appear dead when in fact he or she is in an extreme state of paralysis. This thought becomes all the more frightening when one considers the fact that a person who has been paralyzed by puffer fish poison can still use all of their senses, though in a somewhat limited capacity. Imagine being paralyzed, hearing a doctor say you are dead, and later watching helplessly as the morgue doctor begins your autopsy—all the while, you can still hear, see, and feel *everything*.

Immortal Words _____

Zombi is the root word for the modern English term **zombie,** and refers to a now debunked belief of the Haitian vodun (voodoo) cult. The belief states that a priest has the power to steal a human soul through means of "black magic." A zombi is a person whose soul has been stolen, causing him to become in a state, as if dead. After a time, the vodun priest digs up the body and is said to be able to command it with his will.

The poor victim, believed to be dead, is then buried and later dug up by the priest and told he or she has been brought back to life as a zombie. Often, these "zombies" exhibit rather odd movement, slurred speech, and spacey behavior as a result of brain damage they received during their ordeal. This brain damage comes either from being poisoned or from prolonged oxygen deprivation during the time that they were mistakenly buried alive, or perhaps both. In fact, it is a miracle that anyone has ever survived having this "zombie scam" done to them.

Recent research into this practice has revealed that the voodoo zombie scam has a ridiculously poor success rate. A vodun priest would probably only get about one so-called zombie in hundreds of attempts. So what was once seen as miraculous magic has now been exposed for what it truly is—murder for the sake of some power-hungry scam artist's pride.

The Viral Zombie

Viral zombies are so called because they are caused by the infection and spread of a lethal virus that later reanimates the bodies of those it kills. In some cases, the virus reanimates anyone who has recently died. In others, the virus only affects those who are bitten by a zombie. Either way, these zombies are far creepier and more danger-ous than the voodoo zombie. Why? Because, unlike the voodoo zombie, viral zombies feed on living human flesh! That's right! As soon as viral zombies reanimate, they will attack any living person they come across, even their own friends and family members.

Myth and Metaphor _____

The viral zombie is a common subject of today's film industry and, during the last half-century, has begun to play a large part in pop culture. The viral zombie's creation is often credited to filmmaker George Romero, who created the first successful zombie film, *Night of the Living Dead*, followed by a string of other well-received films such as *Dawn of the Dead, Day of the Dead*, and *Land of the Dead*. The first two mov-ies have been remade in recent years, and Romero has become an icon in the realm of the pop culture zombie.

You can whack away at a zombie all day long and, until you hit the thing in the right spot, it'll just keep on coming! You see, unlike vampires, there is only one sure-fire way to kill a zombie—destroy the brain! How you do it does not really matter. Whether you crush their skulls in with a crowbar or blow their heads to pieces with a shotgun, as long as the brain is splattered, the zombie will go down. Although sev-ering the head might work, most portrayals of viral zombies show that even a severed head will keep chomping away until the brain is destroyed. Believe it or not, there are actually manuals available in the book market to help prepare a person for defending themselves in the event of a zombie virus outbreak!

Oh yeah, and viral zombies have *no* supernatural or magical abilities (aside from the fact that they're dead and walking around)!

The Least You Need to Know

◆ Vlad Tepes, often credited as the "father of vampires," was actually the terribly violent ruler of Wallachia during the mid-fifteenth century.

◆ Some believe Peter Plogojowitz's tale is evidence of the existence of vampires, though it may just be the record of an extreme case of mass hysteria.

◆ Voodoo zombies aren't truly undead, just now-brain-damaged individuals who have been slipped puffer fish poison and dug up before suffocating.

◆ The viral zombie, while frightening, is now the only valid *undead* zombie of modern-day mythology. Fortunately, they haven't shown up yet.

Chapter 21

More Creatures of Myth and Legend

In This Chapter

- The myth of the chupacabra
- The winged Pegasus and burning phoenix
- The terror of the gryphon and Roc
- The Japanese creature of thunder and lightning
- The reason you should never want to dream of Jinni

On a mythological level, the fears, dreams, hopes, and desires of human-kind's collective unconscious often manifest in the form of extraordinary creatures that are so incredible as to defy logic. Although the creatures of this chapter share no common archetypal theme, they are all representations of these inner aspects of the human psyche. The elusive chupacabra represents a modern fear of nature, which is increasingly separate from the world of humans. Our fear of helplessness against death manifests in the form of the giant bird known as the Roc, which lifts men into the air and releases them, sending them falling to their deaths. The gryphon is a symbol of the power to combat greed and protect that which is pure and precious. In all cases, these creatures must be understood to grasp mythology. You may find that they're not as simple as you think.

The Chupacabra (South American)

Although the chupacabra may share the trait of blood drinking with the vampire, it cannot, by definition, be classified as one. Unlike vampires, the chupacabra is not a transformed human and has no magical or supernatural abilities or weaknesses. More animal than humanoid, the chupacabra certainly exceeds the criteria for vampirism.

Immortal Words

Exsanguination is an extreme and fatal loss of blood from the body. Basically, exsanguination is just a long word for "bleeding to death."

The chupacabra is more of a glutinous blood-drinking monster than anything else. The name of the creature comes from the Spanish words *chupa* (to suck) and *cabra* (goat), translating as "goat-sucker." This name originates from early incidents when the creature was blamed for widespread mass mutilations and/or *exsanguinations* of goats.

How Big Is a Chupacabra?

Descriptions of the chupacabra vary. Therefore, because the creature has never been photographed, there is no definitive explanation of what one looks like. Ninety percent of the time, a chupacabra is described as between 3½ feet and 4½ feet tall. However, it isn't clear if this height is measured for a bipedal or four-legged creature. Perhaps this explains why the largest point of contradiction regarding accounts of the chupacabra has to do with the creature's size.

Some descriptions or eyewitness accounts have described a chupacabra as being about the size of a common dog. Other descriptions of the creature claim that it is rather large, just slightly smaller in size than a bear. However, the exact kind of bear a chupacabra is smaller than has not been specified. It could be smaller than a koala bear or just shy of a grizzly bear. The only way to settle this enigma is to see one for yourself. Good luck with that.

How to Spot a Chupacabra

As already stated, the eyewitness accounts and descriptions of the chupacabra vary. However, there are two types of chupacabras that are most commonly described. These two types will be referred to here as Type A and Type B.

The Type A chupacabra is more reptilian or lizardlike in appearance. A good rough description of the Type A chupacabra would be something that looks like a terrifying kangaroo/iguana hybrid. The Type A chupacabra is described as having scaly skin that may be green, black, or in some cases even blue. Down the center of the creatures' backs protrude a number of quill-like spines. The face of the chupacabra is commonly said to have a doglike (though some also say catlike) snout and muzzle. The tongue of the Type A chupacabra is said to be long and forked. This chupacabra's presence can be detected, it is said, by the heavy smell of sulfur that the creature gives off. Also, Type A chupacabras are usually bipedal and stand erect on two legs.

Avoiding the Labyrinth

Most zoologists and scientists believe that eyewitness accounts of Type B chupacabras are actually nothing more than hysterical recollections. They believe that more than likely these people were frightened into delusion as a result of unexpected, late-night encounters with deformed and/or mange-covered coyotes. However, there are some who lean toward the idea that this Type B chupacabra may in fact be an undiscovered species of wild dog or some kind of unknown dog-reptile hybrid that has somehow survived extinction for thousands of years but has been driven closer to humankind due to urban expansion.

The Type B chupacabra descriptions arose more recently in sightings of the creature in regions of Europe and North America, and are not as common as the Type A descriptions. Unlike the two-legged Type A, Type B chupacabras are commonly said to walk on four legs. Also, the Type B chupacabra is more caninelike in appearance. Instead of picturing a cross between a kangaroo and an iguana, imagine something that resembles a grotesque coyote-iguana hybrid. The Type B chupacabra is like a hairless dog with the skin of a lizard.

Trapping a Chupacabra Is a Bad Idea

When trapped, startled, frightened, or threatened, a chupacabra's eyes are said to glow red. Whatever you do, do not look into a chupacabra's eyes! If you accidentally *do* see a chupacabra's eyes, you should prepare to get sick. The glow of the creature's eyes is said to cause nausea, sudden bowel evacuation, and vomiting.

If the stomach-twisting red glow of the chupacabra's eyes is not enough to stop an assailant, the creature has a backup defense. When confronted, the chupacabra is said to let out a long and loud hiss. If you ever hear a chupacabra hiss, you might want to cover your ears. If not, prepare to be deafened. Immediately after hissing (a sound which, some speculate, may actually be from the creature inhaling sharply), a chupacabra will unleash a terrible, high-pitched wail loud enough to deafen any living thing with eardrums that is standing too close. After these defense mechanisms have been deployed, the chupacabra disappears into the nearest tree-line with a single and mighty leap.

Many accounts claim that both the Type A and Type B chupacabra have a set of strong hind legs, which are said to be similar to those of a kangaroo (especially for Type A). However, this creature's leaping ability could put most kangaroos to shame. Some reports claim that the creature is able to jump as far as roughly 7 yards (more than 20 feet!).

A Chupacabra's Blood of Choice

Though the chupacabra is called a goat-sucker, this creature's voracious appetite is not restricted solely to the blood of goats. The chupacabra has been blamed for the exsanguination and mutilation of chickens, turkeys, cows, sheep, and even domesticated dogs.

In most if not all cases of suspected chupacabra attacks on livestock, the animals killed had been almost completely drained of blood. In cases where the murdered livestock had not been completely torn to shreds, they were found to have multiple semi-circular cuts on their skins. This gave rise to the idea that a chupacabra must have long, sharp, semi-cylindrical fangs that act somewhat like straws. After the creature latches onto a victim, it then quickly drains the body of blood similar to soda through a straw.

A Creature of Modern Myth

The chupacabra has become an important part of South American pop culture, somewhat similar to how the sasquatch, or Bigfoot, remains a popular legend of North America—so-called sightings of the creature are common, but to date there is still no physical evidence to support its existence. In fact, no one has ever been able to produce so much as a single photograph of the creature (real or fake).

Despite the fact that the name for these creatures was coined in Mexico and South America, reports of chupacabra sightings in North America (in Texas and the Southwest, primarily) and parts of Europe (mainly in Russia and the Balkans) have also begun to occur. The first reported sightings of the creature began in the early

1990s in Chile, Columbia, Puerto Rico, and Mexico. Later, sightings were even reported in the United States. Despite the fact that the animal's existence has yet to be concretely confirmed, the power of the myth has led to its classification as a *cryptid* by cryptozoologists.

Immortal Words

Cryptid is a somewhat recently coined term referring to animal species that are unconfirmed by factual and/or physical evidence. Some cryptids are believed to be lost to extinction, dying out before they could be preserved or properly documented. Other cryptids, such as the chupacabra, are labeled as such due to the fact that they are known only through the testimony of witnesses or because there is a substantial lack of information to prove they exist. The legendary Loch Ness Monster of Scotland, for example, is also labeled as a cryptid.

There have been a number of incidents where people have found unusual animal remains and turned them over for investigation and DNA analysis. In all cases, scientific tests confirmed that the remains were those of deformed (likely the result of birth defects from inbreeding) and/or mange-covered coyotes. One such case happened as recently as August 2007, when a woman named Phylis Canion believed she found the remains of a chupacabra near a ranch in her hometown of Cuero, Texas. When one sees how horrific these coyotes appeared, it is not difficult to understand how a discoverer might believe that they are monsters. Oddly, not one of the suspected chupacabra remains ever had the tell-tale cylindrical-shape fangs that the Type A creature is said to have, nor the scales of both types.

Gryphon (European)

The gryphon (also spelled griffon or griffin) has its written origins in Greek mythology, where the creature was called *gryphus*, though its actual roots are believed to come from regions further east. The gryphon is often portrayed as a majestic creature, with the body of a lion and the head, wings, and talons of an eagle. In some depictions, the gryphon is confused with the chimera (see next section) and is portrayed as having a tail that is a serpent. Later, during the Middle Ages, this mythological animal became a powerful symbol to the knights of feudal Europe. On the decorations of crusader shields and coats of arms, the gryphon was one of the most popular animals depicted.

In mythology, the gryphons were said to be the natural enemies of horses. Myth tells that the gryphons were the animals that pulled the chariot of the sun, often ridden by Zeus. Nemesis, the little-known Greek goddess of divine retribution, is also said to have ridden this gryphon-drawn chariot. In most legends, gryphons are the guardians of either goldmines or vast collections of *Scythian* gold. Sometimes, the treasures they guard are said to come from India.

Immortal Words

The **Scythians** were a nomadic tribe of horse riders who are believed to have spoken some form of Iranian dialect. Eventually, the Scythians were dominated by the Sarmatians, a closely related tribe also of Iranian origins. It is commonly believed that the concept of the gryphon likely reached Greece from tales about the mythological creatures from the Indo-Iranians. This would also explain why gryphons in Greek mythology are often portrayed as the guardians of Scythian gold.

Chimera (Greek)

In Greek legends, the Chimera was the daughter of a huge monster called Typhon and a half-woman, half-serpent creature named Echidna. Typhon, her father, had to be imprisoned under a volcanic mountain by Zeus. Her mother, Echidna, gave birth to some of the most terrifying monsters of Greek mythology. Needless to say, the Chimera is a fairly terrifying creature herself. In early myths, the Chimera is said to have the head of a lion, the body of a goat, and the tail of a serpent. According to accounts from Hesiod, however, the Chimera had more than just an unusual integration of body parts. In addition, he claims she has three heads—one of a lion, the other a goat, and the third a serpent.

Avoiding the Labyrinth

Wait a minute ... the Chimera fell from the skies? It could fly? Though few depictions of the creature show it as having wings, a number of myths say that the Chimera could, in fact, fly.

Greek myth tells of how this monstrous creature was the terror of humankind. Eventually, her constant ravaging of the Lycian countryside causes their king, Iobates, to send the warrior Bellerophon to fight the creature (actually, King Iobates was hoping that Bellerophon would be killed). Luckily, Athena intervenes and offers her aid to the hero. While he is sleeping in Athena's temple, the goddess appears to Bellerophon and bestows upon him a golden bridle that allows him to mount the winged horse called

Pegasus. When he wakes, the bridle is next to him and before him stands the majestic Pegasus. Upon this winged horse, Bellerophon rides into battle against the fearsome Chimera. When the fighting is over, the Chimera, terror of the Lycians, falls dead from the skies.

Phoenix (European and Near Eastern)

Phoenix is actually the Greek name for an Egyptian mythological bird called *bennu*. Both names, Egyptian and Greek, have the same meaning—"palm tree." A basic description of the phoenix would be a red-orange-yellow/gold-feathered bird that bursts into flames when it dies, often after living for hundreds of years, only to arise reborn from its own ashes. However, the truth of how this myth evolved is not quite so simple.

The Egyptians claimed, according to the writings of Herodotus, a Greek, that the bennu/phoenix actually resided in the lands of the Arabs. However, it would seem that Herodotus was not too inclined to believe this story. It is quite possible that the Egyptians told the Greeks this when they were unable to actually produce a phoenix to show them.

 Myth and Metaphor

The phoenix/bennu was originally a symbol for the rise, fall, and return pattern of the sun. Later, the creature also became a symbol for the human journey of life, death, and rebirth.

According to the account of Pliny, a phoenix died once every 500 years. As this time drew near, the dying phoenix would create a nest from twigs of frankincense and cassia. He would then lie down in the nest and die. From the body of the dead phoenix, a worm would emerge. From this worm grew a new phoenix. However, apparently the Egyptians told Pliny that the bennu/phoenix actually resided in India. After embalming the remains of his father in a ball of myrrh, the young phoenix would travel to Heliopolis (which means "City of Helios" or "City of the Sun").

According to the second half of the myth, which was recorded by Herodotus, the young bennu/phoenix then flew to Heliopolis. The fiery bird would arrive with a ball of myrrh in its beak, within which were the embalmed remains of the bird's father. The young phoenix would then take the ball into the Temple of the Sun, where he buried it. On the walls of this temple, according to the Greek's description, were depictions of a red- and gold-colored bird about the size of an eagle.

Raiju (Japanese)

Raiju is a small-size Shinto demon of thunder and lightning. He is, quite appropriately, a companion of Raijin (sometimes spelled Raiden), the Shinto God of Thunder and Lightning. His name comes from the Japanese words *Rai* (thunder and lightning) and *Ju* (animal or, sometimes, creature), so his name basically means "lightning animal." Often, the Raiju appears in the form of a sharp-clawed animal, such as a badger, cat, or weasel.

The dwelling of the Raiju is often at the tops of trees. Shinto myth says that Raiju becomes excited by thunderstorms, as they are the work of his friend and master, Raijin. When a thunderstorm occurs, Raiju begins leaping from tree to tree, leaving behind gashes or burns on their trunks, if not completely tearing them asunder. In Shinto lore, if one sees a tree that has been gashed by lightning, it is said that it has been scratched by Raiju.

Myth and Metaphor

The Raiju myth is believed to have originally been created to explain the phenomenon of "ball lightning," where lightning travels in what appears to be a massive orb instead of a jagged line. Often, Raiju is depicted curled up as though in the fetal position. When ball lightning hits a tree, it often goes up in flames. As a result of this, Raiju is also associated with the element of fire.

One odd part of the Raiju myth is the fact that he is said to be fond of residing in the belly buttons/navels of humans. However, he often does this so that he can slumber longer than Raijin would like for him to. Therefore, the thunder god shoots "arrows" (thunderbolts) at the belly of the person in which Raiju is sleeping to wake the demon up. Obviously, this can be a rather unpleasant experience for the unsuspecting human who gets pierced through the stomach with a bolt of lightning.

The human navel aspect of the Raiju myth gave rise to a practice that is still performed by some of the more superstitious people of Japan. During a thunderstorm, these individuals will make certain to sleep on their stomachs, making it impossible for Raiju to take his slumber there, thereby avoiding the arrows of Raijin.

Roc (Middle Eastern)

The Roc, also spelled Rukh or Rokh, is a gigantic mythical bird. Often, the Roc is depicted as a vicious bird of prey. However, as a result of its size, its prey is often humans and/or large livestock. In some descriptions, the Roc is said to be an enormous white eagle. In other descriptions, a Roc is said to look more like a giant vulture (either white or gold).

One of the most well-known tales of the Roc comes from *1001 Arabian Nights*, a collection of short stories compiled during the rule of the Caliphate, sometime around the ninth century C.E. In the tale of Sindbad's (sometimes spelled Sinbad) second voyage, of which there are seven total, he becomes separated from his crew and is stranded on a strange island. The center valley of this island is completely covered by large diamonds. Unfortunately, the diamonds are hard to reach, because they are blocked by a ravine filled with poisonous snakes.

Myth and Metaphor

The idea of Sindbad strapping himself to the carcass of a lamb to escape being trapped can be compared to a story of the Greek hero Odysseus, who straps himself and several of his men to sheep to escape the cannibalistic jaws of a one-eyed Cyclopes. In fact, some believe that this tale of Sindbad's escape from the island of Rocs may have been directly influenced by the tale of Odysseus' escape from the Cyclopes' cave in Homer's *Odyssey*.

Sindbad watches, however, as a group of men arrive on the other side of the ravine and toss enormous chunks of raw meat (or whole, skinned lamb carcasses) over the snakes and onto the diamonds. He then watches as a number of Rocs descend on the meal, a fortune in diamonds sticking into the soft flesh of every chunk of the raw meat. The merchants later steal away the meat and harvest the diamonds. Sindbad, who is able to reach the valley of diamonds, straps himself to one of the large chunks of meat and is soon whisked away by the powerful talons of a Roc. His plan almost goes south, however, when the gigantic bird brings him to its nest. Before he is devoured, however, the merchants arrive and rescue him. Sindbad returns home (after a number of other adventures) with a fortune.

Demons of the Desert (Middle Eastern)

Often misspelled in English as "genie," these were the demon spirits of the Arab world. When female, they are called Jinniyah and in plural they are called Jinn. There are said to be five different types of Jinn: ifrit (the most troublesome), jann (the least powerful), jinn (the most powerful), marid (the most evil), and *shaitan* (fallen angels). However, in tales, these distinctions are rarely acknowledged.

Immortal Words

Shaitan is an Arabic pronunciation of the name "Satan," a label which was given to Lucifer in biblical mythology after his fall from Heaven. The shaitan types of Jinn are fallen angels in general. Iblis, the Prince of Evil and leader of the Jinn, is a shaitan class Jinni.

Most likely, the Jinn are a carryover from the pre-Islamic, nature-centered religions of the Arabic and Bedouin tribes. Most evidence suggests that they were originally malevolent demons who were believed to frequent the dark, secluded, and/or cursed places of Arabia. Often, in early depictions, the Jinn assumed the shapes of animals. Myth states that the Jinn also have the ability to appear as mist, or to become invisible.

Avoiding the Labyrinth

The spelling of Jinni as "genie" in English has caused them to become confused with Roman stories involving the concept of mythical beings known as *genii*, a plural form of the word *genius*. The genii were protective spirits of Roman mythology that later became the basis for what has become the common depiction of angels in Christianity. Genii had white wings and wore long, flowing robes or togas which were often white or gold. So the genii protective spirit may have been the mythological origin of the popular Christian concept of "guardian angels." In the modern English language, genius has become a term that refers to a person of extraordinary intelligence, skill, and/or creativity.

When the religion of Islam dominated the Middle East, the Jinn were retained in the new mythology. However, the Jinn's adoption into the evolving region caused them to be altered somewhat. Instead of being viewed as purely malevolent, the post-Islamic Jinn were depicted as having the potential to be both good and evil. Their appearances also became slightly more human, though they did retain some of their original animal traits, often in the form of their appendages. For example, a post-Islamic Jinni or Jinniyah often had a humanlike appearance. However, in the place of its feet were the hooves of a goat, or it might have pantherlike paws instead of hands, or a scaly dragonlike tail protruding from its back. In Arabic lore, the Jinn are led by Iblis, the Prince of Evil. For the most part, Iblis is the Muslim equivalent of Lucifer from Judeo-Christian mythology.

Avoiding the Labyrinth

Because the Jinn were the original demons of the Arab world, the word was adopted into Islam and used to refer to the demons and fallen angels of the Koran. The tale of the Jinn leader Iblis, Prince of Evil, tells of how Allah ordered Iblis to bow before Adam, the first man, in the Garden of Eden. When the powerful and beautiful Jinni refused to obey the command of Allah, he was condemned, cursed, and exiled from grace. Iblis, therefore, is often viewed as the Arabic equivalent of Lucifer.

Most Westerners have become familiar with the concept of the Jinn through the story of Aladdin from *1001 Arabian Nights*. However, they are also said to have appeared to the biblical character Solomon, who was at first terrified by their horrible appearances. In his wisdom, however, Solomon overcame his fear, learned to command the Jinn, and became master over them, thus allowing him to bend these powerful beings to his will.

The Least You Need to Know

- Creatures may be powerful without necessarily being evil.

- The gryphon is often confused with the Chimera, but these are in no way to be thought of as the same creature.

- A spelling error caused the mistaken relation between the Arabic Jinn and Roman genii, but they are not the same.

- Raiju was likely created to explain the phenomenon of ball lightning, the shape of which does not match up with the Shinto idea of normal lightning being the "arrows" of Raijin.

Chapter 22

Comparative Mythology in Pop Culture

In This Chapter

- ◆ The application of comparative mythology
- ◆ The Crow as a modern avatar of Odin
- ◆ The Shinto mythology of *Naruto*
- ◆ Goku and Odysseus: journeys to the underworld
- ◆ Comparing *Star Wars* and *The Last Samurai* to Arthurian legends
- ◆ Mythical representations in *The Matrix*

Mythology, as explained repeatedly throughout this book, is more than just studying a bunch of "old stories." The events and figures in myths are beyond fiction, being larger-than-life representations of the human condition—our fears, hopes, dreams, strengths, desires, weaknesses, virtues, and flaws. The need for such representations still exists, despite the fact that the value of myth is often dismissed by many who do not understand the difference between it and fiction. Now that you have been introduced to world mythology as a subject, you may learn how to begin applying those myths comparatively to the works of recent times. Through an understanding of comparative mythology, you will be able to identify the mythical symbols, heroic ideals, and mythological archetypes (which have existed for thousands of years) still being used in the entertainment media of the modern world.

Understanding Comparative Mythology

Comparative mythology is a fairly young and rather interesting field of mythological study. Primarily, there are two main avenues of approach to mythological comparisons: myth-to-myth/literature and myth-to-pop culture. The younger of these two fields is comparing myth to stories and figures in pop culture. At times, the parallels that exist between the myths of old and the more modern creations of film, literature, animation, and comic books are done purposely. At other times, however, these parallels exist despite the fact that the author/creator did not intentionally use them.

The key to applying the use of comparative mythology with pop culture is to first have a working knowledge of the common themes and figure types that exist in world myths. This book has already provided you with much of that knowledge, though it is still up to you to learn and retain that information. The next step is to be able to identify the subtle and sometimes hidden uses of these same themes and figure types in the various creations of modern writers and other kinds of artists (musicians, filmmakers, painters, and graphic artists). In the sections that follow, you will read through a number of examples where mythological concepts can be applied to icons of modern pop culture.

Odin and *The Crow*

James O'Barr wrote the *graphic novel* titled *The Crow* during an extremely painful and turbulent period in his life. Orphaned at a young age in the tough city of Detroit, Michigan, O'Barr's early life was not an easy one. In fact, though the date of the writer/artist's birth is officially listed as January of 1960, the truth is this was designated as such because his actual date of birth was unknown. A dark and cynical young man, James liked few people and was very much a loner.

Immortal Words _____

A **graphic novel** is similar to a comic book. However, it is a lengthy, illustrated book that tells a novel-like story within a larger number of pages than is seen with comic books. Also, graphic novels are often meant for a mature reading audience, which makes them common subjects for film adaptations. For example, the film *Road to Perdition*, starring Tom Hanks, was based on a graphic novel of the same name by Max Allan Collins, which was in turn a tribute to the long-running Japanese manga series *Lone Wolf and Cub*.

However, all the hardships that O'Barr had endured in his life seemed worth it when, at the age of 16, he met a girl named Bethany who became the love of his life. For years, the two were inseparable and, as they neared graduation, they became engaged. Sadly, Bethany was senselessly killed by a drunk driver shortly before she and O'Barr were to be married. Having suddenly lost the only person in his life who had ever made him feel genuinely loved, O'Barr's world began to fall apart. After a period of self-destructive behavior, the young self-styled artist (he never took a single art class and had no formal training) realized that he would have to make some changes to his life and find a way to channel his anger before it utterly consumed him.

In an attempt to bring some order to his chaotic life, O'Barr joined the U.S. Marines and soon found himself stationed in Berlin, Germany. It was in Germany that O'Barr began working on the graphic novel that is considered by most to be his greatest masterpiece. The music scene he observed during this time heavily influenced the style of *The Crow*, and O'Barr openly admits that the bands Joy Division and The Cure were always in his mind as he drew the work. The first part of the story is dedicated to Joy Division frontman Ian Curtis, who hanged himself at the age of 23. The physical appearance of Eric Draven was based heavily on the face of Peter Murphy of the band Bauhaus, who O'Barr also saw while in Germany, and the body of rock icon Iggy Pop.

At the time it was created, *The Crow* was nothing more than a way for O'Barr to deal with his feelings of anger, rage, frustration, and sadness at what he saw as the senselessness of Bethany's death. The medium for these emotions would be a tragic character he named Eric Draven, and his sad yet heroic story eventually became (and remains to this day) the highest-selling black-and-white graphic novel in history. Even though a number of new and alternate versions of *The Crow* have been made since, none have been as popular or successful as O'Barr's original graphic novel. It is possible that O'Barr himself was not even remotely aware of the parallels to the Norse god Odin that his character would ultimately exhibit.

The Story of *The Crow*

The theme of *The Crow*'s main story came to O'Barr when he was inspired by an article he read in a Detroit newspaper, which told of a young couple who had been murdered by a gang of thugs over nothing more than a $20 engagement ring. The graphic novel tells the story of a young couple in love, Eric Draven and Shelley Webster. Shortly after the two are engaged, they go out for a romantic picnic but, as they return home, become stranded on the side of a rural highway just outside Detroit when Eric's car throws a rod.

Unfortunately, the unsuspecting lovers soon catch the malevolent attention of a car-load of cracked-out gang members who happen to be driving by. The story then takes a tragic turn, becoming one about two people who are simply in the wrong place at the wrong time. Eric is shot in the head and left for dead. Shelley is raped repeatedly and savagely beaten, as Eric lies helpless and dying nearby, until one of the gang members fires a bullet into her head as well.

As Eric dies, a crow flies down to him to usher his soul to the land of the dead. Eric's eyes have been open, however, and he is able to witness the terrible things that the thugs do to his beloved Shelley (despite the crow's urgent warnings that he not look). One year later, Eric unexplainably returns from the grave because his soul is unable to rest as a result of what he saw. He returns to seek vengeance upon the men who destroyed his life and killed his love without provocation or reason.

Avoiding the Labyrinth

Many people are likely familiar with the film adaptation of *The Crow* but unaware that it was ever a graphic novel. It is important to note that the graphic novel is what is being discussed here, not the film. There are a number of distinct differences between the film and the graphic novel, a few of which were the result of the untimely death of the lead actor, Brandon Lee, near the end of production when he was shot while filming a scene. Though it was officially declared a tragic accident, a number of "urban myths" exist surrounding the circumstances of Lee's death (much like those surrounding the death of his father, Bruce Lee). One main difference between the two is that Eric Draven is a rock musician in the movie but a construction worker in the graphic novel. While the same Odin parallels also exist in the movie, it's important not to get the movie confused with O'Barr's original work.

The crow acts as a living vessel for Eric's soul and is his dark guide on the labyrinthine road of postmortem vengeance, revealing to him the hidden truths of matters, as well as leading him to the men he has come to kill. Until justice has been done, Eric's soul cannot rest. Therefore, he will remain separated from Shelley, who waits for him at the threshold of the afterlife. Eric's face is painted in the style of a theater mask to symbolize the emotions within him—irony, pain, and sadness.

Immediate Parallels

When you are attempting to apply comparative mythology to a pair of works, it often helps to first identify the immediate parallels. These should be basic points of similarity which can then be examined, supported, or proven false. For example, in comparing Odin to Eric Draven, the immediate parallels are as follows:

◆ Presence of a crow/raven (blackbird) as guide/advisor

◆ Presence of the feline feminine

◆ The faces of both figures are covered, with Eric's painted in the style of a theater mask and Odin's concealed by either a large hood or wide-brimmed hat

◆ Both figures speak in poetic verse

◆ Both figures have overcome death to return from the underworld

Odin and His Ravens

The interesting thing to note about the similarities between the Teutonic god Odin and the Crow/Eric Draven is that there is no evidence to even suggest that this was something intentionally done by O'Barr. By his own testimony, the story was purely a therapeutic way to vent his negative emotions after his fiancée's senseless death. This makes the similarities even more compelling, especially when you consider the fact that Odin is a God of War, Poetry, Music, and Justice. These are all attributes that Eric Draven exhibits.

The first and most obvious similarity between Odin and O'Barr's character is the presence of a crow/raven (blackbird) that acts as guide and advisor. While Eric Draven is guided by only a single crow, Odin has a pair of them—Hugin (Thought) and Munin (Memory). However, Eric's one crow assumes the roles of both of Odin's ravens. The first raven of Odin, Hugin, always speaks the truth into Odin's ear. The second raven, Munin, allows Odin to accurately recount any memory (his own or, at times, those of others).

After Eric's resurrection, the crow communicates with him telepathically, conveying information to him that he would not be privy to otherwise. For example, at one point in the graphic novel, the crow tells Eric that one of his murderers, whom he has just found, is a morphine addict. The crow even gives exact evidence as to how Eric can be sure of this, pointing out that the man's arms have track marks and that his skin is clean (a *heroin* addict, you see, would have yellowed skin and acne). In other situations, the crow tells Eric when an opponent is armed with a concealed weapon, even going so far at times as to identify the exact type of weapon with which the person is armed. In situations such as these, Eric's crow is assuming a role similar to that of Odin's raven Hugin (Thought).

Throughout the graphic novel, the crow also reminds Eric of who he was in life as well as what happened to Shelley and him. The undead wraith is constantly haunted by self-inflicted visions, dreams, and flashbacks about his former life with his beloved Shelley. These vision sequences always begin happily and beautifully, only to end with images of grotesque horror and death. In situations such as these, the crow is assuming a role similar to that of Munin (Memory), by allowing Eric to have glimpses into the beautiful life he once had (and that he'll never have again) and the horrific and ugly reality that destroyed it all.

Gabriel and the Presence of Freya

As you have already read, Freya (sometimes spelled Frigga) is the wife of Odin as well as the Goddess of Marital Fidelity and Love. One of the animals most commonly associated with Freya is the cat. When Eric returns to his now-dilapidated home upon his return from the grave, he befriends a cat named Gabriel. O'Barr may have given this feline an assumedly male name (Gabriel is the name of one of the seven strongest archangels, which can be found in Chapter 17), but he goes out of his way to make sure the reader knows that the animal is actually a female. Near the end of the novel, Eric leaves the cat in the care of the police captain who was once in charge of his case (though he was unable to solve it), with instructions explaining that she is apparently pregnant and he should be expecting kittens any day now.

The presence of this feline, as with the presence of the crow, can be viewed as a symbol of how marital sanctity (which is Freya's domain) has been violated by the gang members who killed Eric and Shelley. Since the couple is needlessly murdered before their love could be unified by marriage, the cat Gabriel becomes a representation of Freya's presence just as the crow represents Odin's. Since Odin is a God of Justice and his wife is a Goddess of Marriage, it only makes sense that the archetypal animals and images associated with them are present in a story such as *The Crow*, where two engaged lovers are unjustly killed and those responsible have gone free.

> **Myth and Metaphor** _____
>
> Though *The Crow* contains a plethora of imagery and symbolism associated to Christ, the theology of the Christian religion is entirely absent from the graphic novel. This, perhaps, could be an explanation as to why James O'Barr unconsciously included archetypal figures that suggest the presence of two prominent pre-Christian gods from the religions of "Old Europe." Whereas Christianity teaches that one should "turn the other cheek" when transgressed against, the Teutonic culture did quite the opposite. The Teutonic gods are prone to wrathful behavior, which isn't surprising considering that the concept of revenge was a large part of the Norse social and political structures.

Talking in Riddles, Speaking in Rhymes

As a result of drinking the Mead of Poetry that belonged to the giant Suttung (which he had obtained by seducing Suttung's daughter, a giantess named Gunnlod), Odin speaks almost entirely in poetic verse or song. This is one reason why Odin was designated as the God of Poetry and Music in addition to his many other divine titles as leader of the Aesir.

Eric Draven, after returning from the grave as the vengeful Crow, often speaks in rhymes. Sometimes he will directly quote poetry, such as that of Edgar Allan Poe's *The Raven* (which, one must admit, seems rather appropriate). At other times, he quotes song lyrics or riddles when addressing the victims of his wrath. This verbal behavior is undeniably similar to that of Odin.

> **Avoiding the Labyrinth** _____
>
> Odin seems rather fond of seeking, stealing, and drinking liquids that give him special knowledge, powers, or skills. Therefore, it's important not to get the myth of Odin's drinking the Mead of Poetry confused with that of him drinking from the Well of Knowledge (an act which, as you read in Chapter 5, required Odin to voluntarily sacrifice one of his eyes).

Heroes of Death

The final parallel between Odin and *The Crow* is the theme of the hero conquering death. Odin, in Teutonic mythology, is the lord of Valhalla, a realm of the afterlife specially reserved for warriors and/or those who died with bravery or in battle. Odin is immortal and, as far as the myths surrounding him are concerned, will never be killed or otherwise vanquished until the time of the Teutonic apocalypse known as Ragnarok (and even then, some myths are rather uncertain as to whether he will be killed). Odin leaves the afterlife and often travels in the realm of men in order to right wrongs, aid heroes who are in trouble, or otherwise see that justice is ultimately served to the wicked.

> **Myth and Metaphor** _____
>
> Eric Draven's return from the afterlife is a modern-day example of the typical nekyia journey, which you read about in Chapter 7. Eric Draven, as the resurrected Crow, is very much a death hero and therefore falls into the category of a necrotype (which is also explained in Chapter 7). In fact, one could view the web of streets and alleyways through which Eric travels in his quest for revenge as a type of modern labyrinth, a common necrotype found in most nekyia myths.

Eric, like Odin, has conquered death and returned from the afterlife in order to see that justice is served to the wicked men that killed Shelley and destroyed his once happy life. However, since he is not a god like Odin, his conquering of death is only a temporary one. He must, like all living beings, return to the realm of the dead. However, what manner of afterlife Eric will have to exist in upon his return to death is dependent upon him accomplishing his task of vengeance by setting right the wrongs that have been committed.

Sun Wu Kong, Odysseus, and Son Goku

In 1984, Japanese manga artist/writer Akira Toriyama published the first editions of his martial arts–styled action series *Dragonball*. The series was published weekly in *Shonen Jump* magazine and quickly became one of the most successful *manga* series of its time. The *Dragonball* story would continue to run weekly for 11 straight years. The amazing popularity of the *Dragonball* manga over the first two years of its publication led to its adaptation into an anime series, which proved even more successful.

The *Dragonball* series follows the adventures (and sometimes misadventures) of a young martial arts genius named Son Goku (in some English language versions, however, he is simply referred to as Goku). One day, an old warrior hermit happens upon a strange infant with a monkey's tail (Son Goku) and chooses to raise him as his own. Son Goku is an ill-tempered and mean toddler, until one day he accidentally tumbles off a cliff and hits his head. From that day forward, he is the kindest and most good-hearted child any person could ever hope for.

Immortal Words

Manga is a Japanese term for black-and-white, graphic novel–styled comics. Manga is viewed differently in Japanese culture than are comic books in the West where, until recent years, they were still considered by most as something solely for the entertainment of children. In Japan, however, manga is read by people of all ages, from preschoolers to seniors. The most popular manga series are often adapted into *anime*, the Japanese style of cartoon animation which has also become increasingly popular with American audiences over the last two decades.

In all, there are three main installments to the *Dragonball* series:

◆ *Dragonball:* This initial part of the series deals with Son Goku's childhood and his journey to assemble the seven mystical Dragonballs, which summon a magical dragon who has the power to grant any wish.

◆ *Dragonball Z:* This installment covers the events of Son Goku's adult life, and introduces his young son, Son *Gohan,* to the story. At times, he still finds it necessary to assemble the Dragonballs. However, this installment primarily has Son Goku fighting against the evil alien forces that have come to conquer Earth after finding that he has not done as they intended due to his head injury as a toddler.

Immortal Words

The fact that Son Goku names his son **Gohan** is actually a kind of joke. In the Japanese language, the word *gohan* actually means "rice" and is also used to refer to "dinner." There is a running gag throughout the series that Son Goku loves to eat food (and lots of it), so the fact that he has basically named his son "dinner" is a continuation of this joke.

◆ *Dragonball GT:* This is the final installment of the series, which deals with Son Goku learning that his frequent use of the Dragonballs has disrupted the balance of good and evil energies within them. This installment also deals with the adulthood of Son Gohan.

Later in the series, when Son Goku is an adult (the installment referred to above as *Dragonball Z*), it's revealed that the hero is not actually human at all (of course, the fact that he has a monkey's tail probably should have been a big clue). Son Goku finds out that he comes from an alien race of warriors, called Saiyans, when several of them arrive on Earth (expecting to find it void of all human life). It turns out that, as an infant, Son Goku was sent on a mission to kill all sentient beings that inhabited Earth and prepare it to be sold for colonization. You see, to the Saiyans, selling planets was a business.

The fact that Son Goku is an alien explains a lot about why he is the way he is. For starters, it explains why he has a monkey's tail. Also, it explains the superhuman strength he displayed even as a child, as well as why he heals relatively quickly from serious injuries. Lastly, Son Goku being an alien also explains why he transforms into a 50-foot-tall raging gorilla anytime he sets eyes on the light of a full moon.

Immediate Parallels

Again, the first step is to identify the immediate parallels that exist between Son Goku and the mythical figures Sun Wu Kong (the Monkey King) and Odysseus.

For the Chinese Monkey King, Sun Wu Kong, the immediate parallels are:

- Both figures wield a magical cudgel that changes size
- Both figures can fly on a cloud
- Both have monkey attributes (technically, Sun Wu Kong *is* a monkey)
- Both undergo journeys to retrieve special items

Between Son Goku and the Greek hero Odysseus, the immediate parallels are:

- Both must make journeys into the realm of the dead
- Both return from the realm of the dead with special knowledge that assures their success
- Both have sons who, in their absences, journey from home to be trained/counseled by a hero colleague
- Both men have wives who attempt to protect their sons from harm by preventing them from leaving

Son Goku and Sun Wu Kong

The original *Dragonball* series' Son Goku was directly based on a popular character in Chinese mythology—Sun Wu Kong, the rebellious and wild-hearted Monkey King. The parallels between the two are fairly obvious at this stage in the series, the most obvious being that both exhibit physical traits of primates. Son Goku has a monkey tail and turns into a gigantic ape, while Sun Wu Kong is, well ... a monkey. In fact, Chinese mythology and culture seems to have had a heavy influence on Toriyama when he created *Dragonball*.

As you read in Chapter 2, Sun Wu Kong's primary weapon is a magical cudgel. What makes this weapon so special is the fact that he can alter its size with a word. The Monkey King's cudgel can shrink down to the size of a toothpick, and he often keeps it tucked behind his ear. Son Goku has a similar weapon, a cudgel that he can increase the length of at will. However, Son Goku's cudgel only shrinks down to the size of a short stick, which he carries strapped to his back.

Sword and Man

A cudgel is a weapon that is similar to a long staff. However, both ends of a cudgel are reinforced, often with steel spikes or studs. As a result, cudgels can be rather heavy weapons to carry and require a fair amount of upper body strength to wield. This is why having a cudgel that you could shrink down at will, as Sun Wu Kong and Son Goku do, would be pretty handy.

Also, both Son Goku and Sun Wu Kong travel by riding on a cloud. However, later in the *Dragonball Z* section of the series, the cloud begins to be phased out and Son Goku simply acquires the ability to fly by using only the power of *ki*.

Sun Wu Kong journeys to the East in his mission as a warrior protector to the pilgrim Tripitaka in his search of the Buddha's sacred scrolls. In similar fashion, Son Goku journeys the world (and sometimes the universe) in search of the seven Dragonballs which, obviously, are what the story is named after. On Sun Wu Kong's journey, one of his comrades is a gluttonous figure named Pigsy. Similarly, in *Dragonball*, one of Son Goku's companions is a talking pig named Oolong.

Immortal Words

Ki is a Japanese word that means something similar to "energy" or "life force." In Chinese dialects, this is called *chi*, and in Hindu it is called *chakra* (though this term has also come to be more commonly used in the Japanese language in recent years).

Son Goku and Odysseus

The events that take place in the first 10 chapters of the *Dragonball Z* installment of the series bear a number of striking similarities to events that take place in Homer's *Odyssey*. When Son Goku dies following his battle with an evil Saiyan named Raditz, his soul goes on to the afterlife. Luckily, the God of Death also happens to be Son Goku's father-in-law. So Son Goku finds out that he can be resurrected in a year. During this time, he trains under the master warrior of Heaven, Lord Kaio. During Son Goku's absence, his son, Gohan, is trained to fight by Piccolo (in Japanese, they pronounce the name Pee-ko-ro). Piccolo is a green-skinned alien from a sluglike race, and is both Son Goku's rival, fellow warrior, and friend. In order to train Son Gohan, Piccolo takes the boy to a faraway and dangerous land. The training of Son Gohan is a backup measure. You see, if Son Goku is killed in the next battle (which they are aware will be against two Saiyans this time), the only other person left on Earth with Saiyan blood will be Son Gohan (who is half Saiyan, and even has the same monkey tail as his father).

The journeys of Son Goku and Gohan are very similar to those of Odysseus and his son Telemachus. Both Son Goku and Odysseus make journeys into the land of the dead, the latter going to the realm of Hades to consult the dead spirit of the blind prophet Tiresias (among others) on how he can safely and successfully return to his homeland of Ithaca.

While Odysseus is traveling the land across the Styx, his son Telemachus is searching for a way to fight his mother's suitors, most of them greedy and gluttonous men who have taken up unwelcome residence in his father's home. To seek counsel about what to do as well as possible word of his father, Telemachus sails to the lands of King Menelaus (Odysseus's comrade during the Trojan War). It is here that Telemachus is given advice on what to do.

The Samurai and the Knight

The myth of Sir Yvain (also spelled Ivain, Ywain, Owain, Ewein, and Iwein) of King Arthur's Knights of the Round Table was likely initially written by French author Chrétien de Troyes sometime during the mid- to late twelfth century (around 1160–1170 B.C.E.). Though several other written renditions of the Sir Yvain/Knight of the

Lion myth exist, Chrétien de Troyes' version is the most commonly used. Therefore, it is this version that will be used for comparison here. The poem is rather long and complicated, so only the relevant parts are summarized here.

Avoiding the Labyrinth

Aside from Chrétien's Arthurian romance, *Yvain, Knight of the Lion,* there are several other written renditions of this legend. The original or mythical source for Chrétien's work is unknown, but some suspect it was the older Middle English poem *Ywain and Gawain.* Regardless, Chrétien's version became the source for all later renditions of the myth. For example, the German version of the tale, by Hartmann Von Aue, is called *Iwein.* There is also a Welsh version of the legend called *The Lady of the Fountain* (sometimes it is just called *Owein*). Though the basic events remain relatively (if not exactly) the same, it is important not to get them confused. Chrétien's story is also sometimes called *The Knight with the Lion,* depending on the translation.

In *The Knight of the Lion,* Sir Yvain takes on a quest to avenge the shame of his cousin, Calgrenant (sometimes spelled Calogrenant, depending on which translation you are reading from), who has recently lost a battle against a knight in red armor. Calgrenant loses his horse to the red knight but not his life, something that would be cause for great shame to any good knight. This red knight, you see, is charged with the task of attacking and defeating any knight who dares to come near a certain spring outside his castle and pour a bowlful of the spring's water over the magic stone that sits beside it. The red knight is immediately alerted to these challenges, because when the water runs over the rock, it causes the sky to erupt in a terrible storm.

Yvain arrives and pours his challenge upon the rock. The sky turns violent, and soon the red knight appears and rushes at him. The two knights have a fierce battle, both delivering grave injuries to the other, until finally Yvain lands a square and powerful blow to the red knight's helm. Knowing he has been mortally wounded, the red knight attempts to escape and rides full gallop back to his castle with Yvain in close pursuit. When they cross the threshold to the castle, however, Yvain springs a trap that causes bladed gates to come down on both sides of the narrow entryway. He would surely be found and killed once the knights of the castle learned of their lord's death. However, one of the handmaidens to the lady of the castle is indebted to Yvain's father Urien and she recognizes him. Until she can find a way to secure his escape, the handmaiden gives Yvain a special ring that makes him invisible.

Avoiding the Labyrinth

A medieval sword was rarely used for cutting or slashing in battle. Use of heavy plate and chainmail armor made delivering fatal cuts or stabs to the body extremely difficult. Therefore, the most effective way to dispatch an armored knight was to deliver strong blows to the side of his helm. Though made of steel, the inner padding of medieval helms came from crude materials—*very* poor shock absorbers. After receiving repeated hits on the helm with a heavy sword, the vibrations began to take a toll on the brain. Either one strong hit or multiple square blows to the helm could knock a knight unconscious (often causing serious brain damage) or kill him if his helm split or caved (fracturing the skull). The greatest vulnerability of the helm was the eye slit or visor, depending on the armor's style. However, this slit is a small, narrow opening that's next to impossible to hit, as this requires incredible speed and accuracy (both of which are hindered when one's body is covered by 80-plus pounds of metal).

Before the handmaiden can secure his escape, Yvain lays eyes upon the deceased knight's widow and falls immediately in love with her (he is also heartbroken to know he has caused her so much grief). At first, obviously, the lady of the castle is loath to accept Yvain's affection since he is responsible for taking her husband's life. Eventually, however, the handmaiden who assisted Yvain reasons with the lady that Arthur and his knights are on their way to siege the castle and that Yvain is the only knight in the castle strong enough to take her husband's place as lord of the land and protector of the spring. Soon their love blossoms and Yvain assumes the responsibilities and position of the red knight, whom he has slain.

Since he rode out from Camelot to avenge Calgrenant's defeat without the permission of Arthur's court, Yvain realizes that he cannot simply explain the situation when Arthur and his fellow knights arrive. He decides to conceal his identity by wearing the red knight's armor. Soon enough, however, his true identity is discovered and Arthur calls off the siege and forgives all. Later in the tale, Yvain rescues and befriends a mighty lion (hence the title of Chrétien's version), and the animal becomes his loyal ally throughout a number of terrible battles against both men and monsters alike.

Immediate Parallels

Before discussing in detail the mythological comparison between the story of Sir Yvain and that of the character Nathan Algren from the film *The Last Samurai*, it is important to once again outline the immediate parallels first, which are as follows:

- Both men are on a quest for redemption from shame, which they do by choosing to fight a battle not their own.

- During battle, both slay a strong warrior in red armor.

- Both men fall in love with the widow of the warrior they have killed.

- Both men fight to defend the realm of the warrior they killed while wearing his red armor.

- Both men are associated with a large predatory cat: Sir Yvain with a lion and Nathan Algren with a white tiger.

Red Knight, Red Samurai

The 2003 film *The Last Samurai,* starring Tom Cruise and directed by Edward Zwick, tells the story of a tortured former army captain by the name of Nathan Algren (Cruise). Algren is ashamed and tormented by the atrocities he participated in during his service with General Custer's unit and other such "Indian Fighting" missions that were little more than systematic slaughters of entire villages. The need to redeem himself from that shame is comparable to Yvain's need to avenge the shame of his cousin Calgrenant. An unemployed alcoholic, Nathan Algren accepts employment to go to Japan to teach firearms, drill, and Western military tactics to the new Imperial Conscript Army.

The ill-prepared conscripts are ordered into battle against a man named Katsumoto, the leader of a renegade, anti-Westernization group of samurai. Despite being ordered to the rear, Algren chooses to stand at the battlefront with the Japanese officers, as he knows they are not yet prepared to lead their men in actual combat. Despite having firearms and numerical superiority, the conscript forces fall apart when confronted by the chaos, stress, and fear that are the realities of combat. Captain Algren eventually becomes isolated from the main force, which is soon in full retreat, and stands his ground bravely even though he is surrounded.

When a samurai in red armor approaches with his katana to cut off Algren's head, the American shoves a splintered piece of a guide-on pole through his head by stabbing through the opening just under the samurai's chin (a spot not protected by the helmet-and-mask–styled armor of the samurai). In the end, however, Algren succumbs to his wounds and passes out. This situation is comparable to that of Sir Yvain slaying the red knight with a fatal blow to the helm.

Sword and Man

Cutting off a man's head with a katana in only one cut was a skill that took a lot of practice. The human neck is a mass of strong and densely packed muscles and tendons, and cutting through it in one shot is no easy task (this is why European executioners used large, heavy axes). In combat, a samurai presented heads of enemy officers to his lord after a battle as a sign of his value and battle prowess. In formal situations, a special swordsman called a *kaishakunin* was used. In such formal situations, kaishakunin often assisted a samurai committing ritual suicide by cutting the dying warrior's head off when he could no longer continue his self-disembowelment. Sometimes, they also carried out ordered executions. Either way, this was usually witnessed by high-ranking officials. Because of the strength required for a clean cut, severed heads had a tendency to fly toward the witnessing officials. To avoid this, a kaishakunin had to be able to sever the head while leaving uncut a small flap of skin just under the chin. This caused the severed head to fall downward, landing either directly in front of or on the lap of the beheaded.

Red Warrior, White Tiger

Unexpectedly, Algren's life is spared when Katsumoto sees him standing against a number of samurai. The samurai leader realizes that Algren's situation is identical to a vision he had recently during meditation. In Katsumoto's vision, a wounded white tiger was trapped by a number of samurai yet fought with savage ferocity. Seeing Algren, he realizes that the vision had been of the American before him. So Katsumoto orders his men to take Algren prisoner.

The association of Nathan Algren to the white tiger is nearly identical in symbolism to the presence of the lion in Sir Yvain's story. In Asian culture, the white tiger is considered a symbol of purity/virtue, strength, and bravery. In European culture, especially in the Middle Ages, the lion was considered a symbol of knightly virtue, courage, nobility, and strength. Whether this parallel between the two stories of the symbolic use of a large predatory cat was intentional is unclear. Regardless, it is undeniably present.

In the Armor of the Departed

Algren spends the winter in captivity, a "guest" in Katsumoto's village. He is lodged in the home of the very red-armored samurai he killed, and nursed back to health by the fallen warrior's widow. In this time, Algren develops loving feelings for the red samurai's widow and develops an increasingly deep admiration for the ways of the samurai (and the Japanese in general). When spring arrives, Algren is returned to his unit unharmed, though he is a changed man (for the better). He soon learns that the conscript army is now well organized and has just acquired howitzer cannons and Gatling machine guns, which they plan to use to rout Katsumoto's men now that he has been arrested for violating a law that forbids the carrying of swords. Algren helps Katsumoto escape, and they return to the mountain village to prepare for the inevitable assault from the conscript army.

On the morning of the final battle, the fallen samurai's widow dresses him in her late husband's red armor. As Yvain does, Algren dons the armor of the warrior he killed in order to defend a land that is not his. In short, he puts on the armor of the departed and more or less takes his place in the world as warrior, defender, and lover/husband. Yvain eventually married the widow of the red knight and in a similar fashion the final scene of *The Last Samurai* shows Nathan Algren returning to the mountain village to (presumably) live out the rest of his life in peace with the widow and children of the red-armored samurai.

Star Wars and Arthurian Legend

George Lucas' sci-fi fantasy film saga *Star Wars* became an unexpected hit among audiences of all ages when the first movie was released in 1977. These days, it has become fairly common knowledge that parallels exist between characters in the *Star Wars* story and those in Arthurian legends. Lucas has also openly admitted that mythology had a large influence on him in creating the story.

Avoiding the Labyrinth _____

Though many of the characters in the *Star Wars* saga were directly based on figures in Arthurian legend, Lucas does not seem to have based his Jedi Knights on the Western knight. Instead, the ideals and philosophies of the Jedi resemble the warrior orders of Asian cultures. The Jedi fighting styles, clothing, and philosophies resemble those of the Japanese samurai. A number of their philosophical ideas come from Zen/Ch'an Buddhism.

The late Joseph Campbell (see Chapter 7), a renowned mythologist who was a close colleague and myth mentor to George Lucas, discussed the Arthurian parallels of the first *Star Wars* films in great detail in his own works. However, Joseph Campbell passed away on October 31, 1987, before any of the current films had been created (a prequel trilogy that covers episodes one through three, whereas the first three films covered episodes four through six). Therefore, the parallels that will be covered in this section will come from the characters of the three most recent *Star Wars* films: *The Phantom Menace, Attack of the Clones,* and *Revenge of the Sith.*

While some minor parallels do exist between Anakin Skywalker and King Arthur, there are far more that can be drawn between Luke Skywalker and Arthur. Upon close examination, one will find that Anakin Skywalker is the embodiment of the characters Uther Pendragon (Arthur's father) and Mordred (Arthur's illegitimate son with Morgan Le Fey). However, since the father figure (Anakin) is evil while the son (Luke) is good, this causes an interesting role reversal in the father versus son scenario of the Arthur myth.

One Wizard, Three Jedi

The figure of Merlin from Arthurian legend is actually embodied in three separate characters—Qui-Gon Jinn, Obi Wan Kenobi, and Yoda. All three of these characters act as skilled mentors to both father and son (Anakin *and* Luke), just as Merlin acts as an advisor and mentor first to Uther Pendragon and later to his son Arthur. The mythical character of Merlin, traditionally, can be said to change and evolve in a number of very specific stages, which are as follows:

- ◆ **Idealist Prophet Merlin:** Merlin believes, due to his abilities of precognition, that a man will soon rise to bring order to the chaos that engulfs the land, and believes Uther Pendragon is that man. The Jedi Qui-Gon Jinn of *Star Wars* represents Merlin in this stage of his development, as he believes that Anakin Skywalker is the one who will return balance to the force, as prophesied long ago. However, Qui-Gon is slain by the Sith apprentice Darth Maul and at that point Obi-Wan Kenobi assumes the task of training young Anakin.

- ◆ **Disappointed Merlin:** Merlin chooses to help Uther Pendragon, believing he is the one to restore order to the land. First, he helps Uther, Arthur's father, rise to power. Once Uther's ends have been met, however, he proves to be a huge disappointment to Merlin when he uses that power only to serve his own selfish interests. This stage of Merlin is represented by Obi-Wan Kenobi in his relationship with Anakin Skywalker, who eventually becomes a Sith lord and turns to the dark side.

◆ **Hopeful Merlin:** Merlin watches over and becomes the tutor for young Arthur, who grows up unaware of who his true father is. In Arthur, Merlin see the hope of perhaps regaining what was lost when Uther failed to unite the land. At this stage, Obi-Wan Kenobi again represents Merlin in his relationship with Luke Skywalker. Just as it turns out to be Arthur, son of Uther, who fulfills Merlin's original prophecy by bringing order to the land, it is Luke Skywalker, son of Anakin, who returns balance to the force as Qui-Gon prophesied. In both situations, it is the son who fulfills the destiny/prophecy that was failed/betrayed by his father. In both situations, the son also takes up the weapon of his father, Arthur removing Uther's sword from the stone where Merlin had placed it and Luke being given his father's lightsaber by Obi-Wan Kenobi.

◆ **Pessimistic Merlin:** Merlin watches, often with displeasure, at how Arthur changes as he grows into manhood as King of the Britons. His treatment of Arthur becomes far harsher than when he was a boy, and he often scolds his student for failing in his thinking in ways that serve to perpetuate the chaos (such as the idea that the strongest man may commonly win wars, but that does not mean he is always right). Merlin in this stage is represented by Jedi Master Yoda, who is far harsher in his relationship with Luke Skywalker than was Obi-Wan Kenobi. For example, Jedi Master Yoda forces Luke to confront his own negative emotions, specifically his hatred of Darth Vader (who is his father, as this is Anakin Skywalker's title as a Sith Lord), whereas Obi-Wan sought to shield him from the truth (by telling him that Darth Vader *killed* his father).

Father of Darkness, Son of Hope

In the last three episodes of the *Star Wars* saga, the father-son relationship of Anakin and Luke Skywalker shifts from one resembling that of Uther Pendragon and Arthur to one more akin to the relationship of Arthur and his illegitimate son Mordred. For example, Arthur and Mordred are both born under questionable circumstances (related to magic) that are certainly not within the social norms of the time period. Arthur is conceived when Merlin disguises Uther Pendragon as the husband of a woman he covets so that he can have sex with her. Mordred is similarly conceived when Morgan Le Fey (Arthur's half-sister and a powerful enchantress) uses magic to either enchant or trick Arthur into sleeping with her (see Chapter 15). While Arthur grows to be a great king who brings order to the land, Mordred grows up to become the death of Arthur and a bane to the utopia of Camelot. The two eventually kill one another in battle.

In *Star Wars*, Luke (and his twin sister Leia Organa) is conceived as a result of the secret marriage between Anakin Skywalker and Padme/Queen Amidala. Just as Arthur is taken from Uther at birth and looked after/tutored by Merlin, Luke is taken at birth and looked after/trained by Obi-Wan Kenobi's family. In this case, Luke is more like Arthur than Mordred. Also, Luke will grow up to be the salvation of his father, saving Anakin from the clutches of dark side (though he is unable to save his life). So, therefore, the father-son relationship of Anakin and Luke Skywalker is similar to that of Arthur and Mordred, except that the roles have been reversed. In *Star Wars*, it is the son who is good and the father who is evil, while in Arthurian legend the son (Mordred) is evil and the father (Arthur) is good.

Myth and *The Matrix*

There are a plethora of resources that examine the mythological archetypes that exist in the Wachowski Brothers' film series, *The Matrix Trilogy*. The Wachowski Brothers used archetypal figures from mythology rather liberally and extremely broadly. As a result, it is rather difficult if not impossible to draw concrete, direct parallels from any one character of the films to any one character in myth. The parallels that exist are not from any specific myth, but from myths in general. However, it is interesting to examine the presence of archetypes and concepts in *The Matrix Trilogy*.

Neo: The Messianic Archetype

The character *Neo* is very much the epitome of a modern-day messiah archetype. The majority of messianic figures, especially in religion, fulfill a number of very specific criteria, which are as follows:

- The birth/arrival of a messiah is prophesied in advance.

- A messiah figure does not necessarily deny his position, but at times wishes it were not his/her "cross to bear."

- A messiah resists temptation by an opposing evil force encouraging her to use her power to escape suffering.

- A messiah is often betrayed by someone close to him.

- *All* messiah figures *must* fulfill one basic thing—to die in order to save their people or humankind in general.

Neo's "birth" from the matrix is prophesied long before it occurs. In fact, the character Morpheus has been searching for him for some time due to a prophecy he received years ago from a character called The Oracle. The prophecy surrounding Neo's arrival fulfills the first criterion in the preceding list.

Though Neo never immediately or directly denies that he could be "The One," he often expresses his doubts about it. On several occasions, Neo's behavior suggests that he wishes someone would confirm his suspicions and tell him that he is not the messiah Morpheus is seeking, thereby relieving him of the heavy burden of responsibility such a destiny would carry. Neo's full powers, in fact, do not manifest until the moment in the film when he chooses to accept and believe that he is "The One."

Immortal Words

The word **neo** comes from the Greek word *neos*, both of which basically mean "new." In addition, neo is also an anagram of one. Throughout the movie, Neo is referred to as "the one." By analyzing this, one comes to the conclusion that his name has a double meaning, suggesting that Neo is the "new one/messiah."

Early on in the film, Neo is confronted by an "Agent" named Smith, who is actually a sentient program within the matrix. He is offered a way out. If he will only comply and cooperate with Smith's demands, he will be able to go back to his life. Smith also threatens to have Neo thrown in jail for the rest of his life if he refuses. Neo's answer … is a finger (and it's not a nice finger, either). Neo succeeds in the messianic task of resisting temptation by an opposing evil force offering him an escape from suffering.

In the first film, Neo is betrayed by a comrade named Zypher who wishes to be returned to the matrix and made ignorant that anything else exists. He chooses the bliss of an illusion over the bleak truth of reality. This situation is comparable to the betrayal of Jesus, messiah of the Christian religion, by Judas Iscariot (see Chapter 8). However, also like Judas, Zypher does not live to enjoy the reward for which he betrays his messiah.

At the end of the final film of *The Matrix Trilogy,* Neo must commit the ultimate act of all messianic figures—he must sacrifice his life in order to save his people (in this case, what little remains of the human race). In the scene where he does this, the crucifixionlike position of Neo's body makes this reference to him as a messianic figure blatantly obvious.

The Least You Need to Know

◆ In comparative mythology, parallels can be both subtle and blatant.

◆ The obvious nature of parallels is often dependent upon whether the writer/ creator intended them or included them unconsciously.

◆ The first step in applying comparative mythology to any two works is to identify the immediate parallels between them.

◆ The most amazing parallels that one can find are those that seem to have been included unconsciously or are not immediately obvious on the surface.

Glossary of Terms in Mythological Studies

allegory   A story, legend, or myth that is a symbolical representation of a concept, situation, archetype, or idea.

analytical psychology   Carl Jung's analytical theory of psychology which sought to positively influence the deep-seated drives of the human psyche by connecting the psychology of individuals to universal cultural patterns and symbols, referred to as archetypes.

angel   A messenger spirit; a divinely created, nonhuman entity that is not considered a god.

anima   The opposite-sex traits that contrast with the public persona. For men, the *anima* is the inner feminine.

animus   The opposite-sex traits that contrast with the public persona. For women, the *animus* is the inner masculine.

archangel   Warrior angel of the highest rank, led by the Archangel Michael. In Christian mythology, there are 7 archangels; in Islam, there are 4 archangels; in Judaism, there are 12.

archetype   In Jungian psychology, an inherited idea or mode of thought stemming from the experiences of the human race and which are present in the unconscious of individuals.

avatar   A god in a different form, most commonly seen in Hindu Dharma mythology.

Campbell, Joseph   A revolutionary comparative mythologist who further expanded on the works of Carl Jung.

collective unconscious   Part of the psyche that contains the racial memory of humankind and the cumulative experience of all human generations. These cumulative experiences manifest in the form of archetypes.

Cycle of Hero's Journey   The cycle is separation-initiation-return. *See also* Hero's Journey.

demigod   Half-god or part-god offspring, resulting from a union between a god and a mortal. Later, this term also came to be used for lower-level gods.

demon   A malevolent spiritual entity, often cursed, exiled, or banished from grace as a result of its own evil actions.

Depth Psychology   Refers to any psychological approach that examines the depth (meaning "hidden" or "deeper" parts) of human experience.

fatal flaw   In tragedy, a flaw in a hero's/character's personality that leads to his or her ruin or downfall.

Freud, Sigmund   Founder of psychoanalysis; called the "father of modern psychology."

god   In this book, used to refer to all gods in mythology. For Judeo-Christian God, the title YHVH is used in this book to avoid confusion.

goddess   Female god figure.

Great Deluge   A common theme of primal myths all over the world that tells of a great flood that nearly destroyed humankind. Often, this event is credited as the act of or punishment from a god figure.

Harrowing of Hell   A mythological journey into and return from hell or the underworld. Often, this phrase is literally used to refer to the Catholic myth of Jesus' journey into hell during the three days between his death and resurrection.

hell   A word used in Christianity to refer to an afterlife for those who commit certain sins and/or reject YHVH. The term is actually taken from the name of the Teutonic goddess of the underworld, Hel.

hero   Originally referred to a half-god/demigod; however, over time, it came to refer to individuals who act with bravery, integrity, and selflessness.

Hero's Journey   The journey of the hero in the monomyth, consisting of four sub-stages—call to adventure, completing the mission/boon, return to the point of origin, and application of a learned skill/acquired boon.

heroine   The female hero.

Hillman, James   Founder of archetypal psychology.

id   Sexual center of the psyche.

Jung, Carl   Founder of psychoanalytical method of psychology.

libido   Psychic and/or emotional energy stemming from primitive physical urges, usually focused on the attainment of some goal.

Messiah   A savior who sacrifices his or her physical self to aid or rescue humankind.

metaphor   An implied comparison; for example, saying "That guy *is* a bear" to imply that he is large. Often confused with simile, which is indirect.

metaphysical   Having to do with a transcendent/divine/unknown reality, which cannot be perceived or understood within the confines of physical reality.

monomyth   Refers to parallel structures and patterns that are experienced by particular character archetypes in different tales, myths, and legends from all across the globe. The term has also been used as an alternative way to refer to The Hero's Journey cycle.

myth   Commonly misunderstood to mean "false" or "fictitious," this term actually refers to the tales and legends around which cultures, civilizations, and/or religions are built.

mythology   The study of myth.

necropolis   A term used to refer to the underworld; comes from the Greek words *necro* (dead/death) and *polis* (city-state), giving it the literal meaning of "city of the dead."

necrotype   An integration of the Greek word *necro* (dead/death) with the word "archetype" (see earlier entry on Jung). This word refers to universal symbols of the human imagination (i.e., archetypes) catalyzed by the journey to the underworld.

nekyia   Derived from Greek for "dead," *necro*, nekyia was a word used by the Greeks to refer to the eleventh book of Homer's *Odyssey*, in which Odysseus travels into Hades to consult the spirit of the blind prophet, Tiresias, so that he might find out how to get back home. This term is now used to refer to the theory of Dr. Evans Lansing Smith, for universal structures and collective archetypes that make up all journeys to the underworld.

nymph   A lower order of goddesses in Greek mythology, often very beautiful and sexual in nature.

ocean/water   In mythology, oceans/seas/water are archetypal symbols of the unconscious.

persona   Opposite of the *anima/animus*; means "mask," and refers to one's outward self, the person that one shows to others on a social level.

personification   Giving life/personality to that which does not have it.

primal god   A creator god.

primal man   Refers to the first humans created by a god.

primal myth   Myth dealing with the creation of Earth and/or humankind.

psyche   The deep, often unconscious recesses of the human mind. The term is taken from the name of the Greek heroine Psyche, a lover/wife of Eros/Cupid.

psychopomp   A guide to the afterlife/underworld.

religion   An organized system of worship often based on the foundations of myth.

shadow   In Jungian psychology, the shadow is the pre-conscious, animalistic side of human nature.

simile   An indirect comparison; for example, saying "That guy *is like* a bear" to imply that he is large. Often confused with a metaphor, which is a direct comparison.

symbolism   The representation of a concept, situation, or idea by a person, animal, or object.

tragedy   A genre of myth/literature in which a sad or painful chain of events occur as a result of a hero's/character's fatal flaw.

trinity   A three-member group of gods or entities in mythology.

unconscious   In psychoanalytic theory, the repository of repressed desires, memories, and impulses.

underworld   In ancient mythology, a dark realm of the dead with unknown powers and knowledge. This underworld is not an exact equivalent of the modern Western concepts of Heaven or hell.

well   In mythology, a well or spring of water is often associated with the divine feminine. A nymph, for example, often lives near a well, or has one in her home.

Genealogies and Important Names

Greek Names with Latin/Roman Equivalents

Aphrodite/Venus   Goddess of Beauty and Sexuality.

Apollo/Phoebus   God of Light, the Arts, and Intellect.

Ares/Mars   God of War.

Artemis/Diana   Virgin Goddess of the Hunt.

Athena (also, Pallas Athena)/Minerva   Virgin Goddess of Wisdom and War Strategy.

Demeter/Ceres   Earth goddess.

Dionysus/Bacchus   God of Wine, Poetry, Merriment, and Insanity.

Eos/Aurora   Goddess of the Dawn.

Erinyes/Furies   A trio of wrathful, winged, demonlike female creatures that carried out terrible justice on wicked and unjust people.

Eris/Discordia   Goddess of Chaos, Mayhem, and Discord.

Eros/Cupid   God of Love; son of Aphrodite.

Gaea/Tellus   The earth; female in nature.

Hades/Pluto, Plutus, Dis, Orcus   God of the Underworld.

Hebe/Juventas   Daughter of Zeus and Hera, she is the embodiment of youth and acted as cupbearer of the Olympians until replaced by Ganymede.

Hecate/Trivia   A Titaness often associated with witchcraft; she is also the only Titan that was allowed to retain her power after Zeus rose to power.

Hephaestus/Vulcan   God of the Forge and the blacksmith of the gods.

Hera/Juno   Goddess of Marriage and Marital Fidelity; wife of Zeus.

Herakles/Hercules   Half-god/demigod son of Zeus and Alcmene.

Hermes/Mercury   Messenger of the gods.

Hestia/Vesta   Virgin Goddess of the Hearth.

Hypnos/Somnus   God of Sleep.

Kronos/Saturn   Creator god.

Leto/Latona   Titaness who, with Zeus, became mother of Apollo and Artemis.

Nike/Victoria   Goddess of Victory, associated with Pallas Athena.

Odysseus/Ulysses   A Spartan warrior who fought in the Trojan War and is credited with creating the Trojan Horse; also, he is the hero of Homer's *Odyssey*.

Pan/Inuus, Faunus   Demigod of Music, Dancing, Panic, and Fear.

Persephone/Proserpina   Daughter of Demeter and wife of Hades/Pluto.

Poseidon/Neptune   God of the Sea and Earthquakes, called the "Earth Shaker."

Rhea/Ops   Sister and wife of Kronos.

Selene/Diana   Goddess of the Moon.

Tyche/Fortuna   Goddess of Good Fortune.

Zeus/Jupiter   The patricidal son of Kronos as well as the most powerful of the gods; God of Sky and wielder of the thunderbolt.

Basic Genealogy of the Greek Pantheon of Olympians*

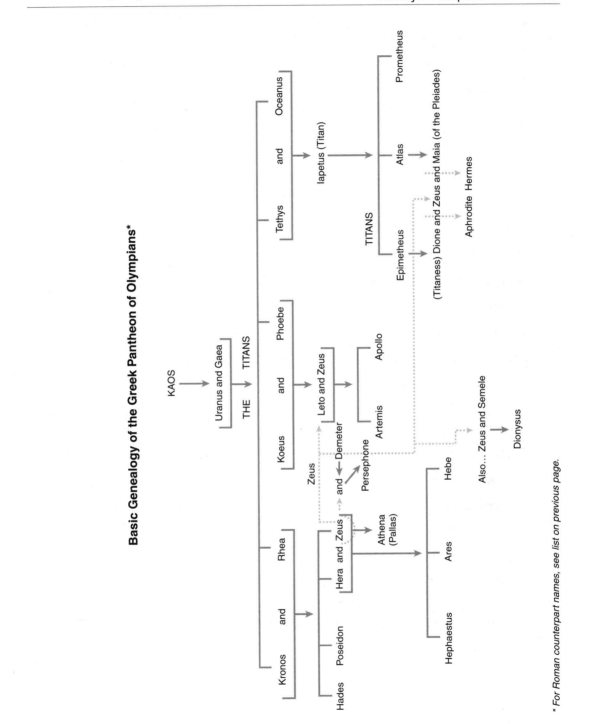

* For Roman counterpart names, see list on previous page.

Primary Teutonic Gods

Aesir   The race of Teutonic gods and immortals.

Balder   God of Death; has the eye of death.

Bragi   God of Poetry and Music and son of Odin.

Freya/Frigga   Wife of Odin; Goddess of Marriage.

Heimdal   God of the Dawn/Sun/Light.

Idunn   Goddess of Spring.

Loki   God of Mischief.

Njord   God of the Sea and Fishing.

Norns   The Fates of Teutonic mythology, they are depicted as three virgins; also, they are responsible for watering the roots of Yggdrasil.

Odin/Woden   Main god of the Teutonic pantheon; God of Wisdom, Poetry, Mead, and Warriors; ruler of the domain of Valhalla.

Thor   Thunder god and son of Odin.

Tyr   God of War, Courage, and the Sword.

Valhalla   Heaven of warriors, where after death the brave live forever.

Valkyries   Battle maidens of the Aesir and the attendants of Odin.

Yggdrasil   The World Tree that connects the three worlds.

Primary Hindu Dharma Terms, Figures, and Gods

Brahma   Creator god of the Trimurti.

Brahmin   Religious ascetic, holy man.

Buddha   In Hinduism, believed to have been the last avatar of Vishnu. Buddhist views of the Buddha, Siddhartha Gautama, differ.

dharma   Hindu concept that all are born into a specific role in life, similar but not equivalent to the Western concepts of fate and destiny.

Durga   A wife of Shiva.

Ganesha   Elephant-headed God of Wisdom and son of Shiva.

Hanuman   Lord of the monkeys and ally to Rama in *Ramayana*.

Indra   War god.

Kaikeyi   The stepmother of Rama in *Ramayana*, responsible for Rama's exile from his home kingdom of Dasarath.

Kali   Goddess of Death, Pestilence, and Destruction; called "The Black One."

Kalkin   The Final Avatar; tenth avatar of Vishnu whose appearance will mean the end of the current cycle of existence.

Kama   A god-servant of Shiva.

karma   A shared concept of Buddhism and Hinduism that all acts result in the accumulation of either positive or negative karma which can affect one's ascension to Heaven and/or reincarnation.

Krishna   Avatar of Vishnu and charioteer of Arjuna in the *Bhagavad-Gita*.

Kurma   The Tortoise Avatar; second avatar of Vishnu

Lakshmi   The Lotus Goddess and wife of Vishnu.

Manu   Hero of the Hindu flood/deluge myth.

Matsya   The Fish Avatar; first avatar of Vishnu.

Mitra   God of the Sun.

Naraka   A Hindu concept similar to but not the equivalent of hell (see Chapter 6).

Narasimha   The Man-Lion Avatar; fourth avatar of Vishnu.

Parasurama   The "Rama with the Axe" Avatar; sixth avatar of Vishnu.

Prajapati   Lord of Creatures, a name that has been applied to multiple Hindu gods such as Indra, Soma, and even Brahma.

Purusha   The primordial being that was sacrificed to create the world.

Rama   Hero of *Ramayana* and the seventh avatar of Vishnu.

Rati   Wife of Kama.

Rudra   A destroyer god later replaced by Shiva.

Rukmini   The wife of Krishna; also an avatar of Lakshmi.

Sarasvati   The wife of Brahma.

Shakti/Sati   Mother Goddess; as the avatar Sati, she was a wife of Shiva and continues to be depicted as such.

Shiva   Destroyer god of the Trimurti.

Sita   Wife of Rama in *Ramayana*; also an avatar of Lakshmi.

Skanda   God of War; General of the Gods and the youngest son of Shiva.

Soma   Sacred drink of the immortals and gods.

Trimurti   The Hindu creator/sustainer/destroyer trinity of the godhead, consisting of Brahma, Vishnu, and Shiva.

Valmiki   Author of the *Ramayana*.

Varaha   The Boar Avatar; third avatar of Vishnu.

Varuna   Supreme ruler of the gods, guardian of cosmic order, and he who bestows the rains upon the earth.

Vishnu   Sustainer god of the Trimurti.

Yama   God of Death; first man to die.

List of Primary Middle Eastern Deities

Ahura Mazda (Ohrmazd)   Supreme God of Zoroastrianism.

Allah   God of Islam.

An   Supreme Sumerian God of the Sky.

Ana Hita   Fertility.

Angra Mainyu   God of the Darkness.

Anu   Father of Gods in the Sumerian pantheon.

Astarte   God of War and Love.

Ba'al   Semitic Storm God.

Dumuzi (Tammuz)   Sumerian God of the Sheepfold, Shepherd King of Ururk.

Enki   Sumerian God of Wisdom.

Enkidu   A being created to act as a friend to Gilgamesh so the hero will stop terrorizing the people.

Enlil   Sumerian God of Earth, Air, and Storm.

Ereshkigal   Sumerian Goddess of the Underworld.

Geshtinanna   Sumerian Goddess of Wine and sister of Dumuzi.

Gilgamesh   King of Uruk and hero of *The Epic of Gilgamesh.*

Gugalanna   The Sumerian "Sacred Bull" God; husband of Ereshkigal.

Inanna   Sumerian Goddess of Heaven and Earth.

Ishtar   Assyrian Goddess of War, a later modification of Inanna.

Ki (Urash)   The Sumerian Earth Mother.

Kur   The Sumerian underworld.

Lugalbanda   Third king of Uruk and father of Gilgamesh.

Lulal   Younger son of Inanna.

Marduk   Slayer of Tiamat; champion and king of Sumerian gods.

Mithras   Primal god figure of Zoroastrianism.

Mohammed   Prophet of Allah in Islam.

Mot   Ancient Semitic Death God.

Nammu   The sea; a Sumerian creator goddess.

Nanna   Sumerian God of the Moon.

Ningal   Sumerian Goddess of the Reeds, called the "Great Lady," and mother of Utu and Inanna.

Ningikuga   Sumerian Goddess of the Pure Reeds, associated with Ningal.

Ninhursag   Sumerian Mother Goddess of Earth.

Ninlil   Sumerian Goddess of Air and a consort of Enlil.

Ninsun (Sirtur)   The Sumerian "Wild Cow" goddess; a Queen of Uruk, wife of Lugalbanda, and mother of Gilgamesh.

Nurgul   Sumerian God of Plague.

Shara   Sumerian God of Submission.

Utu   Sumerian God of the Sun and Justice.

Genealogy of the Sumerian Gods*

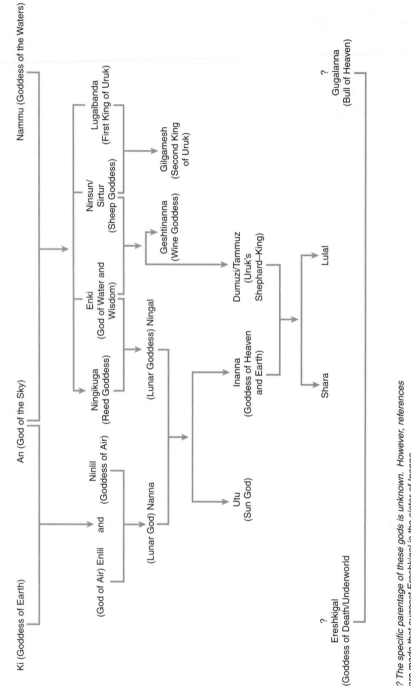

? The specific parentage of these gods is unknown. However, references
are made that suggest Ereshkigal is the sister of Inanna.

*Please note that this is only a basic genealogy, and that the roles, names, and relationships
of these gods changed when the Sumerians were conquered by other cultures.

List of Egyptian Dieties

Anubis   The hound-headed God of Death that carried souls to the afterlife for judgment; son of Isis and Osiris. The center of Anubis' cult could be found at Cynopolis.

Atum-Re   The creator god who later became Ammun-Re. This was the most common supreme, universal god of the ancient Egyptians. His symbol is the Ram and the center of the Ammun-Re cult was found in Thebes.

Geb   God of the Earth or, actually, the earth. His symbol is the human form and the center of his cult was found at the Nile delta. Creator of minerals and vegetation who united with Nut to birth the lower gods.

Horus   The falcon-headed God of Wisdom and Guardian of the Pharaohs' Divinity; son of Isis and Osiris.

Isis   Goddess of Magic and Resurrection; wife of Osiris.

Nephthys   Goddess of Sterility and wife of Seth.

Nut   The Sky itself, who is credited with bringing all lower gods into existence when united with Geb.

Osiris   God of Fertility and Vegetation; husband of Isis.

Seth   God of Evil, brother of Osiris, and husband of Nephthys.

Shu   The divine essence of air and light that united with Tefnut to birth Geb and Nut.

Tefnut   The divine essence of moisture that united with Shu to birth Geb and Nut.

Genealogy of Atum-Re/Ammon-Re (Egypt)

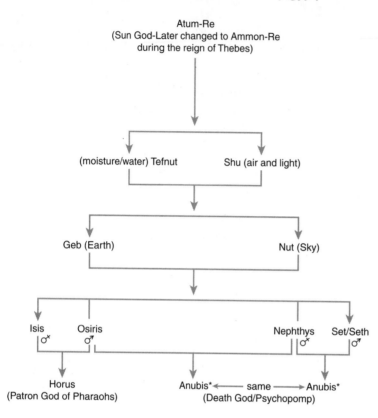

Atum-Re
(Sun God-Later changed to Ammon-Re
during the reign of Thebes)

(moisture/water) Tefnut   Shu (air and light)

Geb (Earth)   Nut (Sky)

Isis   Osiris   Nephthys   Set/Seth

Horus   Anubis* ◄── same ──► Anubis*
(Patron God of Pharaohs)   (Death God/Psychopomp)

*Versions of Anubis' parentage differ. Some say Osiris is
his father while other versions credit Seth as his father.*

Index

B

E

N

Y

Z

Great gifts for *any* occasion!

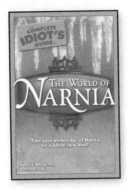